International Review of Social History Supplement 4

"Peripheral" Labour? Studies in the History of Partial Proletarianization

Edited by
Shahid Amin and Marcel van der Linden

T0370651

CAMBRIDGE UNIVERSITY PRESS
Cambridge, New York, Melbourne, Madrid, Cape Town, Singapore, São Paulo

Cambridge University Press
The Edinburgh Building, Cambridge CB2 8RU, UK

www.cambridge.org
Information on this title: www.cambridge.org/9780521589000

First published 1997

A catalogue record for this publication is available from the British Library

Library of Congress Cataloguing in Publication data

Peripheral labour : studies in the history of partial
proletarianization / edited by Shahid Amin and Marcel van der
Linden.
    p. cm. — (International review of social history : v.
41. Supplement : 4)
    Includes bibliographical references (p.   ).
    ISBN 0-521-58900-2 (pbk.)
    1. Working class—Developing countries—History. 2. Marginality,
Social—Developing countries—History.   3. Proletariat—History.
4. Library—History. I. Amin, Shahid. II. Linden, Marcel van der,
1952– . III. Series: International review of social history : v.
41. IV. Series: International review of social history.   Supplement
: 4.
HD8943.P47   1997
305.5'62'091724—dc21   96-50484
                                                              CIP

ISBN 978-0-521-58900-0 paperback

Transferred to digital printing 2007

Front cover illustration: Poster of the VIth World Congress of the
International Federation of Plantation, Agricultural and Allied
Workers (IFPAAW), Lausanne, 26–27 May 1988. Collection IISG.

CONTENTS

Introduction

The proletarians have lost their innocence. A conservative sociologist once described wage labourers as follows:

The worker is *personally free*, i.e. his physical and spiritual-moral powers are completely at his own disposal. [. . .] He *has no property*, i.e. he has no exclusive material power over capital as a secure basis with relative permanency. [. . .] He has neither a stock of consumer goods that enable him to live, nor permanent interests of capital. [. . .] He lives in economic circumstances in which means of subsistence can be obtained only through *economic returns*. [. . .] He is forced to offer personal capacities with an economic exchange value in return for means of subsistence.[1]

The fact that this description – disregarding its formulation – is almost identical to the classical Marxist definition indicates a broad consensus regarding the characteristics of proletarians among intellectuals in the first half of the twentieth century. Implicitly, proletarians were considered to be male, were perceived in isolation from their families or households, and were associated with a "pure" social category: while personally free and without property, they were compelled to sell their individual capacities or skills for money. These proletarians were viewed not as abstract theoretical constructs, but (at least in the advanced countries and in the societies of "really existing socialism") as concrete living people whose number was increasing rapidly by any standard. While some historians and social scientists may have suspected that workers could also be females, might live in families or households that combined several "coping strategies", and sometimes had their freedom severely restricted by debts or other impediments, etc., these insights did not play a significant theoretical role.

Social historians have long been accessories to this misleading conceptualization. Implicitly or sometimes even explicitly, historians have propagated the idea that labour movements (believed to consist of trade unions and workers' parties) were mainly supported by "genuine" proletarians who were preceded (diachronically) or surrounded (synchronically) by "improper" quasi-workers: labour aristocrats, lumpenproletarians, and the like. These stereotypes appear in writings by the US-American Wisconsin School (John R. Commons, Selig Perlman, Philip Taft), the Webbs in Britain, Franz Mehring, Eduard Bernstein and Gustav Mayer in Germany, and Edouard Dolléans in France. As Eric Hobsbawm observed: "classical labour movement history tended to

---

[1] Goetz Briefs, "Das gewerbliche Proletariat", in *Grundriss der Sozialökonomik*, Part IX (Tübingen, 1926), pp. 142–240, 149. The *Grundriss der Sozialökonomik* was the Weimar Republic's standard sociological reference work and included the original edition of Max Weber's *Economy and Society*.

International Review of Social History 41 (1996), pp. 1–7

produce both a model and an accepted version of history, national as well as international, which ranged from an informal but not very flexible to a formal and highly inflexible orthodoxy".[2] E.P. Thompson became one of the first historians to develop a new approach when he stressed the social variety and heterogeneity of the working class in early nineteenth-century England.[3]

About twenty-five or thirty years ago, the old stereotypes created serious problems for the incipient interest among Western scholars in the social history of the so-called "Third World". Robin Cohen, one of the most important protagonists of African and Caribbean labour history, has rightly observed that a restrictive definition of the workers ignores the widespread presence of ambivalent class positions: "There is [. . .] a large group of the population which is simultaneously and ambiguously 'semiproletariat' and 'semipeasant' [. . .]. Equally, within the *favelas* and shantytowns, large numbers of individuals who are sometimes described as 'unemployed' or as 'sub-' or 'lumpenproletariat' are in fact intermittently employed performing services or in small workshops employing a handful of workers and apprentices. In the case of this group, the ambiguity arises from the fact that it comprises people who can at the same time be considered self-employed or employees."[4]

In the urban sphere, anthropological and historical studies started to reveal a wide range of so-called "marginals". Surveying the research, Peter Worsley, for instance, identifies not only industrial workers, but also workers in sweatshops, putting-out work in the home, self-employed artisans, domestic enterprises using family labour, street vendors, pedlars, hucksters, domestic servants, casual wage labourers (car-washers, etc.), refuse-collectors and beggars.[5] All these categories are fluid: households may combine several of the activities listed and may alternate between coping strategies.

Studies of the rural world also revealed an increasingly complex picture. As early as the 1960s, Eric Wolf described some of the numerous economic and social variations characteristic of agricultural life in his seminal little book on *Peasants*.[6] Later studies have added an array of other types of labour relations. The reconstruction of forms of agrestic servitude and the inadequacy of terms such as debt bondage were particularly important in providing a satisfactory explanation for the

---

[2] "Labour History and Ideology" (1974), in E.J. Hobsbawm, *Worlds of Labour. Further Studies in the History of Labour* (London, 1984), pp. 1–14, 4.

[3] E.P. Thompson, *The Making of the English Working Class* (London, 1963).

[4] Robin Cohen, "Workers in Developing Societies", in Hamza Alavi and Teodor Shanin (eds), *Sociology of "Developing Societies"* (London, 1982), pp. 279–286, 279–280.

[5] Peter Worsley, *The Three Worlds. Culture and World Development* (London, 1984), pp. 194–202.

[6] Eric Wolf, *Peasants* (Englewood Cliffs, NJ, 1966).

phenomenon of bonded labour.[7] Gyan Prakash's article in this volume is a forceful reminder that classificatory systems are fine as long as they do not impede the actual task of comparison by a preoccupation with identical sets of phenomena. Prakash's interpretation of the history of agrestic servitude from the North Indian state of Bihar calls for an "undoing of the discourse of freedom". As he notes: "if servitude was the form that the capital-labour relationship was compelled to assume in the process of its universalization, then colonial servitude must be included in the account of free labour."

Gradually, it has become clear that pure "free wage labour" in the double Marxian sense[8] is an ideal type, the conceptual nucleus of far more complicated historical realities. Pure free wage labour – i.e. the exchange of labour power for money implying "no other relations of dependence than those which result from its own nature"[9] – forms a kind of analytical core surrounded by numerous rings of labour relations that we would like to call intermediary. We might construct a triangle with three "poles": pure free wage labour, unfree labour and independent labour (self-employment).

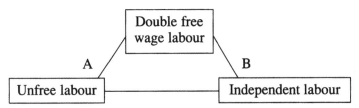

Here we are especially interested in the "grey zones" A and B surrounding double free wage labour. The number of variations within these zones is probably infinite. On line A we may, for instance, distinguish:

● formally "free" wage labourers tied to a particular employer through loans (truck systems, etc.), housing facilities, etc.;
● indentured labourers tied to a particular employer through long-term contracts;
● unfree labourers hired out by their owners to other employers in exchange for wages.

[7] On the genesis of bonded labour as a general category, see Gyan Prakash, *Bonded Histories: Genealogies of Labor Servitude in Colonial India* (Cambridge [etc.], 1990), pp. 1–12.
[8] The worker is "free in the double sense that as a free individual he can dispose of his labour-power as his own commodity, and that, on the other hand, he has no other commodity for sale". Karl Marx, *Capital*, vol. 1, trans. Ben Fowkes (Harmondsworth, 1976), p. 272.
[9] *Ibid.*, p. 271.

On line B we may, for example, distinguish:

• disguised wage labourers whose work products are regularly appropriated partly by an employer without these persons being official
employees of the firm;
• dependent workers who do not perform wage labour but are dependent upon an employer for credit, rental of premises, etc.

Although it can be argued that "proletarianization is the most significant process in the contemporary world",[10] developments in the so-
called "Third World" can be understood only if these intermediary
forms of wage labour (indicators of partial proletarianization) are taken
seriously. History in general and the history of labour in particular is
not a unilinear process embodying an ongoing transition from "traditional" to "modern" forms. "Modern" capitalism may involve the reconstitution of slavery (as can be seen in countries as diverse as Burma,
Brazil, or India), as well as the reconstitution of older forms of
industry.[11]

The careful study of these intermediary forms may also shed new light
on the history of the labouring classes in the so-called core countries. Not
only have the debates on proto-industrialization[12] and worker-peasants[13]
shown that intermediary forms of wage labour have been of continuous
importance in European history over the past three or four centuries, but
"pure free wage labourers" in advanced countries are at times clearly
forced back into alternative activities through which they can sustain their
subsistence margins in times of unemployment.[14] Alain Faure's contribution on Parisian ragpickers in the nineteenth century is a fitting case study
of a partially proletarianized occupational group usually considered typical
of the "Third World".

It probably makes sense to regard the intermediary forms of wage labour
not as relationships existing outside the true working class, but as articula-
tions of a worldwide segmentation of the labour force. In this segmented
labour force, some workers (mostly in the core countries) are relatively
free, well paid and secure, while other workers, both in the core countries
and especially along the periphery, are less free, poorly paid, and "float-

[10] B.R. Roberts, "Peasants and Proletarians", *Annual Review of Sociology*, 16 (1990),
pp. 353–377, 354.
[11] See Ronald Aminzade's case study "Reinterpreting Capitalist Industrialization: A Study
of Nineteenth-Century France", *Social History*, 9 (1984), pp. 329–350.
[12] See the survey of these debates in *Continuity and Change*, 8 (1993), pp. 151–252.
[13] Douglas R. Holms and Jean H. Quataert, "An Approach to Modern Labor: Worker
Peasantries in Historic Saxony and the Friuli Region over Three Centuries", *Comparative
Studies in Society and History*, 28 (1986), pp. 191–216.
[14] See the example of the workers laid off in Pittsfield, Massachusetts, in the 1980s in
June Nash, "Global Integration and Subsistence Insecurity", *American Anthropologist*, 96
(1994), pp. 7–30.

ing".[15] The boundaries between the two segments are vague and constantly shifting. Further exploration of the differences between segments might benefit from additional class criteria, like Max Weber's notion of the "market position of labour" and the worker's control over the work process. These criteria may also enable us to analyse gender-specific aspects more accurately.[16]

Recent work in labour history has stressed the question of "multiple identities" among the working class.[17] Starting with the classic issues of the development of capitalism and of "abstract labour", historians in the "Third World" have begun to emphasize the historical and analytical relevance of Marx's notion of "concrete labour" and of labour power "as it exists in the personality of the worker".[18] This approach requires careful consideration of both the culture and the material conditions of the working class.

Religion, caste, gender and region (long-distance migrants from culturally dissimilar catchment areas to mines, plantations and factories) have become important issues in recent works on "Third World" labour history.[19] This interest has given rise to particularistic histories, where the operation of familiar Western machinery in far-flung corners of the globe is often pushed aside by accounts of specific groups of working women and men struggling to reproduce their cultural selves away from "home". The value of such histories lies not just in enriching the study of labour in different "Third World" locations – accretions to knowledge that can be accessed when the need arises to understand the working-class history of one or several non-Western societies. Some scholars have argued boldly

[15] Frances Rothstein, "The New Proletarians: Third World Reality and First World Categories", *Comparative Studies in Society and History*, 28 (1986), pp. 217–238. See also Anibal Quijano Obregón, "The Marginal Pole of the Economy and the Marginalised Labour Force", *Economy and Society*, 3 (1974), pp. 393–428; June Nash, "Ethnographic Aspects of the World Capitalist System", *Annual Review of Anthropology*, 11 (1981), pp. 393–423; Eric R. Wolf, *Europe and the People without History* (Berkeley [etc.], 1982).
[16] Kyung-Sup Chang, "Gender and Abortive Capitalist Social Transformation: Semi-Proletarianization of South Korean Women", *International Journal of Comparative Sociology*, 36 (1995), pp. 61–81, 65.
[17] David Roediger, "Race and the Working-Class Past in the United States: Multiple Identities and the Future of Labor History", in Marcel van der Linden (ed.), *The End of Labour History?* (Cambridge [etc.], 1993) [*International Review of Social History*, Supplement 1], pp. 127–143.
[18] Marx, *Capital*, 1, p. 678.
[19] See, for example, Rajnarayan Chandavarkar, *The Origins of Industrial Capitalism in India: Business Strategies and Working Classes in Bombay, 1900–1940* (Cambridge [etc.], 1994), esp. chs 3–5; Dipesh Chakrabarty, *Rethinking Working Class History: Bengal 1890–1940* (Princeton, 1989); Gail Herstatter, *The Workers of Tianjin, 1900–1949* (Stanford, 1986); Emily Honig, *Sisters and Strangers. Women in the Shanghai Cotton Mills, 1919–1949* (Stanford, 1986); Charles van Onselen, *Studies in the Social and Economic History of the Witwatersrand, 1886–1994*, 2 vols (Harlow, 1982); Michael T. Taussig, *The Devil and Commodity Fetishism in South America* (Chapel Hill, 1979).

that the experience of industrialization and proletarianization along the "periphery" has the potential to reveal the cultural characteristics of much of Western labour history itself.[20]

Erick Langer's perceptive study of nineteenth-century Bolivian mine labour addresses three crucial issues: the implications of mechanization, the sources of labour and the effects of agrarian rhythms on labour supply. One of the author's striking observations is that "modern" mining enterprises were combined with haciendas and maintained a kind of peonage arrangement in which resident workers were obligated to pay for their access to lands by toiling in the mines. Such an arrangement obviously contradicts simple models of unilinear progress.

Juan Giusti-Cordero's essay on canefield labour in early twentieth-century Puerto Rico describes another example of the intricate unity of the historical peasant-proletarian relation. In a careful analysis of the Piñones region, Giusti-Cordero argues that the sugar cane workers were neither "peasants", nor "rural proletarians", nor a combination of the two. Rather, they were a social group *sui generis* demanding a fundamental reconceptualization.

The "Indian" papers in this volume also contribute to the rethinking of categories. Each focuses on grasping the colonial situation from a slightly different perspective. Dilip Simeon's detailed reconstruction of the life, work and hazards of coal miners in Jharia is predicated on an engagement with that "historical and moral element" that Marx identifies as a factor in determining the value of labour power. Though deeply concerned with one set of coal pits (the largest in India), Simeon's essay is a plea for situating the concept of "relations of production" within the "histories of given societies".

The two papers by Madhavi Kale and Samita Sen deal with the imperial and colonial contexts within which large-scale, long-distance migration was organized from the north Indian villages to the sugar plantations of the British Caribbean and the tea gardens of Assam. Kale touches upon a host of important issues in Caribbean history: the link between the planters' and the empire's interests, the crucial role played by Indian indentured labour in the plantation economies, the essentialist categories through which the coolie was perceived, and the fluid socialization that sea voyage and plantation life facilitated and encouraged. She highlights the plight of and the opportunities available to single woman migrants on board the ships and in the colonies.[21]

---

[20] See Dipesh Chakrabarty, "Class Consciousness and the Indian Working Class: Dilemmas of Marxist Historiography", *Journal of Asian and African Studies*, 28 (1988), pp. 21–31; idem, *Rethinking Working Class History*; Raj Chandavarkar, "Industrialization in India before 1947: Conventional Approaches and Alternative Perspectives", *Modern Asian Studies*, 19 (1985), pp. 623–668.

[21] For a splendid recapitulation of some of these experiences, see V.S. Naipaul, "Prologue to an Autobiography", in his *Finding the Centre: Two Narratives* (London, 1984), esp. pp. 62–67.

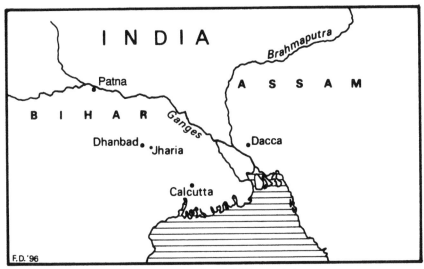

Figure 1. Northern India, showing the regions of Bihar and Assam

Samita Sen applies important new theoretical insights in her investigation of the question of migration by single women to the Assam tea plantations within India. Faced with the difficult problem of facilitating migration by "good women" from north Indian villages without unsettling patriarchal control over females (both married and unmarried), the colonial state opted for an ingenious compromise. While the freedom to enter into wage contracts independently of male guardians was denied to women in law, the magistrates were "encouraged to wink at [. . . such . . .] illegal recruitment". The alternative of facilitating family migration was not seriously entertained, as this choice would have stripped peasant agriculture and the colonial economy, more generally, of its widespread familial base. Such a process would have been contrary to the interests of both colonial capital and the colonial state. As Dilip Simeon remarks, "the hut in the village and the colliery lines became adjuncts of a household in which the rural location of one effected savings on infrastructure for capital in the other."

Shahid Amin and Marcel van der Linden

Colonialism, Capitalism and the Discourse of Freedom

GYAN PRAKASH

In the history and historiography of labour servitude, the ideology of modernity and progress looms large. Thus it was with bitter irony that a British officer described the miserable condition of a labourer in late nineteenth-century colonial India: "Steam, the great civilizer, has not done much for this man, although the railroad runs within a few hundred yards of his door."[1] The persistence of the miserably poor existence was bad enough, but truly appalling was the fact that the introduction of modern industry had not set the labourer free. The poor labourers, or *kamias* as they were called locally, had seen modernity whizz past them without carrying them along in its journey to progress and freedom.

The expectation that the abolition of unfreedom, even if it was "a very long time in coming", was bound to happen with "the advance of modern ideas, open communications and opportunities for industrial labour" was part of an ideology rooted in the post-Enlightenment belief that freedom constituted the natural human condition.[2] This post-Enlightenment discourse enunciated two fundamental propositions. First, that free labour was the natural and the normative form. Thus, even as the Enlightenment *philosophes* offered a tortuous defence of the enslavement of Africans, they also represented freedom as the essence of humanity and servitude as its negation.[3] Indeed, Adam Smith attacked slavery as a system of restraints that stifled the slaves' pursuit of their self-interests and impeded the development of free labour.[4] From this followed the second proposition according to which the purpose and meaning of History was to release human beings from the burdens imposed by the past and usher them into the realm of freedom because anything other than free labour was the suppression of an anterior human essence, because servitude was a deviation from the natural course of human evolution.

However, as Marx pointed out, the emergence of free labour required the dispossession of petty producers so that they could become "free"

---

[1] India Office Library and Records (IOL): Proceedings of the Government of Bengal, Scarcity and Relief Department, January 1874, File 13–76, Letter from the Officiating Collector of Monghyr.
[2] Bihar State Archives (BSA): Proceedings of the Government of Bihar and Orissa (Land Revenue), November 1919, Nos 6–10, Report by W.H. Lewis.
[3] David Brion Davis, *The Problem of Slavery in Western Culture* (Ithaca, 1966), pp. 391–421 *passim*.
[4] Adam Smith, *The Wealth of Nations* (1776; New York, 1937), pp. 80, 364–367.

International Review of Social History 41 (1996), pp. 9–25

to sell their labour power as a commodity. To project the universalization of free labour as the *raison d'être* of history, therefore, was to stage the bourgeois mode of production as History. Thus, even as capital reinforced and profited from slavery, it composed the servile relations of production in the inverse image of free labour. Whether it was slavery and indenture on the "New World" plantations, or bonded labour on the Indian subcontinent, they were constituted as the Other of free labour; what marked them was an economy of restrictions – restraints on the mobility of labourers, impediments on their ability to choose and change employers, controls over their culture, etc. With labour power turned into an exchangeable commodity, capitalism constituted other social forms of labour as the opposite of free exchange. As Eugene Genovese writes: "The power of slavery as a cultural myth in modern societies derives from its antithetical relationship to the hegemonic ideology of bourgeois social relations of production."[5]

To the extent that servitude has come to be defined in opposition to free labour, as the suppression of an innate condition of freedom, its position resembles the position repression occupies in the modern discourse of sexuality. According to Michel Foucault, the "repressive hypothesis" represents power only as a system of restraints, as a thing that represses an innate sexuality, as a force "that only has the negative on its side, a power to say no; in no condition to produce, capable only of posting limits [. . .]"[6] Similarly, capital enacts servitude as the suppression of a prior human essence, as a system of *restrictions* on freedom to exchange labour power as a commodity. Power is banished from the realm of free labour and manifests itself in servitude alone; it becomes visible only in its juridical form, not in the realm of the economy but as "extra-economic coercion" – as an economy of suspended rights and suppressed essence. Such a naturalization of free labour conceals capitalism's role in constituting bondage as a condition defined in relation to itself, and presents servitude as a condition outside its field of operation, as a form of social existence identifiable and analysable as alien and opposed to capitalism. It is thus that the analysis of bondage, servitude and slavery as different degrees of unfreedom appears as a purely descriptive exercise, as self-evident distinctions unconnected to the force of the global spread of capital.

If the stage of history forms one site for the powerful emergence and functioning of the discourse of freedom, the pages of historical writings are another. Instituted by the workings of capital and writings of the Enlightenment *philosophes*, the discourse of freedom claims universal

---

[5] Eugene Genovese, *Rebellion to Revolution* (Baton Rouge and London, 1979), p. xiii.
[6] Michel Foucault, *The History of Sexuality, I: An Introduction*, trans. Robert Hurley (New York, 1980), p. 85.

applicability. With free labour disguised as a natural condition and a universal human destiny, not a specific historical form, social relations across history become representable by this discourse. It is thus that the free-unfree dichotomy has come to invade the understanding of societies ranging from ancient Greece to the Thirteen Colonies in North America. The condition of servitude in the Greek city-states is readily differentiated from bondage under medieval Islamic regimes and from slavery and indenture on sugar and tobacco plantations in the Americas, but the belief persists that they share something in common. Of course, as David Brion Davis suggests, there are grounds for identifying commonality. Certain institutional features, such as the treatment of the slave as a thing, legal codes and regulations, a system of restrictions, and the moral-ideological problem these posed, have existed throughout slavery's history.[7] Orlando Patterson's analysis of slavery across time and space as a system of domination predicated on the "social death" of slaves also makes a persuasive case for continuity.[8] But continuities in slavery as a system of domination cannot mean the persistence of unfreedom. As David Brion Davis writes, though "we automatically contrast slavery with free labor or with various modern ideals of individual autonomy", through "most of history such antonyms would have appeared absurd or contradictory".[9] In classical societies, slave and free represented legal statuses connected with the classification and ranking of people as barbarians and citizens: free status was associated with citizenship, wealth and membership in the community, whereas slavery was imposed on the poor and foreigners who were identified as barbarians.[10] Slavery enjoyed acceptance from philosophers, such as Plato and Aristotle, who regarded it as a "natural" institution.[11] In pre-modern societies, generally speaking, "the salient characteristic of slavery was its antithetical relationship to the normal network of kinship ties of dependency, protection, obligation, and privilege".[12] But in spite of the accumulated evidence demonstrating that the free-unfree opposition is the product of a specific historical moment, the belief in the universality of the slave-free opposition persists. The assumption endures that there is a brute, material

[7] Davis, *The Problem of Slavery*, pp. 30–31.
[8] Orlando Patterson, *Slavery and Social Death* (Cambridge, Mass., 1982).
[9] David Brion Davis, *Slavery and Human Progress* (New York, 1984), p. 15.
[10] Thomas Weidemann, *Greek and Roman Slavery* (Baltimore and London, 1981), pp. 15–31 *passim*.
[11] Robert Schlaifer, "Greek Theories of Slavery from Homer to Aristotle", in M.I. Finley (ed.), *Slavery in Classical Antiquity: Views and Controversies* (New York, 1960).
[12] Davis, *Slavery and Human Progress*, pp. 15–16. Here it is worth mentioning the well-known argument of Suzanne Miers and Igor Kopytoff that in African societies the opposite of slavery was not freedom but "belonging". See their "African 'Slavery' as an Institution of Marginality", in Suzanne Miers and Igor Kopytoff (eds), *Slavery in Africa: Historical and Anthropological Perspectives* (Madison, 1977).

level at which unfreedom transcends history; that there is a *"de facto"* level at which unfree labour can be identified independent of its historical configuration.[13]

The universalization of capital's historical definition of servitude as a system of restraints, as the denial of a prior human essence, has a colonial genealogy. For it was through colonialism that capital constituted irreducibly different forms of social relations as its Other. As the history of *kamias* in colonial India demonstrates, it was British rule that universalized capital by reconstituting a range of unequal relations of dependence as unfreedom. To the extent that these social relations of dependence – by no means egalitarian or non-exploitative – were defined as unfree, they came to embody India's otherness and served to authorize colonial rule as a project of reform. The establishment of railways, modern industry and education, law and legislation, came to function as technologies of colonial modernity projected to deliver India from its backwardness, from the horror of servitude. The emergence of slavery and bondage in colonial India, therefore, is inseparable from the discourse of modernity.

My essay explores this connection between servitude and freedom in the context of the history of *kamias*, a group of agricultural labourers distinguished by their long-term ties to landlords known as *maliks*. The labourers were drawn from outcastes while the *maliks* belonged to upper castes, although by the late nineteenth century low-caste rich peasants had also begun to employ *kamias*. A *kamia* worked all his life for the same landlord, earning wages for the days he was employed and expecting assistance in times of need. For his son's marriage, he received some grain, money and a small plot of land from the landlord. Following this transaction, called *kamiauti*, the son, too, became the *malik's kamia*. Women also became attached to the same master through the labour relationship of their husbands. These relations were structured as dependent ties that represented the landlord as a munificent patron and the labourer as his dependent subject. This *kamia-malik* relationship, classified as slavery and serfdom initially, was reformulated as debt-bondage after the abolition of slavery in 1843. Advances of grain, money and land became loans, and the *kamias* came to be reported and administered as bonded labourers.

---

[13] Thus Tom Brass, after making the reasonable argument that capitalism is not opposed to unfree labour, ends up endorsing the concept of unfreedom as a condition outside of its historical context of emergence so as to assert the superiority of his self-described Marxist interpretation over the the palpable idealism of my alleged "symptomatically postmodern outside-of-discourse/language-there-is-nothing view". Thus he invokes the notion of *"de facto* unfreedom"*, distinguishing it from the *"ideology* of unfreedom,"* to defend the concept of unfreedom as a form independent of its historical conditions of existence. As a result, Marx gets dragged in to vindicate the representations of capitalism and colonialism through appeals to a supposedly "materialist" notion of unfreedom. See

Slavery and otherness

When the East India Company conquered eastern India in the mid-eighteenth century, its primary aim was to secure its trading and political interests. Thus it saw itself as a neutral force with respect to indigenous traditions that it pledged to respect. But this commitment to uphold traditions meant that these had to be first discovered. Officials made these discoveries as they set out to administer the newly conquered territories. It was thus that the existence of slavery was reported, as was its basis in native laws. Attempts to regulate slavery followed the discovery of the indigenous basis for the suppression of freedom, setting off a process that reconstituted the *kamias* as bonded labourers.

The story of the *kamias*' transformation begins in the late eighteenth century when, following the direction of the Governor-General, Warren Hastings, the Provincial Council at Patna issued a declaration in 1774 stating that the right of masters over their slaves should not extend over a generation.[14] The declaration was directed at slavery in general, and it mentioned two specific forms of servitude – "Moolzadeh" and "Kahaar". The first, according to the Provincial Council, concerned Muslims and referred to the enslavement of enemies defeated and captured in wars. The second referred to the property in a group named and ranked by the Hindu caste system as palanquin bearers. Despite this difference, what mattered was the lack of freedom. Therefore, any variation in the conditions of slavery became intelligible in terms of unfreedom alone. Thus, referring to the "Kahaars", the Council remarked that while they "belong[ed] to one person or another", they were "allowed to intermarry & labour for themselves and at their own discretion, almost as if no bondage existed". The equation of the ability to marry and labour at "their own discretion" with "almost as if no bondage existed" is significant because it suggests the definition of slavery as unfreedom, rendering any deviation from slavery representable only in relation to a state of bondage.

Just as surely as the Company equated slavery with unfreedom, it also attributed the absence of freedom to Indian religions and customs. Important in this process was the interpretation of classical texts by British judges and Orientalist scholars, often one and the same. These interpretive efforts, designed to locate the indigenous basis of slavery in India, entailed reading the discourse of freedom into classical Hindu and Islamic texts. Consider, for example, the Hindu laws on slavery. These were found primarily in Narada's texts, translated in H.T. Colebrooke's *Digest of Hindu Law on Contracts and Successions* (1801).

Brass, "Some Observations on Unfree Labour, Capitalist Restructuring, and Deproletarianization", *International Review of Social History*, 39 (1994), pp. 255–275.
[14] IOL: Bengal Revenue Consultations, 16 August 1774, No. 442, letter from the Provincial Council at Patna to Warren Hastings, dated 4 August 1774. For a more detailed treatment of this process, see Gyan Prakash, *Bonded Histories: Genealogies of Labor Servitude in Colonial India* (Cambridge, 1990), pp. 142–148.

The fifteen categories of "slaves" found in Narada's texts by British scholar-officials and Hindu pundits were actually called *dasas*, whose condition was distinguished by the fact that they were required to perform ritually polluting labour.[15] Basing the classificatory system on the nature of work that people were required to perform, the *dasas* were distinguished from *karmakaras* who were assigned only non-polluting tasks. The colonial discourse of freedom, however, appropriated this mode of classification, reading the identification of different groups by the ritual rank of their assigned work according to the free-unfree divide. Thus interpreted, classical texts were made to speak of *dasas* as unfree persons.

The identification of the source of unfreedom in Indian religions had contradictory implications. On the one hand, the supposedly religious roots of slavery expressed the Indian "temperament". On the other hand, the fact that these laws provided for the enslavement of persons regarded as innately free meant that Indians could not after all escape the application of "natural" laws. Entangled in this contradiction until slavery was abolished in 1843, the British both tolerated what they viewed as religiously-sanctioned slavery and applied laws they considered to be humane and just in areas where Hindu and Muslim laws were silent. As the *Report from the Indian Law Commissioners*, appointed in 1835, revealed, local officials administered Hindu and Muslim laws while also applying principles of equity and justice.[16] This had three important effects: first, they helped create an indigenous "tradition" of slavery as unfreedom; second, by regulating slavery with "just and equitable principles" in order to ensure that slaves were treated kindly, they juridically privileged non-corporeal slavery; and third, their actions created a space for the definition of the *kamias*' condition as "voluntarily entered" bondage, which was then placed in the slave-free continuum.[17]

The operation of these effects was visible in the abolition of slavery. When the government abolished slavery in 1843, it saw itself eliminating practices sanctioned by indigenous religious laws. Now that slavery, a condition marked by the master's power of life and death over the slave's body, was illegal, the stage was set for "voluntarily entered" servitude to receive full judicial focus and appear as debt-bondage.

From *kamias* to bonded labourers

The emergence of "voluntary servitude" based on leases and contracts neatly dovetailed the increasing importance that the transactions of

[15] H.T. Colebrooke, *A Digest of Hindu Law on Contracts and Successions* (Calcutta, 1801), II, pp. 321–340.
[16] *Report from the Indian Law Commissioners* (hereafter *ILC*), 54–55, in Great Britain, Parliamentary Papers, 1841, 28 (262), *Slavery (East Indies)*.
[17] For examples of the regard shown for "voluntarily entered" bondage, see *ILC*, Appendix II, No. 73, pp. 318–320.

money, grain and land acquired in the relationship between landlords and labourers. Although there is no reason to rule out the existence of these transactions in pre-colonial times even if they cannot be documented, the oral traditions of *kamias* do not mention them. In fact, their traditions represent *kamia-malik* ties as a relationship of power between a royal patron and his dependent subjects, suggesting that, while these may have existed in earlier times, they did not bear the entire burden of representing *kamia-malik* relations.[18] During the nineteenth century, however, written records document the growing importance of money, grain and a small plot of land that the *malik* gave his *kamia* on the occasion of his son's marriage. This objectification of labour relations in things formed part of a more general transformation that gathered momentum in the nineteenth century. By this time, the consolidation of private exclusive property ownership in land, the commercialization of agriculture, and the emergence of a land market, facilitated by colonial land tenure and economic policies, had loosened agrarian relations from the grip of social hierarchies. As land became the object through which social groups formed themselves and their relationships, free individuals marked only by their differing property claims replaced hierarchy and graded ranks. These claims were put to work in agriculture, in stabilizing and consolidating landed property, and in integrating agricultural production with the market. These required, however, a control over labour.

If tenurial laws provided a weapon of control over peasants, the figuration of *kamia-malik* relations around transactions of things emerged as the means of dominance over the landless labourers. Singled out as the basis of landlord-labourer relations, the transactions of money, grain and land that had previously functioned as means for reproducing *kamias* and *maliks* as ranked groups now became things with which even low-caste rich peasants could exercise labour control. In fact, the figure of the landlord as a powerful and munificent patron and the labourer as his dependent subject became reified, much like other rights and obligations in the countryside, into instruments of labour control. Both landlords, who strove to expand their directly-cultivated estates, and rich peasants, who sought to prosper while still burdened by rental exactions, seized upon the old shell of dependent ties and forged in it a new system of ordering and controlling *kamias* as unfree labourers through the power of things.[19]

The staging of the growing power of things as debt-bondage, however, was the work of the official discourse. This discourse was not separate from those transformations in the agrarian structure that objectified social relations. The act of describing, documenting, administering and

---

[18] On these oral traditions, see Prakash, *Bonded Histories*, ch. 2.
[19] See *ibid.*, pp. 162–169.

legislating transactions of money as "loans" formed part of a context characterized by the growing importance of ownership, rather than hierarchy, in social relations. In this sense, the official reformulation of *kamiauti* transactions as loans was one element of a discourse that functioned in a range of social spaces, spilling and circulating from one to another. It is this feature that rendered the colonial discourse of freedom powerful and enabled it to exercise a constitutive influence over *kamia-malik* relations.

We can observe the beginnings of the formulation of the discourse of debt-bondage in Francis Buchanan's surveys of 1809–1812 in which the earliest reference to the importance of *kamiauti* transactions occurs. A sprawling account of land and society in several districts of Bihar, Buchanan's reports favoured luxuriant description over frugal classification; he lingered over variations, rather than rushing to draw common patterns. Consequently, even as he drew attention to *kamiauti* transactions, he suggested enormous variation. Writing about the southern part of Bhagalpur district, where he first came across these labourers, he noted that in return for cash advances, *kamias* worked every ploughing season for the landholders and received a small amount of coarse grain as their daily allowance. In Patna and Gaya districts, the *kamias* were sometimes also given, in addition to cash advances, small plots of land. They cultivated these lands with their *maliks'* ploughs, but had to supply seeds themselves and paid half the produce as rent to their masters. These transactions were not new in origin; Buchanan was told that "in some places in the district [Patna-Gaya] [. . .] within the memory of man the price necessary to be advanced to servants [*kamias*] has doubled".[20] He noted, however, that the practice of cash advances was not followed everywhere, and that they did not always demand hereditary servitude.

Such details illustrate Buchanan's attention to diversity and change, and they complicate what his focus on *kamiauti* transactions sought to achieve. For, if the purpose of this focus was to explain the long-term ties between *kamias* and *maliks*, what are we to make of his observation of a considerable variation in the practice of giving advances and in the length of service they commanded? His description suggests that, while in some places advances of money led to hereditary bondage, not everywhere was the *kamia-malik* relationship centred on transactions of objects, nor did money exercise uniform effects. This tacitly questioned his own premise that money caused bondage. His description, militating against its own assumptions, suggested a much more flexible system than the focus on *kamiauti* transactions warranted; it indicated that the objectification of the labour relationship was far from a complete process

---

[20] Francis Buchanan, *An Account of the Districts of Bihar and Patna in 1811–12* (Patna, [1936]), II, p. 556. For Bhagalpur, see his *An Account of the District of Bhagalpur in 1810–11* (Patna, 1939), p. 46.

in the early nineteenth century. Rather than money exercising an inherent and uniform power, the *kamia-malik* relationship was negotiable.

Later, official accounts suppressed such ambiguities. Thus, reading Buchanan's work in 1841 in the light of an overriding concern with slavery, the *Report from the Indian Law Commissioners* distorted his nuanced descriptions of *kamias* to fit the straitjacket of the free-unfree opposition. Describing the *kamias* under a section entitled "Conditional Slavery and Bondage", this report used Buchanan's reports, available in manuscript and in Montgomery Martin's haphazardly edited *History, Antiquities, Topography, and Statistics of Eastern India* (1838), to define them as "conditional slaves".[21] It attributed the *kamias'* "unfreedom" to their "debts", and understood variations in the relationship described by Buchanan as differences in the length of servitude.

Interestingly, it did not escape the notice of some officials that the emergence of "voluntary servitude" based on "loans" was related to the general impression that, with the sale and import of slaves prohibited, servitude provided by leases was still legal. Thus, even before the abolition of slavery in 1843, landlords had begun representing their relations with labourers as conditional leases based on loan transactions because government rules and court decisions had sent a signal to Indians that contractual servitude was legitimate. Judges ruled to enforce lease deeds stipulating that labourers serve their employers for ninety years as provided in their contracts because such transactions conformed to English laws on contractual obligations.[22] Undoubtedly, such rulings signalled to the landlords the value that courts placed on contracts, and they took to executing creditor-debtor deeds to legitimize the *kamia-malik* relationship and to use it as an instrument against their labourers.

If a poor man when in debt objects to write a bond binding himself to slavery, the creditor prosecutes him in our courts; and as the claim has always some foundation although the amount is often exaggerated, finds no difficulty in getting a decree in his favour, after which the threat of imprisonment in execution of the decree speedily compels the unfortunate debtor to agree to the terms required, and he executes the bond.

After 1843, once slavery was outlawed, *kamia-malik* disputes were frequently represented and brought before the courts as creditor-debtor disagreements.[23] The landlords entered contract deeds on stamped legal paper and produced them in the court "with the more confident air as if they were perfectly certain of being upheld".[24] Lower courts frequently ruled to enforce these contracts. In fact, one magistrate even issued a

[21] *ILC*, pp. 44–47.
[22] *Ibid.*, p. 14; Appendix II, No. 75, p. 322.
[23] Government of Bengal, *Bengal Zillah Court Decisions, Lower Provinces* (Annual Series), 1854, p. 57; 1856, pp. 1–2.
[24] IOL: Bengal Judicial Proceedings, 17 March 1859, No. 290.

general order in 1855 instructing labourers to honour their contracts and asking the railway officials to dismiss those workers whom the landlords claimed as their *kamias*.[25] Such practices authorized and enforced the constitution of *kamiauti* transactions as loans and the labour relationship as debt-bondage.

Just as the fiction of loans centred the *kamias'* obligation to serve on the magical power of money, the functioning of the British land tenure regulations objectified labour relations. This objectification formed part of a general transformation of agrarian relationships, and its origin reaches back to the eighteenth century when the reification of land rights emerged as a powerful tendency. British rule reinforced and extended this tendency as its land tenure policies yoked social hierarchy to control over land. Over the nineteenth century, as the legal and institutional foundation established by the British combined with the extension of markets to render land rights transferable, the acquisition and exercise of land rights, rather than direct claims over people, became the basis of unequal agrarian relations. Much like money, land came to be seen as an object endowed with power, with an intrinsic force capable of anchoring and ordering social relations.

The objectification of social relationships in land surfaced with powerful effects on *kamia-malik* relations during partition disputes. The main quarrel in such disputes, as a report from 1886–1887 stated, was over the *kamias'* homesteads. Rival landed claimants asserted that the repudiation of ownership over these homesteads denied them their share of the *kamias*. Confronted with these disputes, the officers devoted "much labour and misplaced ingenuity in giving each shareholder his fair share of serfs", succeeding in enforcing the power of land to bind labourers to landlords.[26] However misplaced, such efforts succeeded in enforcing the power of land to bind the labourers to landlords. So, three decades later, when another report noted disputes over homesteads, it described the claim over the *kamia* through land control as an accomplished fact.[27] Accordingly, this report described the meticulous attention revenue officials paid in recording rival claims and settling disputes, reflecting the prevailing assumption that land control was the key to labour control.

With slavery abolished and agrarian relations objectified in land, the *kamias* and *maliks* constituted their relations in terms authorized and enforced by the colonial administration. When colonial officials, in turn, encountered the *kamias* as bonded labourers, they were unable to see their own role in shaping the relationship they described. To them, the labourers' bondage and its foundation in the power of things appeared

---

[25] *Ibid.*, 27 September 1855, Nos 62–63.
[26] IOL: Bengal General Department Proceedings (Miscellaneous), November 1887, File 153 and 1/2, "Annual General Report, Patna Division; 1886–87".
[27] Government of Bihar and Orissa, *Final Report on the Survey and Settlement Operations in the District of Gaya, 1911–18* (Patna, 1928), p. 64.

as transparent as the natural right to freedom. Thus, by the 1870s, hereditary debt-bondage, in contrast to Buchanan's early nineteenth-century descriptions, had reportedly become the general form.[28] As a description from 1906 stated:

there is a section of the community known as *kamiyas*, i.e., labourers who sell themselves to a master and whose position is that of mere serfs [. . .] Formerly the *kamiya* used to sell both himself and his heirs into bondage for a lump sum down; now this practice having been declared illegal, he now hires himself, in consideration of an advance or loan to serve for 100 years or more till the money is repaid.[29]

While the conviction grew that the *kamias* were debt-serfs, these "loans" were peculiar in so far as they neither accrued interest nor demanded repayment. The landlords secured long-term domination, as the two specimens of *kamiauti* bonds included in the appendix (see p. 24) suggest, by rendering the repayment of the loan impossible. Thus, the first agreement, recorded in 1855, specified a considerably greater sum than the Rs. 25 cash advance as its repayment; in addition to paying Rs. 100, the *kamia* agreed to hand over the produce generated by the working of one plough on cash-rent (*nakdi*) and produce-rent (*bhaoli*) lands. The second agreement, too, specified impossible conditions for the repayment of the "loan" by stipulating that it be repaid in June, a time of the year when funds were particularly low. Such stipulations were aimed at precluding the possibility of the "loan's" repayment, and available records indicate that neither did the landlords attempt to secure repayment, nor did the labourers try to settle their accounts. These transactions used the language of loans to represent long-term dependent ties as creditor-debtor relationship, but their object was labour control, not usury. They used the fiction of loans to establish the landlords' control over the labourers, to secure the labourer's agreement to "willingly and voluntarily" bind himself to plough the lands of the landlord, to "assist the agriculturist", to perform, along with his wife, "all the work of a *kamia* in agricultural operations". Labourers were to be paid wages, not work in lieu of interests on the "loan". The question of "interest" was ordinarily suspended, and posed only, as it was in the second agreement, if the labourer wished to dissolve the relationship. Furthermore, even though the *kamia* never repaid the "loan" and remained forever "indebted", he received a fresh "loan"

[28] Thus a report from the 1870s concluded that the "half-enslaved *kamia* form the landless day-labourers of these parts. For the sake of a few rupees, a man will bind himself and his family to work for a year, on the understanding that [. . .] the debts of the father do not cease with his death, but are inherited by the son. Thousands of these debts are never paid, and the landlord claims for generations the work of his dependents." Cited in W.W. Hunter, *A Statistical Account of Bengal* (London, 1877; rpt. Delhi, 1976), XII, p. 72.
[29] L.S.S. O'Malley, *Bengal District Gazetteers: Gaya* (Calcutta, 1906), p. 153.

when his son was to be married. *Kamiauti* transactions were, therefore, "loans" which were never expected to be repaid by either side, which never accrued interest either in money or labour because the labourers received wages for their work.

How could the "loan" be a fiction and yet secure bondage? The explanation for such a mode of functioning of "loans" can be found in what Marx identified as the fetishism of commodities which represents the relations between people as relations between things. To be sure, whereas commodity fetishism refers to free market exchange, debt-bondage restrains it. But the power that the notion of debt-bondage attributes to money both naturalizes free labour and invests inanimate objects with a capacity to order social relations. The juridical representation of *kamia-malik* ties as debt-bondage, therefore, performed an important function: it advanced the rule of capital, naturalizing free exchange and manifesting the power of things, while simultaneously permitting the appropriation of irreducibly different social relations as unfreedom. Thus, to the extent that things advanced to the *kamias* anchored social relations, the labourers confronted a power contained in the very intrinsic property of the thing. Their congealed labour – contained in the products appropriated by the landlords and advanced as loans – appeared as things animated with a power derived from within. On the other hand, because these things were not exchanged for other objects – the *kamia* labour did not constitute a repayment of loans – the *kamia-malik* relations did not appear as the relation of things exchanged in the market. When treated as loans, the money advanced to the *kamias* appeared to be permanently unrequited; once advanced, its constant presence rendered any further payment from the landlord representable as generous support from a munificent patron rather than as payment of wages. The labourer's daily work on the fields, for which he received wages, could not count as partial payment of his liabilities because this would have eventually terminated the relationship. Thus, the functioning of *kamia-malik* relations as dependent ties was written into the juridical constitution of these relations as debt-bondage. Constituted in this manner, the effect of concluding debt-agreements was to give landlords long-term control over labour. Through such an operation, capital invaded the countryside and, utilizing the power of money, it secured control over dependent labour ties, appropriating them as debt-bondage, as an unfreedom that belonged to another time, another place.

Convinced of the otherness of debt-bondage, and confronted with the mounting evidence of servitude, the government proceeded to enact a new law in 1920. Called the Bihar and Orissa Kamiauti Agreement Act, this legislation stated that one year's labour was to be considered adequate for the repayment of the principal and interest. Therefore, all labour engagements of longer duration were illegal.[30] While designed to abolish the *kamia*'s bondage, it accomplished very little. This failure convinced the British that bondage was so deeply rooted in India that no law could change it. Any change in the *kamias'* position, the British concluded, was "primarily a question of psychology".[31] This evoked the nineteenth-century beginnings of the colonial complicity in the constitution of the *kamias*. Then, British officials and Orientalists had attributed slavery to Indian otherness, to its religious customs and laws. Now, too, they believed that the absence of freedom was to be explained by the otherness of the *kamias* – by their lack of desire for freedom. But this was no simple return to an earlier time because much had changed since then. The indigenous religious basis of slavery had been constructed and suppressed; and the *kamias* had acquired a half-enslaved status when, after the abolition of slavery, contractual bonds centring on things placed them in a continuum extending from freedom to slavery. Shaping, and shaped by, these transformations since the early nineteenth century, the discourse of freedom was faced with new objects, new contexts. Having released the *kamias* from religious subjectivity and constituted them juridically, the discourse of freedom confronted bondage as a different object for which it had to provide another explanation. If the *kamias* were no longer ruled by religious customs and prescriptions but were constituted by a modern regime of law that defined them as free, then what could account for their enslavement? It was at this point that the discourse of freedom rearticulated its universality by identifying another difference – "the question of psychology". The invocation of cultural difference as an explanation for the persistence of unfreedom preserved the status of free labour as an expression of freedom from power. This manoeuvre allowed power to surface only in slavery and bondage, which was sustained by the *kamias'* lack of desire for freedom. It was in this fashion that colonialism universalized capital, appropriating and placing the *kamias* in a continuum extending from slavery to freedom, and projecting free labour as the modern destiny.

The emergence of capitalism as a global system marks the formation of the modern world since the sixteenth century. This process of capital's universalization, however, entailed the forcible capture, transportation and deployment of labour, asymmetrical patterns of intercontinental migrations, territorial conquests, economic exploitation, racist domina-

---

[30] Government of Bihar and Orissa, Revenue Department (Revenue Department) Proceedings, November 1919, Nos 6–10.
[31] Government of Bihar, Revenue Department (Land Revenue) Proceedings, July 1941, Nos 1–4.

tion, and political, social and cultural oppressions organized by colonial and imperial systems under Euro-American dominance. Instituted by territorial conquests and political domination, the universalization of capital entailed its displacement in the irreducibly different social relations, political structures and cultural forms it confronted and was forced to inhabit. Inseparably connected to historical forms within which it arose and functioned, the rule of commodities and markets took shape in and profited from structures ranging from peasant production to plantation slavery, though it represented them as its opposite. In this sense, the history of unfreedom is the history of capital in disguise.

The history of the *kamias'* transformation into bonded labourers bears witness to the complicity of capital in the emergence of debt-bondage. What mediated this complicity in India, however, was colonialism. For it was the colonial discourse and transformations generated by British rule that reconstituted a range of dependent ties in the inverse image of free labour. Although the free-unfree opposition formed part of the bourgeois political economy, British administrative and judicial practices were critical in identifying dependent social ties as slavery and in "discovering" Indian otherness as the basis for the suppression of natural freedom. Although the British regarded slavery as synonymous with unfreedom, they did not abolish it until 1843 because they were pledged to protect "traditions". They did, however, regulate its operation by applying principles of "equity" and "justice". In this process, a space was opened for "voluntarily entered" servitude based on contracts and leases. It was this space in which *kamia-malik* relations were placed after the abolition of slavery. Colonial officials defined advances of grain and money, and grants of land by landlords to labourers as contractual transactions requiring the *kamias* to work for their masters. As the state gave its stamp of approval to contracts stipulating lifelong and even hereditary labour service – adjudicating *kamia-malik* disputes as debtor-creditor disagreements – landlords took to representing their ties with labourers as contracts founded on advances of loans. The objectification of social relations contributed to this process. As this objectification gathered increasing force by the late nineteenth century, founding social relations in transactions of things, the official discourse constituted these transactions as loans and the *kamia* as an indebted serf. The *kamia* became an innately free person enslaved by debt. The moment of his emergence as a free person, however, was punctuated by his reconstitution as a person with suspended rights. The discourse of freedom represented him as a "half-enslaved" labourer whose servitude persisted in spite of the introduction of railways.

To recognize in the history of unfreedom in colonial India the history of free labour in disguise is to question the absolute separation maintained between the two, and to dismantle the opposition between the history of free labour in the West and unfree labour in the non-West.

As old as the discourse of freedom, the vitality of this opposition is visible in scholarship. There exists a long-standing scholarly separation between those who study slavery and those who study freedom. While the former tend to place social relations contemporaneous with free labour alongside ancient and medieval servitude, the latter treat the history of free labour as autonomous and self-contained, denying the coevalness and the intertwined history of freedom and unfreedom. This pattern normalizes free labour, and places the burden of explanation on servitude. Slavery and bondage have to explain themselves, not free labour because it is represented as a natural condition denied only in less enlightened times and places. Not surprisingly, comparative studies group together colonial servitude in Asia, Africa and the Americas with medieval serfdom and ancient slavery in order to develop analytic insights and concepts. Seldom do we witness the history of free labour placed in such an odd comparative group because that would undo the discourse of freedom's careful exteriorization of servitude from the life of capital.

This is not to suggest that labour relations defined as unfree and free were ever the same, but that their histories since the sixteenth century are impossible to disentangle. They arose in the course of Western expansion, slavery and colonization, which harnessed together their different conditions of existence and trajectories so violently and irreversibly that they cannot be conceptualized as discrete, autonomous categories. Although the dominant scholarship has tried to treat them as separate, the history of servitude cannot be written without taking into account its functioning as an Other through which the notion of free labour as a self-contained, autonomous domain arose. Because servitude has operated as a constitutive Other of free labour, an exteriorized "inside" of freedom, its history can only be written by unravelling the discourse of freedom.

My interpretation of the history of *kamias* calls for precisely such an undoing of the discourse of freedom. For if servitude in the colonies was the alienated image of metropolitan free labour, if servitude was the form that the capital-labour relationship was compelled to assume in the process of its universalization, then colonial servitude must be included in the account of free labour. Because slavery and bondage contain the displaced history of freedom, the history of unfreedom in the colonies must be written into the history of freedom in the metropole. Such a rewriting of the history of servitude would contribute to the re-narrativization of the dominant narrative that Stuart Hall defines so eloquently in another context as a strategy that "displaces the 'story' of capitalist modernity from its European centring to its dispersed global 'peripheries'; from the transition of feudalism to capitalism (which played such a talismanic role in, for example, Western Marxism) to the formation of the world market, to use shorthand terms for a moment; or rather to new ways of conceptualizing the relationship between these different 'events' – the permeable inside/outside borders of emergent 'global' capitalist modernity".[32]

Appendix

I

Sohan Bhuiyan, resident of mauza Diha, pargana Pahra, in the district of Bihar, do hereby acknowledge to have taken an advance of Rs. 24-14-0 for agreeing to work as a *kamia* and as a menial servant from Jainu Singh, by caste Rajput, of Diha. In this document which I execute, I willingly and voluntarily bind myself to plough on *nakdi* [cash-rent paying] and *bhaoli* [produce-rent paying] lands of Jainu Singh, and to grow cotton, sugar cane, etc., for him, and to work wherever the lands of Jainu Singh may be situated. I and my descendants for ever bind ourselves to be ready to perform any work given to us, and to perform all duties of a menial servant without objection. If at any time I abscond I shall be liable to be brought back before the said Jainu Singh by force and offer no objection, and if I refuse to return or offer resistance I shall be liable to pay the *nakdi* and *bhaoli* produce of one plough and Rs. 100 in cash and then I and my descendants can be released from our obligations. I shall be paid the same diet allowance or wages as is customary in this village and around. If I cause any other work of the aforesaid Jainu Singh to suffer he shall have the authority to administer justice as he thinks proper. For the above this document is executed by way of *Sewaknama* so that it may be of use where occasion requires.

Dated 15 Asarh 1262 [1855]

II

I, Somar Rajwar, son of Geyan Rajwar, of Andherbari, pargana Jarra, district Gaya, am by profession a labourer and a *kamia*. As I have to pay off the debt of Babu Bhikhari Singh of the aforesaid village, to make some clothes and to incur expenditure on food, and which cannot be done without recourse to borrowing, and because nobody gives a loan without my executing a Kamiauti document, I requested Babu Dhanpat Singh, son of Babu Gajadhar Singh, deceased, of village Andherbari, by profession agriculturist and service-holder, to advance a loan of Rs. 13-4-0 on Kamiauti terms and to get a document executed by me on stamped paper. To this the aforesaid Babu agreed. I therefore, of my own free will, have taken a loan of Rs. 13-4-0 (half of which

[32] Stuart Hall, "When was 'the Post-Colonial'? Thinking at the Limit", in Iain Chambers and Lidia Curti (eds), *The Post-Colonial Question: Common Skies, Divided Horizons* (London and New York, 1996), p. 250.

comes to Rs. 6-10-0) from the aforesaid Babu Dhanjpat Singh of the above-mentioned village and have put the money to my personal use. I, therefore, bind myself and execute this document agreeing to assist the agriculturist with my wife in all the work of a *kamia* and in the agricultural operations, e.g. sowing, etc., I shall receive antia, dinopra, and wages as per custom of the village and shall raise no objection. I shall also have to repay the money at a lump in Jeth of the year 1916, when I shall take back the stamped document. And so long as I do not repay the money, I shall always discharge my duties, and if I happen to go away elsewhere I shall pay to the said Babu Dhanpat Singh interest at one anna per rupee per month until the aforesaid loan is paid off. On my failing in this the said Babu Dhanpat Singh shall be entitled to realize the money from any of my properties that he may find, and to this neither I nor my descendants or successors-in-interest shall have any objection. I have therefore executed this document concerning interest to be made use of later on if required. Be it noted that if I have to go elsewhere for a day or two I shall put my son in charge of the said agriculturist as my substitute and the said agriculturist will have authority to take work from my son.

	Rs.	a.	p.
Total	13	4	0
Half of which	6	10	0

Dated 2 August 1914

Source: Final Report on the Survey and Settlement Operations in the District of Gaya, 1911–18, Appendix xxiii.

The Barriers to Proletarianization: Bolivian Mine Labour, 1826–1918

ERICK D. LANGER

Labour history in Latin America has, to a great degree, followed the models set by the rich historiography in Europe and North America. Other than a justifiable concern with the peculiarities in production for export of primary goods, much of the Latin American historiography suggests that the process of labour formation was rather similar to that of the North Atlantic economies, only lagging behind, as did industrialization in this region of the world. However, this was not the case. The export orientation of the mining industry and its peripheral location in the world economy introduced certain modifications not found in the North Atlantic economies. The vagaries of the mining industry, exacerbated by the severe swings in raw material prices, created conditions which hindered proletarianization and modified the consciousness of the mine workers.[1]

Mining was in some ways an exceptional activity, but it shows in sharp relief the peculiarities of Latin American economic development and subsequent differences in the process of labour formation. In mining, labour specialization was especially marked and also levels of capitalization were much higher than in agriculture or virtually any other export activity. After all, mining production involved, even in the nineteenth century, a mix of skilled and unskilled labour, extensive supervision, the use of a considerable amount of machinery and production schedules that mimicked industrial processes.

Unfortunately, relatively little scholarly work has been done on the history of Andean mine labour from the nineteenth century until the recent past. There is a long and distinguished series of works on colonial mine labour in Bolivia, since the mines of Potosí and its environs represented some of the most important output of silver in the world and contributed mightily to financing the Spanish imperial enterprise.[2]

---

[1] Among recent works, Charles Bergquist has taken seriously the export orientation of Latin American economies and its effects on labour formation. See his *Labour in Latin America: Comparative Essays on Chile, Argentina, Venezuela, and Colombia* (Stanford, 1986). For a critique of Western-based models of labour formation, see Dipesh Chakrabarty, *Rethinking Working-Class History: Bengal 1890–1940* (Princeton, 1989).

[2] For colonial mining labour demands, see Peter J. Bakewell, *Miners of the Red Mountain: Indian Labour in Potosí, 1545–1650* (Albuquerque, 1984); Jeffrey A. Cole, *The Potosí Mita, 1573–1700: Compulsory Indian Labour in the Andes* (Stanford, 1985); Enrique Tandeter, *Coercion and Market: Silver Mining in Colonial Potosí, 1692–1826*, trans. Richard Warren (Albuquerque, 1993); and Ann Zulawski, *They Eat From Their Labour: Work and Social Change in Colonial Bolivia* (Pittsburgh, 1995).

International Review of Social History 41 (1996), pp. 27–51

However, most of the studies on the colonial period bear little direct
relevance to the republican period, since the infamous *mita*, a type of
forced mine labour in which Indian communities in a vast region around
the mines participated, ceased to exist after independence. A brief
attempt at revival of the *mita* in the late 1820s in the administration of
Andrés de Santa Cruz, changed to the "voluntary mita", was ineffective.[3]
Nevertheless, the close connection between agriculture and the mining
industry persisted even after the abolition of the *mita*. The heavily
peasant countryside remained the primary labour reserve for the mines
until the twentieth century. While mining in many ways was different
from other export activities, the reliance on the peasant economy for
labour was a general characteristic found throughout many Latin American export economies.

I wish to address three issues that are crucial for understanding the
development of mining labour in the nineteenth century: the level of
mechanization in the mines and its implications for labour; sources of
mine labour in the nineteenth century; and the effects of agrarian
rhythms on mine labour supply. Each one of these issues is central to
how labour conditions changed in Latin America, especially in the
heavily capitalized export sector. Through the examination of these
topics I hope to redefine our understanding of mining labour in nineteenth-century Bolivia, as well as help to categorize the changes of
labour in Latin America in general.

There are three basic problems with the still developing historiography
on Bolivian mining. First, the emphasis has been on the largest and
most efficient mining companies, distorting our understanding of the
levels of mechanization and labour control in the vast majority of
the mines. The take-over of the Bolivian mining industry by a new,
export-oriented elite was a pattern common throughout Latin America
in the second half of the nineteenth century. Whether it be coffee
growers in Central America, cattle ranchers of the Argentine pampas,
or cotton farmers of the northern Peruvian coast, an influx of foreign
capital, a change in government policies towards *laissez-faire* liberalism,
and the willingness of the new elites to supply raw materials to the
burgeoning and industrializing North Atlantic economies, made possible
a vast transformation in production and, thus, in the relations of production.[4] In the case of Bolivia, the new mining elite in the second half of
the nineteenth century went beyond reforming the mining sector to
reorganize rural property relations as well. This became possible as mine
renovations and the finding of new, productive silver veins brought about
a boom lasting from the 1860s into the 1890s. The silver miners gained

---

[3] Antonio Mitre, *Los patriarcas de la plata: Estructura socioeconómica de la minería
boliviana en el siglo XIX* (Lima, 1981), pp. 141–142.
[4] For one of the latest additions to this vast literature, see for example Victor Bulmer-
Thomas, *The Economic History of Latin America Since Independence* (Cambridge, 1994).

Figure 1. Bolivia

political ascendancy by the 1860s, taking over direct political control of the country by the 1880s. One of the most important efforts was the abolition of the Indian communities and the effort to settle frontier lands, an effort to bring market forces into the countryside and make it more responsive to the demands of the mining economy.[5]

[5] The idea that the abolition of Indian communities, what one scholar has called the "First Agrarian Reform", was part of a liberal-inspired plan to foster development of the mining export sector and was first developed by Tristan Platt in *Estado boliviano y ayllu*

One of the distinguishing features of the mining boom in the late nineteenth century throughout Latin America was its high level of mechanization. This was the case in certain mining firms in Bolivia as well, especially as the price of silver began to drop towards the latter part of the century. A principal reason for high silver output in Bolivia in the second half of the nineteenth century was that new owners, with the aid of Chilean and British capital, invested heavily in new machinery, modern transportation networks and production processes. An influx of mining engineers, many from Germany, accelerated this process of modernization. Thus, the German Francke brothers created a new refinement process which improved the amount of mineral recuperated from the ore. Later, the Franckes would become partners in one of the most successful mining companies in Bolivia, Aramayo, Francke and Company, based in Tupiza, in southern Bolivia.[6]

This process of increasing mechanization, while especially marked in the mining industry, was not unique to it. Throughout the nineteenth century Chilean agriculture, for example, was highly mechanized, with Chilean estate owners enamoured with the new machines purchased in Britain and other European countries. Likewise, the purchase of steam engines for the Tucumán sugar refineries in Argentina revolutionized the industry, bringing about a lengthy boom period in sugar production. In Mexico, silver and copper mining also increased, with heavy US investments.[7]

While the new technology was a vast improvement over the colonial methods, the new historiography has overemphasized the modernization of mining technology in the nineteenth century. This is certainly the case for Bolivia. Recently, Tristan Platt has shown that there was a mining boomlet reaching its peak around 1840 in the ancient colonial mines around the city of Potosí. According to Platt, innovations in technology, especially in the processing of ores, made this possible.[8]

andino: Tierra y tributo en el Norte de Potosí (Lima, 1982). Its extension to frontier lands is discussed in Erick D. Langer, *Economic Change and Rural Resistance in Southern Bolivia, 1880–1930* (Stanford, 1989), pp. 21–22.

[6] For an overview of this modernization, see Mitre, *Los patriarcas*, pp. 90–108, 112–137; also Gustavo Rodríguez Ostria, *El socavón y el sindicato: Ensayos históricos sobre los trabajadores mineros siglos XIX–XX* (La Paz, 1991), pp. 36. The Franckes' specific contributions are discussed in Ramiro Condarco Morales, *Aniceto Arce: Artífice de la extensión de la revolución industrial en Bolivia* (La Paz, 1985), pp. 265–268.

[7] For Chile, see Gabriel Salazar Vergara, *Labradores, peones y proletarios: Formación y crisis de la sociedad popular chilena del siglo XIX*, 2nd ed. (Santiago, 1989), pp. 156–172; for Tucumán see Daniel J. Santamaría, *Azúcar y sociedad en el Noroeste argentino* (Buenos Aires, 1986), pp. 9–22; for Mexico, see for example Mark Wasserman, *Capitalists, Caciques, and Revolution: The Native Elite and Foreign Enterprise in Chihuahua, Mexico, 1854–1911* (Chapel Hill, 1984), pp. 71–94.

[8] Mitre, *Los patriarcas*. For the Potosí mining boomlet, see Tristan Platt, "Producción, tecnología y trabajo en la Rivera de Potosí durante la república temprana", Paper presented at the Encuentro Internacional de Historia "El siglo XIX, Bolivia y América Latina", Sucre, 25–29 July 1994.

Platt's study in certain ways is characteristic of the studies on mining, where an emphasis on the industry leaders (a significant but small minority of companies) preponderates. Because of Antonio Mitre's path-breaking study, many have taken the Huanchaca Company, the largest and best-capitalized mining company in nineteenth-century Bolivia, as the model with which to understand silver mining in Bolivia at that time. Huanchaca was the exception rather than the rule. While the company might have produced a large portion of the total silver in late nineteenth-century Bolivia (according to one estimate about 46 per cent of all silver exported in 1882),[9] in terms of technology and thus in the number of labourers employed, it was hardly a typical mining operation. The emphasis on mining technology innovation, which was a relatively exceptional behaviour, also bedevils other studies eager to show Bolivia's technological capabilities in the nineteenth century.[10]

Another problem in studies of Latin American export industries is the emphasis on large enterprises (often foreign-run), because they were efficient enough to leave historians copious documentation. This has distorted our understanding of export industries in general, for the export sectors often consisted of medium or small companies as well. Some might have fitted into the interstices of the export economy, as Florencia Mallon has shown for the mining region of the Central Highlands of Peru, whereas others, such as the coffee estates in Central America, were often run by smallholders.[11]

It is also necessary to take into account regional variations, for they have proved very important. Witness, for example, Friedrich Katz's seminal article on the regional variations of Mexican labour, in which he showed that wages, debt peonage arrangements and labour supply diverged greatly, based on degrees of coercion, competition for labour among different sectors, as well as types of economic development.[12] For Bolivia, mining labour regimes also have a regional dimension. In terms of labour access, it is possible to distinguish four types of mining operations.[13] One was the mining centre located in the high *altiplano*

---

[9] Ernesto Rück, "Bolivia: Su producción actual de plata en 1882, segun cálculo del suscrito", Colección Rück 541, p. 4, Archivo Nacional de Bolivia [hereinafter ANB].

[10] Mitre, *Los patriarcas*. Condarco Morales's study, *Aniceto Arce*, does likewise.

[11] Florencia Mallon, *The Defense of Community in Peru's Central Highlands: Peasant Struggle and Capitalist Transition, 1860–1940* (Princeton, 1983); William Roseberry, Lowell Gudmundson and Mario Samper Kutschbach (eds), *Coffee, Society, and Power in Latin America* (Baltimore, 1995).

[12] Friedrich Katz, "Labour Conditions on Haciendas in Porfirian Mexico: Some Trends and Tendencies", *Hispanic American Historical Review*, 54:1 (1974), pp. 1–47.

[13] As far as I know, there is no serious study of mining in northern Bolivia (in the La Paz district) for the nineteenth century except for Gustavo Rodríguez Ostria, "Vida, trabajo y luchas sociales de los mineros de la serranía Corocoro-Chacarilla", *Historia y Cultura*, 9 (1986), pp. 151–167. This region might provide a different model of labour access about which we have no knowledge at present.

or in extremely high altitudes, where agriculture was non-existent and the Indian communities that surrounded the mines were sparsely populated and consisted essentially of herders. This was the case with the Huanchaca Company, positioned in one of the most infertile regions of the high *altiplano*. The Huanchaca Company has been taken as the model of nineteenth-century silver mining because of the superb study by Antonio Mitre.[14] The second type of mining operation, about which most of the writing on colonial mining has focused, was located near large urban centres founded in colonial times to service these mining districts. The important mining centres were located adjacent to the cities of Potosí and Oruro. The third type, most studied in northern Potosí department (Chayanta), was the mining district located close to Indian communities whose numerous members worked largely in cultivating fields of the high valleys. The fourth type, prevalent in southern Potosí provinces, such as Chichas and Porco, incorporated mines with nearby haciendas. Access to labour and different types of labour available in the different regions determined to a large extent the amount of mechanization of the silver mines, the degree of self-sufficiency of the mines (and thus their costs), as well as the relationship between the countryside and the mining centres. (For a table of all mining companies mentioned, their owners and their relative locations, see Appendix, p. 51.)

Most studies have focused on either the heavily indigenous northern Potosí districts or the *altiplano* type such as the Huanchaca Company. This ignores the southern Bolivian type of mining-agricultural complex, which indeed was in many ways more representative of Latin American export industries. After all, vertical integration, diversity in production, the maintenance of a large labour reserve, were all characteristics of many Latin American export sectors, especially if one takes into account smaller enterprises. In the south, the most important mining enterprises functioned in conjunction with the surrounding countryside, often firmly in the hands of the mining company itself. As we shall see, the problems of labour access (recruited primarily from the peasants on the surrounding haciendas) and of supplying the mines with foodstuffs, fuel and other goods were very different from those mines that were not integrated into an agricultural enterprise.[15]

The third basic problem of the historiography is the idea of progress in the labour force, from poorly organized part-time miner-peasant to a fully conscious proletarianized labour force that, by the mid-twentieth

---

[14] Mitre, *Los patriarcas*.
[15] Only Ramiro Condarco Morales, in his voluminous study of the silver oligarch and Bolivian president Aniceto Arce, notes this type of mixed agricultural-mining enterprise, but does not follow up on the implications for the operation of the mines located within the agricultural estate. See his *Aniceto Arce*, pp. 597–598. Curiously, Condarco discusses the "ecosymbiosis" of Arce's haciendas, but fails to take into account Arce's southern mining possessions. Instead, like Mitre, he concentrates on the Huanchaca Company, an atypical mining enterprise as noted above.

century, constituted one of the most radical and powerful labour movements in the world. While Guillermo Lora, the Trotskyist labour historian, most fully represents this trend, others have borrowed the ideas of
labour development from E.P. Thompson and Eric Hobsbawm to create
a similar progression. This is the case with Gustavo Rodríguez Ostria,
who, while rejecting many of Lora's ideas about the weak political
development of nineteenth-century miners, still accepts the idea that
there was a type of linear development of labour relations from the
paternalistic nineteenth century to the tin mining regimes in the early
twentieth century under which the Bolivian labour movement became
fully politicized.[16] However, recent studies have questioned this progression. Tristan Platt, for example, has shown how mine workers in the
late twentieth century continue to worship earth deities, called the *tío*
(uncle) in the mines. Offerings to the *tío*, such as cigarettes, coca leaves,
and other ritually charged objects are placed at shrines within the mine
shafts, to receive permission to take the earth's bounty. These offerings
take place within a context of a highly capitalized enterprise where,
presumably, the workers themselves are ideologically committed to the
historical materialism of a Trotskyist strain.[17] As Dipesh Chakrabarty
has posited, the use of European models often does not fit realities in
other parts of the world. While the development of labour consciousness
in Bolivia has some similarities to the European case, the class consciousness of the Andean miners melded with strains of powerful religious
beliefs far predating this class consciousness.[18]

Given these problems in the historiography, let us now look in greater
detail at the issues of capitalization and mechanization, access to labour,
and agrarian rhythms with a sensitivity to the four regional variations
about which we know in nineteenth-century Bolivia.

Labour and the mechanization of mines

Mechanization is often a response to labour scarcity. In Latin America,
this has not usually been the case. Instead, employers tried to tie workers

---

[16] Guillermo Lora, *A History of the Bolivian Labour Movement, 1848–1971*, trans. Christine
Whitehead (Cambridge, 1977); E.P. Thompson, *The Making of the English Working Class*
(London, 1966); Eric Hobsbawm and George Rudé, *Captain Swing: A Social History of
the Great English Agricultural Uprising of 1830* (New York, 1975); Rodríguez Ostria, *El
socavon*.
[17] Tristan Platt, "Conciencia andina y conciencia proletaria: Qhuyaruna y ayllu en el
Norte de Potosí", *HISLA: Revista latinoamericana de historia económica y social*, 2 (1983),
pp. 47–73. Platt argues that the *tío* represents old Andean deities rather than what Michael
T. Taussig, in *The Devil and Commodity Fetishism in South America* (Chapel Hill, 1979),
described as a representation of the devil, which for the workers meant a symbol of their
own capitalist exploitation. See also June Nash, *We Eat the Mines and the Mines Eat Us:
Dependency and Exploitation in the Bolivian Tin Mines* (New York, 1979).
[18] Dipesh Chakrabarty, "Postcoloniality and the Artifice of History: Who Speaks for
Indian Pasts?", *Representations*, 37 (1992), pp. 1–26.

to their enterprises through debt or coercive measures, ignoring the modernization of machinery as a solution to this dilemma.[19] Mechanization occurred primarily in activities directly tied to exports, such as mining. Unlike agrarian estates or textile mills, mining enterprises in Latin America had to compete in the world market and remain as efficient as possible. Thus, levels of mechanization remained relatively high, as recent research on mining has shown.[20]

Much has been made of the introduction of machinery in Bolivian mines, as well as the extension of the transportation revolution, through the building of railways, in the second half of the nineteenth century.[21] The impact of railways, however, was more limited than might appear at first glance. The principal beneficiary of the railway between Antofagasta on the Pacific coast and the Bolivian highlands was the Huanchaca Company and its impact was relatively late. It reached Oruro in 1892, just as the silver mining boom reached its close with the financial crisis engendered by the bankruptcy of the Bank of Potosí and the rapid fall of international silver prices. Moreover, the vast majority of silver mines were at no time close enough to the rail lines to benefit effectively from the new transportation network.[22]

This meant that most mining operations depended upon the time-honoured method of moving their products by llama or by mule, both the ore from the mine to the grinding and refining mills, as well as the refined mineral to the coast or, in the last few years of the silver era, to the railhead in Uyuni. As one observer noted in 1908, "[j]ust as in earlier times, the transport of minerals from these mines is done exclusively by llamas or mules, which constitutes a great inconvenience for the miners".[23] Moreover, the mines depended upon animal transport to supply them with important inputs into the mining operations, such as salt, wood, foodstuffs and fuel. Tristan Platt has shown how in the 1840s the mines in the south-western corner of the country (in the first type of region, the high *altiplano*), depended upon the Indian community members of López province to transport with their extensive llama herds the minerals and supplies such as salt and fuel required by

[19] There is a vast literature on this topic for rural estates in Latin America. See for example Magnus Mörner, "The Spanish-American Hacienda: A Survey of Recent Research and Debate", *Hispanic American Historical Review*, 53:2 (1973), pp. 183–216 and Eric Van Young, "Mexican Rural History since Chevalier: The Historiography of the Colonial Hacienda", *Latin American Research Review*, 18:3 (1983), pp. 5–61. For *obrajes*, the textile mills, see for example Alberto Flores Galindo, *Arequipa y el sur andino, siglos XVIII–XX* (Lima, 1997), pp. 36–44.
[20] Mitre, *Los patriarcas*; also see Manuel Contreras, *Tecnología moderna en los Andes: Minería e ingeniería en el siglo XX* (La Paz, 1994) and Alberto Flores Galindo, *Los mineros de la Cerro de Pasco, 1900–1930* (Lima, 1974).
[21] See especially Mitre, *Los patriarcas* and Condarco, *Aniceto Arce*.
[22] See Langer, *Economic Change*, pp. 25–29.
[23] William van Brabant, *La Bolivie* (Paris, 1908), pp. 272.

the mines.[24] Transportation costs were a high proportion of total mining costs, and the number of individuals employed in this task was relatively large. In the case of the Guadalupe Company, the third largest silver mining company in the country, in 1888 just the cost of taking the ore from the mine head to the refining plants, the *ingenios* nearby, cost 27.57 Bolivianos [Bs] per box [*cajón*] of metal, or about 10 per cent, out of a total of 292.06 Bs per box in total expenses. While some authors have made much about the fact that mine owners introduced carts to bring the ore to the *ingenio*, freeing themselves from the expense of the llama drivers, this does not appear to have been the case here. That year, the Guadalupe Company paid llama drivers 17,398 Bs for their services, while expending 4,806 Bs for the carts and draft animals.[25]

These costs did not include the transportation of the silver to the rail line that at this time was approaching Uyuni. Once the railhead arrived in the *altiplano* town, all mine owners other than those of the Huanchaca Company still had to hire pack animals to take the metal bars to the railway. This entailed significant costs as well as a large number of pack animals. Only the Colquechaca Company, the largest mining operation in northern Potosí, in 1890 needed 2,000 to 3,000 llamas monthly to transport its metals to Uyuni. This was a large number of pack animals, if one multiplies that several times to include the demands of the smaller companies that proliferated throughout the region. Although in some cases the companies employed mules which could take a larger burden, competition for the pack animals and the greater expense of mules over llamas made the companies prefer the latter animals over the former.[26]

In addition to problems with utilizing the railways, mechanization lagged in significant aspects in most mining enterprises. Few Bolivian

[24] Tristan Platt, "Calendarios tributarios e intervención mercantil. La articulación estacional de los ayllus de Lípez con el mercado minero potosino (siglo XIX)", in Olivia Harris, Brooke Larson and Enrique Tandeter (eds), *La participación indígena en los mercados surandinos: Estrategias y reproducción social. Siglos XVI a XX*, (La Paz, 1987) pp. 502–516.

[25] Compañía Guadalupe de Bolivia, *Memoria presentada a la Junta General de Accionistas* (Sucre, 1889), pp. 12, 10, Be 162, XIII, Biblioteca Nacional de Bolivia [hereinafter BNB]. For the argument that carts diminished the dependence on llama drivers, see Gustavo Rodríguez Ostria, "Los mineros: Su proceso de formación (1825–1927)", *Historia y Cultura*, 15 (1989), p. 89 and Rodríguez Ostria, *El socavón*, p. 36.

[26] For the needs of Colquechaca Company, consult Lucio Leiton to Jacobo Aillon, Potosí, 15 January 1890, "Copiador Cartas Abel Vacaflores 1889. Libro No. 2", Fondo Vacaflores, Archivo de la Sociedad Agrícola, Ganadera é Industrial de Cinti (La Paz) [hereinafter FV]. I have estimated that a llama can carry one *quintal*, or about 100 pounds. For competition over pack animals, see Leiton to Justino H. Balderrama, Potosí, 21 January 1890; Leiton to Guillermo Leiton, Potosí, 25 February 1890; Leiton to Balderrama, 25 February 1890, *ibid*. The use of llamas and mules and the cost of the latter is documented in Leiton to Néstor Villa, 29 January 1890; Leiton to Sr Prsdte de la Ca Aullagas, 1 February 1890; and Leiton to G. Leiton, 18 March 1890, all *ibid*.

mining companies actually had the wherewithal to adopt new machinery
into the productive process other than the most highly capitalized, but
exceptional companies studied most intensively by scholars. In addition
to the Huanchaca Company, the Colquechaca and Guadalupe companies
attained a certain level of mechanization. Whereas the Guadalupe company owned five steam motors with a combined power of 120 hp in 1889
(two of which were out of service), this was an unusually well-mechanized
operation.[27]

Moreover, the records at our disposal often make historians concentrate on only a particular phase of mining production in which mechanization was most likely.[28] The long period of exploration for a productive
vein, during which the company employed the most primitive type of
technology, has been largely ignored. Exploration in the nineteenth
century entailed getting men to hack away at the earth with pickaxes,
with the occasional use of black powder and later, dynamite. If the
records of Compañía Consolidada de Colquechaca (a smaller successor
to the Colquechaca Company discussed above) from the early twentieth
century might be used to indicate nineteenth-century patterns, independent contractors performed much of the exploration work. These independent contractors owned few tools – they often borrowed the mining
companies' shovels, picks and wheelbarrows – and took part of their
pay in the ore they came across while digging the shaft. This was the
case with the Andacaba Company as well, where in 1887 the administrator hired four Italian contractors to dig the shafts to the main vein
of silver ore. This payment in kind was similar to the *kajcha* arrangements
in the colonial period, where workers took the richest ore to supplement
their meagre wages. In other words, at least in the exploration phase,
when mine owners had little or no income to offset expenses, colonial-
type relations continued to persist in nineteenth-century mining.[29]

---

[27] Compañía Guadalupe de Bolivia, *Memoria (1889)*, pp. 12–13. Gabriel Salazar makes a
similar point for Chilean mining operations. See his *Labradores*, pp. 214–216.

[28] All studies thus far for the nineteenth century are almost exclusively based on the
mining companies' annual reports. There are several problems with this type of source.
First of all, the annual reports, printed in neat folios and often with extensive ornamenta-
tion, privilege those companies that were wealthiest and most highly capitalized. Reports
come into existence usually only when significant progress had already been made and
the company produced some kind of ore. Secondly, the company reports, which were not
only reports to stockholders but also pieces of propaganda to lure new investors, as in
stock reports today, tended to emphasize the high technology employed and the successes.
Only with the weekly reports written by the mine administrators to company headquarters
is it possible to get a real sense of how these companies worked.

[29] For a revealing look at issues facing a mining company in the exploration phase, see
"Cartas Copiadores, Cía Colquechaca, Sep. 30, 1907 a Nov. 1913". For example, in
September 1912 the company paid 865 Bs to contractors and only 266.90 Bs for wages.
Only 9 Bs were used for materials, out of a total of 1147.80 Bs total expenditures. See
ff. 546–547. For the Andacaba Company, see Libro No. 3, f. 87, Fondo Aniceto Arce,

In contrast to the heavily capitalized Huanchaca Company, the administrator's reports show a different picture for the much smaller Andacaba operation, certainly more typical of nineteenth-century mining operations than the former. At the height of mining activity, between 29 October and 4 November 1888, the Andacaba Company employed 80 individuals working on four different shafts. In addition to the administrator and his servant, a blacksmith and five carpenters, the company employed 28 *barreteros*, miners who dug into the walls and extracted the ore, nine peons and nine *palliras*, women who broke up and sorted the ore according to its quality. To transport the ore from the depths of the mine to the surface was the task of six *carreros*, men who handled the animal-driven carts, as well as 20 *chasquiris*, who stood in line to hand sacks of mineral or perhaps water buckets to drain the mine from one to the next. Soon afterwards, the company added a contingent of *torneros*, by March 1889 eighteen men, who were responsible for turning a large wheel in the mine rigged to pull sacks of mineral or buckets of water out of the mine shafts. By March 1890, the height of production with 125 labourers (40 of whom were *barreteros*), the lack of machinery was even more noticeable. Only three *carreros* were left, while the number of men pumping increased and those carrying buckets jumped to 35.[30] The distribution of jobs, which shows the high proportion of men occupied in the backbreaking labour of simply hauling bags of ore, pumping water by hand, or carrying buckets of water, shows the lack of mechanization in a mine owned by one of the most forward-looking miners of the silver era.

Labour remained by far the largest expenditure for most mining companies. Typical in this respect are the accounts for Andacaba in July 1888 when the company spent 617.29 Bs on materials, whereas 1,256.76 Bs went on labour.[31] In other words, mining costs broke down to 67 per cent for labour and only 33 per cent for materials. In Guadalupe, where, as noted above, operations were relatively mechanized, in 1889 labour costs constituted 87 per cent of the costs of producing silver. By 1895 the Guadalupe had reduced the percentage attributable to labour down to 43 per cent.[32] This was in stark contrast to mining costs in the Huanchaca Company, where according to Antonio Mitre labour

ANB [hereinafter FAA]. For an excellent treatment of nineteenth-century *kajchas*, see Gustavo Rodríguez Ostria, "Kajchas, trapicheros y ladrones de mineral", *Siglo XIX: Revista de Historia*, 8 (1989), pp. 125–139.

[30] See Libro No. 3, ff. 227, 261, 371, FAA. For definitions of the various occupations, see Frédrique Langue and Carmen Salazar-Soler, *Diccionario de términos mineros para la América española (siglos XVI-XIX)* (Paris, 1993).

[31] Libro No. 3, ff. 192, 196, FAA.

[32] Compañía Guadalupe de Bolivia, *Memoria (1889)*, p. 11; *Memoria presentada á la Junta General de Accionistas* (Sucre, 1896), p. 45, Bd 253, BNB.

represented 23 per cent of total costs for extracting the ore from the mine in Pulacayo.[33]

Similar patterns existed throughout Latin America, as in the second half of the nineteenth century increasing mechanization brought down labour costs. Virtually all activities, and especially agriculture, saw employers cutting labour costs. In the case of Chile, mechanization in the countryside was accompanied by a shift from permanent labourers to hiring mostly day labourers. This also led to an increasing number of peons migrating to the mines in the north of the country, where low wages created high mobility rates among workers too.[34]

Access to labour

Providing enough labourers for working the mines had been a problem since colonial times. The colonial state utilized forced labour recruited from a wide swath of the Andes, though there were important exceptions, such as the flourishing silver mines in Oruro, just north of Potosí.[35] In the republican period it proved impossible to reinstitute the *mita*, and thus miners had to try different methods. First, much of the silver produced came not from production by the owners, but by independent contractors, called *kajchas*, whose activities frequently shaded into outright robbery of ores.[36] In 1827 *kajchas* contributed about half of all output; by 1850 these contractors still provided a third of all silver production. *Kajcha* production tapered off in the following decades, only to arise again very briefly in the last few years of the nineteenth century when silver mining entered into crisis before being replaced by tin.[37]

The use of independent contractors (and thus the possibility of mineral theft) was virtually inevitable, however, given the demands of the initial phases of mining production. In the exploration phase of the mining process, when mine owners nervously analysed the earth they cut through for signs of ore, the administrators kept costs as low as possible and hired as few men as possible. As soon as a vein tapered off into less valuable minerals, they again laid off workers to conserve resources. This was the case with the Andacaba operation, where in April 1887 the mine occupied only 30 workers to cut a shaft to the principal vein and clean out air ducts (*chimineas*). Where metal was found in the *chimineas*, a few *palliris* – seven out of the total – sorted out the best

---

[33] Mitre, *Los patriarcas*, p. 154. With such a divergence in figures, it is likely that Mitre's calculations factor in additional costs which the other records do not reveal, but still the difference must have been significant.

[34] Salazar, *Labradores*, pp. 216–219.

[35] Zulawski, *They Eat from the Mines*.

[36] Rodríguez Ostria, "Kajchas, trapicheros"; also see Mitre, *Los patriarcas*, pp. 138–145.

[37] *Ibid.*, p. 145; Rodríguez Ostria, "Kajchas, trapicheros"; idem, *El socavon*, pp. 47–49.

pieces for processing. In contrast, by May 1890 the mine was producing in full swing, employing over a hundred workers, with fourteen *palliris*.[38]

It is necessary to distinguish between short-term swings in labour demand and supply as well as long-term trends, such as the increase in labour supply in the second half of the nineteenth century. Regional variations and differential levels of capitalization must be taken into account too. The highly capitalized Huanchaca Company hired fewer labourers because of mechanization, especially since the surrounding countryside was largely devoid of human habitation. In turn, the late nineteenth-century growth of towns in the northern Potosí mining district made it less necessary to depend on the surrounding Indian communities whose economy remained resolutely oriented towards agrarian subsistence. Nevertheless, during the nineteenth and even early twentieth centuries the distinction between town and country was not that great, for town residents usually had their own plots of land somewhere or worked that of their extended families. After all, the vagaries of the mining cycle might at any time bring about the loss of their job; keeping their options open by returning to the fields when jobs disappeared could keep their families alive. Only in the mining regions next to a major city such as Potosí or Oruro was it possible to survive in an urban occupation while waiting for the mines to hire again. Perhaps more importantly, the cyclical nature of international mineral prices and Bolivia's dependence on international economic forces forced the mine labour force not to proletarianize completely lest they starve when the mines went into cyclical decline.

Not only mine labourers, but many important mining companies also tried to hedge their bets when playing in the export market, where they had no real control over prices. One important way was to combine landed estates with mines. This was a common strategy throughout Latin America, where vertical integration took some of the risks out of a poorly developed infrastructure. For example, Warren Dean, in his book on the industrialization of São Paulo, shows how large enterprises engaged in these kinds of practices.[39] The largest mining enterprise in southern Bolivia, the Guadalupe Mining Company, used such an approach. It owned the haciendas of Oploca and Salo to the north of Tupiza, a silver refinery in Guadalupe, and mines in nearby Tatasi, Chocaya and Guadalupe. Altogether, the company owned almost 25,000 square miles of land, most of it rocky and mountainous, but with some prime agricultural lands suitable for growing fodder and other crops tucked into the lower valleys. In 1892 the estates of Oploca and Salo had 2,915 peons living on the land, of which 987 were adult men and 947 were adult women. These peons owned 17,966 llamas and 4,384

---

[38] Libro No. 3, ff. 9, 459, FAA.
[39] Warren Dean, *The Industrialization of São Paulo, 1880–1945* (Austin, 1969).

donkeys for transporting ore, salt, fodder and fuel for the company.[40] It was a combination that Aniceto Arce, principal shareholder of Huanchaca and one of the most progressive silver miners, utilized, purchasing the estates that had made up the old Condado de Oploca, a vast landholding in southern Bolivia. Arce's friend and political rival, Gregorio Pacheco, in the 1880s purchased Arce's stock to become the largest shareholder in this agro-mining enterprise. Aniceto Arce apparently did not abandon the model of combining agricultural estates with mining, because in 1889 he used the peons from his newly purchased hacienda of La Lava (south of Potosí city) to work in the silver mines of his Andacaba Company.[41] It is likely that other mining concerns also attached agricultural estates to their companies at the end of the nineteenth century, but our lack of knowledge about the workings of the vast majority of nineteenth-century mining companies prevents us from quantifying this trend.

There were many advantages to combining large landholdings with mining enterprises. The haciendas produced income from agriculture that were independent of the vagaries of the mining cycle, and thus propped up the mining portion in times of low production. This was the case for the Guadalupe Company, which in 1888 lost 74,371.04 Bs in mining operations. In turn, the haciendas attached to Guadalupe Company earned 36,486.99 Bs which, combined with other earnings, diminished total losses to 28,525.22 Bs. Earnings from the haciendas came primarily from the sale of fodder crops and rents paid by the hacienda peons for their plots. The company also used many of the products produced on demesne lands for the mines, such as a portion of the fodder, as well as to stock the company stores with foodstuffs.[42]

The estates also provided the mine owners with other services from the landholdings' large service tenantry. All estates in highland Bolivia (as well as elsewhere in the Andes) maintained a peonage arrangement in which resident workers were obligated to pay for their access to lands through a combination of rental payments in cash, in kind (such as providing wood for fuel, a small portion of their livestock, eggs, etc.), as well as a certain number of days of labour and transportation of

[40] Compañía Guadalupe de Bolivia, *Memoria (1889)*. Guadalupe was the third largest silver mining company in the country in the late nineteenth century. See Rück, "Bolivia", Colección Rück 541, p. 4, BNB. For descriptions of the Guadalupe estates, see Compañía Guadalupe de Bolivia, *Estadística general de las propiedades de la Compañía Guadalpue de Bolivia* (Sucre, 1892), Bd 338, XI, BNB; and William L. Schurz, *Bolivia: A Commercial and Industrial Handbook* (Washington, DC, 1921), p. 131.

[41] Arce's purchase of Oploca is documented in Condarco, *Aniceto Arce*, pp. 597–598. By 1889, Gregorio Pacheco was the majority stockholder, with 2,000 out of 3,000 shares, whereas Arce had no stock at all in the company. See Compañía Guadalupe de Bolivia, *Memoria* (1889), p. 2. References to the use of peons from Hacienda La Lava first appear in Eduardo Vallalba to José Ma. Goitia, 19 July 1889, Libro No. 3, f. 283, FAA.

[42] Compañía Guadalupe de Bolivia, *Memoria (1889)*, pp. 10, 13, 14.

crops to market, for which the landlord had to pay at stipulated, but usually below-market rates.[43]

The mining companies that owned haciendas changed labour obligations from working on the farm to the mines. The haciendas, in essence, presented vast and inexpensive labour reserves for the mining enterprises in boom times. Thus, owning haciendas was advantageous to mining enterprises because the mining company could keep its workers from year to year, but without having to pay them extra during the low points of the mining cycle. After all, the hacienda provided the workers with land (for which they paid rent, another source of income) and absorbed labourers who became relatively skilled at their mining jobs. These workers were theoretically always available, unlike the floating population of the mining towns, where labourers drifted from one mining boom to the next. In the case of the Guadalupe Company, the peons from Hacienda Oploca performed virtually all types of tasks in the mines, from the relatively unskilled jobs of llama drivers, ore carriers, suppliers of fuel to the ovens (*leñadores*), and ore mixers in the mills (*mortiris*), to the more specialized jobs of ore cutters (*barreteros*) and oven operators (*horneros*). For Andacaba, the recent addition of Hacienda La Lava's "Indians" (*indios*), as they were invariably described, for the period for which we have records, did not permit them to be used other than in the most unskilled jobs, such as ore and water carriers, water pumpers and llama drivers.[44] According to Gregorio Pacheco, administrator of Guadalupe in the last decades of the nineteenth century, using peons as miners also had the advantage that the remuneration they received "facilitates the payment of their rents".[45] As a result, the mining companies recouped part of their labour costs through the rental payments the peons had to make to the company for the usufruct of its land.

Moreover, the wages in the mines and the earnings from transporting minerals must have had a profound effect on the economy of the hacienda peons. The sums that this employment pumped into the peasant economy were significant, at times much larger than the rents the peons

[43] For a discussion of the hacienda labour system in nineteenth-century Bolivia, see Langer, *Economic Change*, pp. 54–61.
[44] Gregorio Pacheco, *Compañía Guadalupe de Bolivia: Informe que el Delegado del Directorio de dicha compañía presenta á la Junta General de Accionistas* (Sucre, 1889), p. 7, Be 156, VII, BNB. For Andacaba, see Libro No. 3, ff. 283–434, FAA. Unfortunately, we do not know the percentage of hacienda peons who worked in Guadalupe's mines and refining establishments. The Andacaba Company records, where the relationship between hacienda and mine was more recent, suggest that the proportion of workers was significant, but did not represent the majority. During the period from 16 March to 27 April 1890, the only time-span for which we have this type of documentation, an average of 31 out of 97 workers in the Andacaba mines were hacienda peons from La Lava, or about a third of all workers. It is likely that this was a lower percentage than in Guadalupe, where the relationship between the mines and the landed estates was much more ancient.
[45] Pacheco, *Compañía Guadalupe de Bolivia*, p. 7.

had to pay for the usufruct of hacienda land. For example, while for the Guadalupe Company in 1888 the amount paid out to transport minerals and the amount brought in for rent were roughly equal (17,389 Bs versus 17,590 Bs respectively), in 1896 just for the transport of minerals the company spent 62,643 Bs, whereas the total amount of rent charged was only 16,718 Bs.[46] If one includes the money peons earned as mine workers as well, this must have constituted a significant sum that the mining company pumped into the peons' household economies.

Early in the nineteenth century owners paid a high proportion of wages in kind, not in money. In 1826 and 1827 the mine owners of Cochinoca and Aranzazu paid approximately 60 per cent of their wages in goods, presumably recovering some of their costs in this way.[47] By the late nineteenth century workers still took goods in lieu of wages, but a much smaller percentage. For the seven accounts we have for the payment of La Lava hacienda peons in early 1890, on average workers only received 16 per cent of their wages in merchandise rather than cash.[48] In the case of Guadalupe Company, the administrator in 1888 complained in the annual reports that the company stores were not very well stocked and that they had to buy their merchandise from the nearest city of Tupiza rather than directly from Europe. Nevertheless, he insisted that the store was there to prevent the abusive pricing of outside merchants rather than a means of making more money.[49]

Despite these relatively benevolent practices, labour discipline remained a problem throughout the nineteenth and early twentieth centuries. In part, the blame lay on the hybrid quality of the labour force on these agro-mining enterprises, which was needed both as agriculturists as well as miners. The records of the Andacaba Company show that mine administrators fought continuously to get the number of workers they required from the hacienda. Moreover, many of "the Indians" of La Lava fled when they could, to return to their families and fields. From the beginning, the peons, according to the frustrated Andacaba administrator, left when they felt like it. While they could be charged for the goods they had received from the company store, they did not return to the mines once they had decided to go back to the hacienda.[50] At other times, many of the workers sent from La Lava

---

[46] Compañía Guadalupe de Bolivia, *Memoria (1889)*, pp. 7, 8, 10; *Memoria de 1896*, pp. 11, 35, 36.

[47] William Lofstrom, *Dámaso de Uriburu* (La Paz, 1982), 36–37.

[48] Libro No. 3, ff. 374–375v, 385–386v, 397v–398, 407–408v, 413–414v, 424–425v, 433–434, FAA.

[49] Compañía Guadalupe de Bolivia, *Memoria (1889)*, p. 14; Pacheco, *Compañía Guadalupe de Bolivia*, p. 8.

[50] Libro No. 3, Emilio Benavidez to José Ma Goitia, Andacaba, 19 July 1889, f. 283, FAA.

did not show up or showed up a few days late for work.[51] When they did not receive their *socorros* (their payment in food and goods), many simply abandoned the mines and returned home. Some simply refused to do the most onerous tasks. This was the case in 1890, where the administrator could not prevent the rise of water in the shafts "because the Indians working the pumps decided all to get sick".[52]

It is possible that the problems in labour discipline were attributable at least in part to Hacienda La Lava's recent integration into the mining regime, but it is likely that at least some of these problems persisted even in the Guadalupe Company and other agro-mining enterprises where integration was long-standing. The reason for the lack of discipline was that it was difficult for the companies to enforce their mine labour demands on the hacienda peons. After all, the peons had their own agrarian base which served as their primary means for subsistence. If they invested in livestock, it made them relatively independent of the demands for mine labour, for they could serve in another valuable function, that of transporting the ores. The companies had little incentive to throw peons off the farms, for in a labour-intensive and poorly capitalized agrarian economy the number of workers on a farm was the primary determinant of the properties' worth. A diminished labour force was also not in the interest of the company, for in the agro-mining complex the hacienda peons had to do double duty, that of mine and agricultural labourers. The Guadalupe Company was aware of these problems, even in the 1890s purchasing agricultural machinery to lower costs and, not incidentally, make the hacienda workers more available to work off their labour obligations in the mines.[53] This might have been a successful experiment, but it did not bear fruit as soon afterwards the company ceased production because of the precipitous decline of silver prices in the last years of the nineteenth century.

It is also likely that the mining companies found it very difficult to expand work obligations beyond those that were traditionally required of the peons. As I have shown elsewhere, Andean hacienda workers, in common with many other pre- and proto-industrial workers throughout the world, had an acute sense of what could be required of them and what was customary. In the case of Bolivia and other Andean countries, this was closely tied to the peasants' conceptions of the peculiarly Andean notions of reciprocity. Leadership and legitimacy were tied to the show of redistribution of goods by leaders. Hacienda owners as well as mine owners understood this need to show their largesse, though the creole elites often couched their understanding of reciprocal relations in

[51] See for example Libro No. 3, Indalecio López to Benavidez, Andacaba, 19 and 22 February, and 2 March 1890, ff. 330, 333, 354, FAA.
[52] Libro No. 3, López to Benavides, Andacaba, 2 March 1890, f. 354; López to Mauricio Pidot, Andacaba, 21 March 1890, f. 379, FAA.
[53] Compañía Guadalupe de Bolivia, *Memoria de 1896*, p. 14.

paternalistic terms. During festivals, for example, landlords provided not only food and drink, but also participated in rituals where their workers would come up one by one and kiss the hand of the landlord and present him with a chicken or something similar. In turn, the landlord would provide the worker with a token of his leadership by presenting the latter with a bolt of cloth or perhaps a ready-made shirt.[54] Given the close ties between countryside and mine on the agro-industrial enterprises, this reciprocal symbolism remained strong in the mines as well. We see the importance of these concepts when the employer did not fulfil his obligations. It is likely that, for example, this sentiment was behind the peons' abandonment of the Andacaba mines in early March 1890 because they did not receive their accustomed *socorros*.[55] Custom, such an important ingredient in the daily contestation of power between hacienda owners and their labour force, must have been an important barrier to labour discipline in the agro-mining enterprises.

Agrarian rhythms

A striking characteristic of mining in Latin America until the late twentieth century was the well-nigh universal seasonal scarcity of mine labour. Indeed, as coercive practices in obtaining mine labour declined after the colonial period, mine owners suffered acutely from the agrarian rhythms imposed by their peasant-based mine labour force. This was the case in Peru, where in the nineteenth century this problem remained a constant complaint. Workers would simply return to their communities when the harvests were ready to pick. Even the mighty Cerro de Pasco Corporation in the Central Highlands, financed by large US mining interests, could not attract workers during certain times of the year in the early twentieth century.[56]

Complaints from mine administrators about the seasonal lack of labour were well-nigh universal in nineteenth-century Bolivia as well. Dámaso de Uriburu, an Argentine mining entrepreneur, had problems of this kind in 1826. One knowledgeable contemporary observer blamed the lack of work in the mines in the mid-1840s on the disappearance of the professional mine labourers during the chaos of the independence wars. The same problem continued, however, throughout the nineteenth cen-

---

[54] For a discussion of labour relations in southern Bolivian haciendas, see Erick D. Langer, "Labour Strikes and Reciprocity on Chuquisaca Haciendas", *Hispanic American Historical Review*, 65:2 (1985), pp. 255–277.

[55] Libro No. 3, López to Benavides, Andacaba, 2 March 1890, f. 354, FAA.

[56] For nineteenth-century Peru, see Carlos Contreras, *Mineros y campesinos en los Andes: Mercado laboural y economía campesina en la Sierra Central siglo XIX* (Lima, 1987). For an intriguing study of this problem for Cerro de Pasco, see Elizabeth Dore, "Social Relations and the Barriers to Economic Growth: The Case of the Peruvian Mining Industry", *Nova Americana*, 1 (1978), pp. 245–267.

tury. In 1895, a few generations later, Gregorio Pacheco complained that his mines were not working "because of the harvests, workers are not to be found".[57] In addition, as Gustavo Rodríguez Ostria has written extensively, miners were frequently absent during festivals such as carnival and other such celebrations. The correspondence from the Andacaba mines corroborates this impression. During carnival in 1890 the administrator reduced the mine labour force to a skeleton crew of eight to ten workers, but to only those "worthy of confidence". This proved necessary after the company suffered through various drunken fights, one outright dismissal of a mine worker, and putting labourers to work in the mines very late in their shifts, after they had slept off their hangovers. Even in the early twentieth century the vast Uncía and Llallagua mining complexes in Chayanta virtually shut down during the week of All Saint's Day because the workers simply left to celebrate in their home towns.[58]

Of course, the agricultural and festival cycles did not just impinge upon work in the interior of the mines. During certain seasons, pack animals owned by community members were also not available, because the Indians were on their yearly migrations to the lowlands, to exchange salt and other highland products for maize in the valleys.[59] Even professional muledrivers were often agriculturists on the side and simply disappeared during the sowing and harvest seasons, though at times it was possible to compensate for the lack of Indian-owned llamas by contracting mestizo owners of donkeys to transport the ore.[60]

Regional differences were very important. Mining companies close to cities had little problem with seasonality. The documentation available for the Real Socavon de Potosí Company, with its mines in the huge mountain that towered over the city of Potosí and had given life to it, never mentions a seasonal lack of labour.[61] In turn, mining regions far from large urban centres, such as those in Chayanta or Chichas, had a serious problem with mine workers wandering off to their homesteads during the harvest season. This was especially the case with small

---

[57] Lofstrom, *Dámaso de Uriburu*; Pacheco quote in Rodríguez Ostria, *El socavon*, p. 31. For the 1840s, see José María Dalence, *Bosquejo estadístico de Bolivia* (La Paz, 1975 [1848]), pp. 259–260.

[58] Rodríguez Ostria, *El socavon*, pp. 27–29. For Andacaba, see Libro No. 3, López to Benavidez, Andacaba, 6 February 1890, f. 313; López to Jerardo Azurduy, 7 February 1890, f. 315; López to Benavidez, 8 February 1890, f. 318; López to Benavidez, 9 February 1890, f. 321, FAA. For All Saint's Day, see Zacarias Ponce to German Zelada, Colquechaca, 26 October 1907, f. 10, "Cartas Copiadores Cía Colquechaca, Sep. 30, 1907 a Nov. 1913", Archivo Giménez (Sucre) [hereinafter AG].

[59] Platt, "Calendarios tributarios".

[60] Lucio Leiton to Guillermo Leiton, Potosí, 18 March 1890, "Copiador de Cartas Abel Vacaflores 1889: Libro No. 2", pp. 491–492, FV.

[61] See the company's various *Informes*, stretching from 1860 to 1877, preserved in MSS Rück, Minas, Cía Bolívar, Potosí 1820–1840, BNB.

companies, where the insecurity of mining and the subsequent swings in the number of employees made it necessary for mine labourers to have access to fields so that they could survive when the inevitable lay-offs occurred. The small companies, with their small capital, also were most vulnerable to the swings in the prices of minerals.

While a few large-scale mining companies such as the Huanchaca Company, with their large and stable mining production were probably not as affected by seasonal labour fluctuations, the hacienda-mining complexes were extremely vulnerable to this type of problem. Indeed, the contradictory needs of mining and agriculture formed the greatest weakness of these types of enterprises. The problem of seasonality bedevilled even the largest agro-mining enterprise, the Guadalupe Company. For example, Gregorio Pacheco noted in 1889 that "there are seasons, such as those for sowing and harvest, in which there is a scarcity of [mine] workers, given that they are the same *arrenderos* (hacienda peons) who cannot stop attending to agricultural work".[62]

In addition, these agro-mining enterprises suffered from contradictory capital investment demands in an effort to attenuate the seasonal labour shortages. The Guadalupe Company attempted to introduce agricultural machinery on its lands as a means to free up peon labour for the mines, but the mining complex also demanded large amounts of capital for the upkeep of machinery and the introduction of new labour-saving technology. Thus, in 1889 Gregorio Pacheco prohibited any capital improvements in the company's haciendas, permitting only those expenditures "*absolutely necessary* for the preservation" of the farms.[63] By 1896 the company had, however, invested in a new dam and irrigation canals, as well as a Whitman pressing machine for fodder, and some harvesters for the alfalfa crop despite losing almost 150,000 Bs in mining operations.[64] The investment in agriculture rather than using the money to switch over to tin mining possibly brought the company to the verge of bankruptcy, for shortly thereafter it was purchased by Chilean interests and the headquarters moved to Santiago, Chile.[65] Thus, efforts to provide a more consistently available labour force were not always successful, given the conflicting demands for capital between agricultural and mining enterprises.

Problems with seasonal labour scarcity continued well into the twentieth century, showing that the process of proletarianization had not finished in the mines even in very fundamental aspects. Records are scarce for the period before World War I and little has been written about labour conditions in the crucial transitional period from silver to

[62] Pacheco, *Compañía Guadalupe de Bolivia*, p. 7.
[63] *Ibid.*, p. 10. Emphasis in the original.
[64] Compañía Guadalupe de Bolivia, *Memoria de 1896*, pp. 14, 12.
[65] Schurz, *Bolivia*, pp. 130–131.

tin between 1895 and 1918.[66] Even in northern Potosí, the region where labour union development and proletarianization of the labour force was presumably the highest, seasonality was very important. The records of the Consolidada Company of Colquechaca for the period between 1907 and 1918, in the northern Potosí region, help us to fill this gap. The company was one of the last and best hopes of the post-silver boom Sucre elites to compete with the new multinational corporations that were beginning to dominate the tin mining industry.[67]

The image presented by the Consolidada Company during this time is very different from the image we have of tin companies after World War I. The Consolidada Company operated primarily with independent contractors rather than hiring its own workers as a means of keeping down expenses. Theft in the mines was endemic, indicating that many independent or perhaps occasional miners existed and that a market for contraband ores continued to exist. Indeed, in 1907 the administrator admitted that the contractors worked more with the *kajchas*, or mine thieves, than with the company, causing serious losses. At other times contractors switched between *kajcha* and contracting, depending on what mines were accessible.[68]

The problem with labour discipline and keeping workers from disappearing during fiestas and other unofficial holidays was one of the company's major problems and did not change appreciably over the period for which we have records. In late October 1907 the administrator suspended work in the mines because "I don't try to fool myself that I can have work done next week until after All Saint's Day". He also reported that the large mining centres in Uncía and Llallagua had shut down as well.[69] In early 1908 workers again disappeared before carnival

[66] See for example Rodríguez Ostria, *El socavon*, the best recent mine labour history, which jumps from the late nineteenth century to 1918. Likewise, Antonio Mitre, *Bajo un cielo de estaño: Fulgor y ocaso del metal en Bolivia* (La Paz, 1993) largely skips over this period. The only important contribution is Manuel E. Contreras C., "Mano de obra en la minería estañífera de principios de siglo, 1900–1925", *Historia y Cultura*, 8 (1985), pp. 97–134.

[67] I am extremely grateful to Pilar Giménez Domínguez, who made these records available to me. For an overview of the Sucre elite's attempts to get into the tin mining industry, see Langer, *Economic Change*, pp. 46–47. Most studies on Bolivian mine labour have focused on northern Potosí. For a representative sample, see Olivia Harris and Javier Albó, *Monteras y guardatojos: Campesinos y mineros en el norte de Potosí*, rev. ed. (La Paz, 1986); Nash, *We Eat the Mines*; Platt, "Conciencia andina"; Godoy, *Mining and Agriculture*.

[68] The records indicate that independent contractors composed the vast majority of the labour force, especially in the rubrics of exploration and shaft digging, the most labour-intensive activities. Unfortunately, the letters only record relations with the general contractors rather than with the individual labourers, making it impossible to determine the composition of the contractors' workforce. For *kajchas*, see Ponce to Zelada, 29 February 1907, f. 59; 2 May 1908, f. 87, "Cartas Copiadores Cía Colquechaca, Sep. 30, 1907 a Nov. 1913", AG.

[69] Ponce to Zelada, 26 October 1907, f. 10, "Cartas", AG.

and were not expected to return until well into March. In April workers
were scarce because of Easter celebrations. In June the Corpus Christi
festival seriously restricted exploration activities, while in September the
people of the village of Aullagas tore down the wooden gates to the
mines to use as firewood for the feast of Saint Michael.[70]

Over a decade later similar problems persisted. A new administrator
warned the company's directorate that there were "many difficulties that
one encounters in this place, such as the scarcity of working people in
certain seasons".[71] In April of that year "work has been paralyzed during
all the days of Holy Week and Easter", and "there is a complete scarcity
of muledrivers, which is why the delivery of our products has been
totally paralyzed". Only in mid-May did the labour shortage due to the
feast days disappear. Whereas in 1912 the administrator could boast that
"despite the inconveniences because of the [August 6th] patriotic holidays
of the past week, I have succeeded in making our contractors work
without any stoppage", in 1918 for the 6 August national holidays
workers had not reappeared by 8 August. Again, in late October
"because of the feasts of All Saint's Day, there has been a loss of five
to six days of work in all sections of the company".[72]

Festivals were not the only worries of the company, for workers
continued to disappear during the harvest season as well. In April 1908
"the scarcity of people continues [. . .] because they have begun to
go to the countryside for the harvest". By June even the *barreteros*, the
most specialized and highly paid mine workers, quit *en masse* to go to
work in the cornfields of the valleys.[73] In April 1913 the administrator
tried to increase wages and keep the workers in the mines to finish
their labour contracts by force instead of going to the harvest, but by
early May the miners had disappeared to harvest their crops anyway.
A month later most workers reappeared, but only after having completed
the harvest.[74] In 1918 "day by day our production diminishes because
of the lack of workers [. . .] this is occurring in all sections [. . .]
because all are retiring to the countryside [for the harvest]".[75]

Increasingly, however, complaints centred on competition between
various mining enterprises for workers, leading to a rise in wages or

[70] Ponce to Zelada, 21 March 1908, f. 73; 11 April 1908, f. 80; 20 June 1908, f. 114; 12
September 1908, f. 140, "Cartas", AG.
[71] Francisco Leaño to Directorio, n/d, f. 2, "Letters", AG.
[72] Leaño to Zelada, Colquechaca, 4 April 1918, f. 41; 25 April 1918, f. 71; 16 May 1918,
f. 103, "Letters"; Ponce to Zelada, Colquechaca, 12 August 1912, "Cartas"; Leaño to
Zelada, La Gallofa, 8 August 1918, f. 231; Armando Seoane and Leaño to Zelada, La
Gallofa, 31 October 1918, f. 344, "Letters", AG.
[73] Ponce to Zelada, Colquechaca, 25 April 1908, f. 85; 13 June 1908, f. 112, "Cartas",
AG.
[74] Leaño to Zelada, Colquechaca, 21 April 1913, f. 696; 5 May 1913, f. 711; 2 June 1913,
"Cartas", AG.
[75] Leaño to Zelada, Colquechaca, 18 April 1918, f. 61, "Letters", AG.

contractors' fees throughout the region. In April 1918 a new mining company took away workers by raising wages.[76] Competition was even more marked for pack animals. In northern Potosí, where mining companies were among the most heavily capitalized in the country in the twentieth century, the vast majority of transporters of minerals continued to be members of the numerous Indian communities of northern Potosí and the *altiplano* around Lake Poopó in Oruro. This continued to bring problems, for in July 1918 most Indians had disappeared into the valleys with their llamas, in their age-old voyage to trade salt and folk medicines for lowland maize. Mine owners had complained about the same problem seventy years before, prior to the advent of the railways.[77] While competition brought about higher transport prices, even the stimulus of increased profits could not always move the Indians to change their traditional activities. In September and October 1918 the company sent agents to the towns of Macha and Pocoata to offer high payments to transport goods from the railhead at Challapata to the mines and take tin bars in return, but did not get any takers. Presumably, the llamas had recently returned from their trip into the valleys and their owners preferred to have them rest rather than returning to the road.[78]

Transportation bottlenecks remained an important problem for much of Bolivian mining. Miners had to rely heavily on Indian community members for transporting their ore and other goods. Only in the 1930s, with the construction of vehicle roads and the widespread introduction of trucks, did reliance on Indian peasants for transportation diminish.[79] Within the mining enterprises the proletarianization of workers proceeded somewhat more rapidly. During World War I and especially in the 1920s the tin industry consolidated into a small number of companies that dominated the country's mining until the Bolivian Revolution of 1952. Although the top three companies were presumably owned by Bolivian nationals, in fact they relied very heavily on foreign capital and acted as multinational firms in ways that the silver mining companies had not.[80] The high levels of capitalization, possible through the participation of important US, French, British and Chilean interests, created a situation in which new transportation methods and mechanization brought about great changes in labour conditions. The migration of Cochabamba peasants to the northern Potosí mines largely severed the

[76] Leaño to Zelada, Colquechaca, 11 April 1918, f. 54, "Letters", AG. Also see Contreras, "Mano de obra".
[77] Leaño to Zelada, Colquechaca, 4 July 1918, f. 185, "Letters", AG. For patterns in the 1840s, see Platt, "Calendarios tributarios".
[78] Seoane to Zelada, La Gallofa Colquechaca, 26 September 1918, ff. 298–299; Leaño to Zelada, La Gallofa, October 17 1918, f. 321, "Letters", AG.
[79] For a detailed discussion of the transportation problem, see Mitre, *Bajo un cielo*, pp. 72–102.
[80] *Ibid.*, pp. 202–213.

links between the surrounding countryside and mines that had existed previously. What remained was an Andean consciousness, expressed in the belief of underground deities that controlled access to mining riches in the shafts.[81]

However, one must take into account regional differences even here. Indeed, scholarly attention on the northern Potosí case has been so great because the largest firm, Patiño Enterprises, had its largest mines there and because labour union activity first surged in the Uncía-Llallagua sector. Unfortunately, we do not have much information on the fate of the great agro-mining complexes, but it is highly likely that labour relations were rather different there. Although a Chilean syndicate purchased the Guadalupe Company in 1907, the presence of peasant-miners living on the company's estates must have retarded proletarianization in ways that were not possible in northern Potosí. Suggestive of the persistence of the combination of peasant and miner is a recent characterization of the mine worker of Chichas (where the Guadalupe Company is located), in which the author asserted that

the miner of Chichas works occasionally in the mines when there is no work in his fields, for this [reason] especially in the sowing season he abandons the work of the mines to sow, although he only has a tiny plot of land, sufficient to take part in the *huackes'* [a sowing festival particular to Chichas]. The authentic miner is from Potosí or Oruro who does not leave his work all year around; they are poorer than those who alternate [mine] labour with agricultural tasks, these [latter] have maize, potatoes, meat, etc.[82]

Conclusion

The case of Bolivian mining labour, while unique in certain respects, helps us to understand better the changes and continuities in labour relations throughout Latin America. Although the mining sector was relatively heavily capitalized and mechanized (especially compared to agricultural enterprises), the development of labour consciousness did not follow European patterns. This was due in large part to migration by mine labourers to the agricultural sector and back into mining, depending on job possibilities and seasonal labour demands. Other than the very exceptional Huanchaca Company, more heavily capitalized and mechanized than any other mining syndicate and located in the desolate reaches of the *altiplano*, few companies succeeded in proletarianizing the labour force. Indeed, certain Andean rituals and concepts from the agrarian sector were important in keeping the mine labour force content as well. Belief in and propitiation of the *tío*, an ancient deity of the

[81] Nash, *We Eat the Mines*; Taussig, *The Devil*.
[82] Francisco Salazar Tejerina, *Leyendas y tradiciones de Tupiza*, 2nd ed. (La Paz, 1981), p. 12.

underworld, also shows the penetration of Andean concepts despite the workers' apparently "modern" political beliefs.

Not only were workers exposed to deproletarianization due to the vagaries of a particular mining enterprise, but the vulnerability to the swings of the international price regime made it prudent to cultivate ties to the countryside. Even large mining companies such as the Guadalupe Company recognized this problem when they combined mining concerns with agricultural enterprises. Virtually unstudied and relatively common in the important southern mining districts, these enterprises shifted from agriculture to mining and vice versa as prices varied. Likewise, hacienda peons became mine labourers and then went back to their fields after their turn to work in the shafts. Not only did this hinder the development of a class consciousness, but brought about severe labour discipline problems. Nevertheless, this was a rational means of dealing with the intractable problem of the swings in the mining economy. As shown above, these problems were not unique to the Bolivian mining sector. In fact, examining how workers in peripheral regions such as Latin America hedged their bets as they tried to protect themselves from the brutal realities of the global market-place will bring about new insights into the process of labour formation in much of the rest of the world.

Appendix

Regions, mining companies and mine owners mentioned in the text

Region (and towns)	Mining company	Principal owner
Northern Potosí (dep.) (Uncía, Llallagua, Colquechaca)	Colquechaca Company Consolidada Gallofa de Colquechaca Company	Jacobo Aillon Various (Sucre elites)
High altiplano	Huanchaca Company	Aniceto Arce
Near cities (Oruro, Potosí)	Real Socavon de Potosí	Avelino Aramayo
Agro-mining enterprises (Tupiza, Portugalete – Chicas Province) (Porco Province)	Guadalupe Company (Haciendas Oploca, Salo) Andacaba Company (Hacienda La Lava)	Gregorio Pacheco (initially Aniceto Arce) Aniceto Arce

Labour, Ecology and History in a Puerto Rican Plantation Region: "Classic" Rural Proletarians Revisited

JUAN A. GIUSTI-CORDERO

The sugar workers of large-scale capitalist plantations in the Caribbean are familiar figures in social history. As portrayed in Sidney Mintz's landmark research in southern Puerto Rico,[1] sugar workers are manifest rural proletarians: landless wage labourers exploited by "land-and-factory combines". In Mintz's studies, Puerto Rican sugar workers became the classic case of modern rural proletarians.[2] Such rural proletarians are the dichotomous opposite of peasants: hence given rural populations are *either* peasants or rural proletarians.

Other studies, including later work by Mintz, discern Caribbean rural groups that are *both* rural proletarian and peasant, or *neither* one.[3]

[1] Sidney Mintz, "Cañamelar: The Sub-culture of a Rural Sugar Plantation Proletariat", in Julian Steward *et al.*, *The People of Puerto Rico* (Champaign-Urbana, 1956), pp. 314–417; idem, *Worker in the Cane. A Puerto Rican Life History* (New Haven, 1960).

[2] Out of his research on Puerto Rico, Mintz is most directly responsible for the use of the concept in contemporary social science. Richard Adams, "Rural Labour", in J.J. Johnson (ed.), *Continuity and Change in Latin America* (Stanford, 1964), p. 49. Beyond the Caribbean, Mintz's work on "rural proletarians" became influential in the blossoming field of Latin American studies, in Brazil and the Andean zone. See especially Harry W. Hutchinson, *Village and Plantation Labor in Northeast Brazil* (Seattle, 1956). Anthropologist Thomas C. Greaves referred to Mintz's work on the rural proletariat as his "pioneering contribution": "The Andean Rural Proletarians", *Anthropological Quarterly*, XL (1972), p. 66. At the same time, and while it was invoked with some frequency in social science research in the 1960s–1970s, the concept of rural proletarian was not enthusiastically received – in sharp contrast to "peasant" – and has been something of an ugly duckling in social science (perhaps because of its Marxist ancestry). According to Greaves, research on rural proletarians remained "uneven" and "not the product of a long-term, broadly shared research concern among Andeanists": Greaves: "The Andean Rural Proletarians", p. 66. Curiously, Greaves claimed that only the Andean zone came closest to developing "a significant corpus of ethnography" on rural proletarians: *ibid.* And yet, accepting the conceptual underpinnings of "peasant" inherently carries, I would argue, acceptance of "rural proletarian". In Mexico, the concept of rural proletariat generated broad discussion in the 1970s, though Mintz's work was not addressed and the concept was referred directly to Marx and Lenin. See, for instance, Luisa Paré, *El proletariado agrícola en Mexico: ¿campesinos sin tierra o proletarios rurales?* (Mexico, DF, 1977), and for a more historical approach Arturo Warman, "El problema del proletariado agrícola", in Paré (ed.), *Polémica sobre las clases sociales en el campo mexicano* (Mexico, DF, 1979), pp. 85–96.

[3] Richard Frucht, "A Caribbean Social Type: Neither Peasant nor Proletarian", in Michael Horowitz, *Peoples and Cultures of the Caribbean* (Garden City, 1971), pp. 190–197; Sidney Mintz, "Petits cultivateurs et prolétaires ruraux aux Caraïbes", in Centre Nationale de la Recherche Scientifique (CNRS), *Problèmes agraires de l'Amérique Latine* (Paris, 1967). In research that is especially apposite to Piñones, Michael Taussig found that the Cauca Valley's sugar cane labourers were neither peasants nor "full-fledged wage-earning rural

International Review of Social History 41 (1996), pp. 53–82

Mintz has also written of a "plantation-peasant relation" that seems closest to the "both" approach.[4] In any case, attempts to recombine these concepts can go no further than their own deeply dichotomous structure.[5] "Peasant" and "rural proletarian" first enrich, then constrain our vision. We need to move beyond, towards an elusive history.[6] The "either"-"neither"-"both" conundrum suggests some of the stark limitations of Western social science.

My research on a Puerto Rican sugar plantation zone in the nineteenth–twentieth centuries, Piñones (Loíza), reveals historical labour patterns and social relations that challenge the "peasant" and "proletarian" categories.[7] The labourers' continuing relation to cropland and other ecologies, autonomous production activities, labour-gang organization, face-to-face relations among themselves and with foremen, non-cash wage relations, non-union activism and old cultural forms shape patterns that may perhaps be characterized as "peasant-proletarian".

"Peasant-proletarian" is a critical approach open to local particulars; it goes beyond essentialist, dichotomous, mutually exclusive categories,

proletarians"; they were "liminal beings [. . .] neither what they are, nor what they will become": Taussig, "The Evolution of Rural Wage Labour in the Cauca Valley, Colombia, 1700–1970", in Kenneth Duncan and Ian Rutledge (eds), *Land and Labor in Latin America* (Cambridge, 1977), p. 423; idem, *The Devil and Commodity Fetishism* (Chapel Hill, 1980), pp. 92, 103. Elsewhere, Taussig characterized the "outlaws" of the Cauca Valley as "black peasants [who] formed a new social class that stood *outside* society": Taussig, "Black Religion and Resistance in Colombia: Three Centuries of Social Struggle in the Cauca Valley", *Marxist Perspectives*, VI (1979), p. 102; emphasis added.

[4] Sidney Mintz, "The Plantation as a Socio-Cultural Type", in Pan American Union, *Plantation Systems of the New World* (Washington, DC, 1959), pp. 42–50. Mintz's late approaches suggest a reaffirmation of the earlier dichotomy, if now from the point of view of a "*peasant*" optic. See his critique of a 1978 paper in which Rodney struck a "rural proletarian" note ironically reminiscent of "Cañamelar": Mintz, "Descrying the Peasantry", *Review*, VI (1982), pp. 609–625. Mintz did not register Rodney's changed perspective in *A History of the Guyanese Working People, 1881–1905* (Baltimore, 1981). In this lucid parting work, Rodney characterized post-emancipation sugar plantation labourers as "a permanent hybrid of peasant and proletarian": *ibid.*, p. 218. This suggests a "both" perspective quite different from the 1978 paper, and movement beyond dichotomies and linear history.

[5] Juan A. Giusti-Cordero, "Labour, Ecology and History in a Caribbean Sugar Plantation Region. Piñones (Loíza), Puerto Rico, 1770–1950" (Ph.D., State University of New York-Binghamton, 1994), ch. 2.

[6] The concept of "plantation" shares fundamental methodological premises with "peasant" and "proletarian" in that its landholding pattern is defined as large-scale and virtually monopolistic in a zone: hence its labourers are deemed to be either slaves or rural proletarians.

[7] Giusti-Cordero, "Labour, Ecology and History". Of course, discussion on peasants and rural proletarians is charged with cultural and political implications. See Arturo Warman, "Los estudios campesinos: veinte años después", *Comercio Exterior*, XXXVIII (1988), p. 658. Peasants and proletarians are far more than "economic adaptations": see Mintz, "From Plantations to Peasantries in the Caribbean", in Sidney Mintz and Sally Price (eds), *Caribbean Contours* (Baltimore, 1985), p. 135.

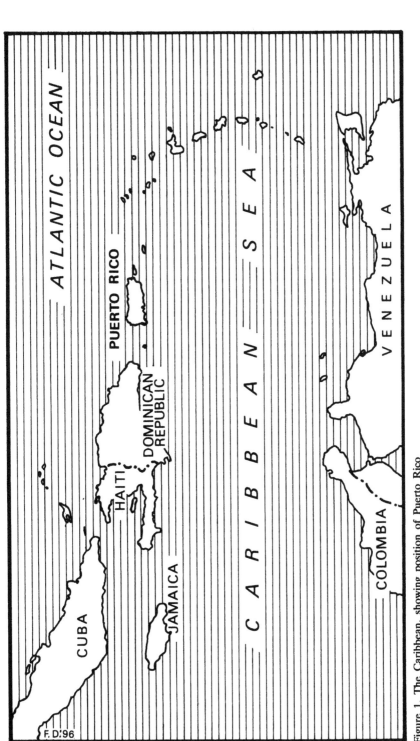

Figure 1. The Caribbean, showing position of Puerto Rico

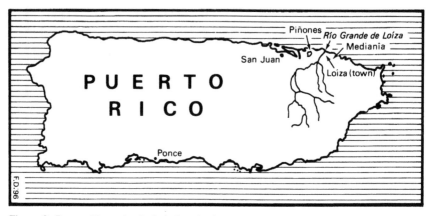

Figure 2. Puerto Rico; the Loízal river basin and littoral

in favour of a conceptually alert *and* more historical perspective. Through my study of Piñones, I aim to focus on the categories of "peasants" and "rural proletarians" not as social types but as dimensions of social life.

Puerto Rico is an especially significant terrain for a joint re-exploration of these categories, as both "rural proletarian" and "peasant" began their trajectory in contemporary social science in the landmark *The People of Puerto Rico* project. This project, directed in the late 1940s by Julian Steward, included among its field researchers both Mintz and Eric Wolf.[8] Mintz and Wolf, who would be lasting collaborators, wrote their dissertations in tandem out of their Puerto Rico research.[9] At the time, Puerto Rico was an "Inter-American or international pilot object,"[10] a "prototype".[11] Puerto Rico was a showcase for US-promoted development and social change. The island's apparent simplicity and straightforwardness made it especially attractive as a research site for US social scientists.[12] The Steward team were among the few to realize the island's complexity, if only to establish five component "subcultures"

---

[8] Steward *et al.*, *The People of Puerto Rico*.
[9] Mintz, "Cañamelar: the Culture of a Rural Puerto Rican Proletariat" (Ph.D., Columbia University, 1951); Wolf, "Culture Change and Culture Stability in a Puerto Rican Coffee Growing Community" (Ph.D, Columbia University, 1951).
[10] Antonio Lauria-Perricelli, "A Study in Historical and Critical Anthropology: the Making of *The People of Puerto Rico*" (Ph.D., New School for Social Research, 1989), p. 7.
[11] Richard Weisskoff, *Factories and Food Stamps: the Puerto Rico Model of Development* (Baltimore, 1985), pp. 85–90. "There is a vast bibliography on Puerto Rico": Gordon Lewis, *The Growth of the Modern West Indies* (New York, 1968), p. liii. W. Arthur Lewis abstracted his interpretation of, significantly, rural-to-urban proletarianization in Puerto Rico in the widely influential "Economic Development with Unlimited Supplies of Labour", *Manchester School* (May 1954), pp. 139–151.
[12] Michael Lapp, "The Rise and Fall of Puerto Rico as a Social Laboratory, 1940–1965", *Social Science History*, XIX (1995), pp. 169–199.

that were themselves depicted in rather oversimplified ways, effectively negating the existence of a Puerto Rican national identity.

The heart of the Steward project, and behind the gamut of six subcultures, was the conceptual dichotomy between peasant and rural proletarian. Mintz researched "rural proletarians" in the island's south coast while Eric Wolf studied "peasants" in the highlands, the two being in frequent consultation between themselves and with other team members.[13] The other two rural subcultures studied in *People of Puerto Rico* were variants of the basic peasant or rural proletarian models (one each).[14] "Peasant" and "rural proletarian" were thus reciprocally constructed as paired opposites in Puerto Rico. *People* essentially canonized the "either" perspective, but its strategy more fundamentally set down the dichotomous architecture of the whole approach.[15]

In Puerto Rico, more than 100,000 sugar cane field labourers formed the largest occupational group in the early twentieth century, and between a third and a half of the agricultural labour force in then-rural Puerto Rico.[16] By the early 1940s, the Puerto Rican sugar industry was

[13] "San José: Subcultures of a 'Traditional' Coffee Municipality", in Steward *et al.*, *The People of Puerto Rico*, pp. 171–264. The root of the "peasant" concept in contemporary social science is said to lie in the important 1955 paper by Wolf, "Types of Latin American Peasantry: a Preliminary Discussion", *American Anthropologist*, LVII (1955), pp. 452–471. Sydel Silverman, "The Peasant Concept in Anthropology", *Journal of Peasant Studies*, VII (1980), pp. 54, 63. In his 1955 paper, Wolf defined peasants as agricultural producers who control their land and who produce for subsistence, a conception fairly close to that of the *jíbaro*. Wolf authored this paper not long after he wrote up his research in Puerto Rico, and while he remained working with Steward at Illinois. On the process beneath and around *The People of Puerto Rico*, see Lauria-Perricelli, "A Study in Historical and Critical Anthropology". In Wolf's best-known characterization of peasants, to be sure, the focus is on social and political subordination, through appropriation of surplus product, and at least latent social antagonism: Wolf, *Peasants* (Englewood Cliffs, 1966). Yet the dichotomous construction of peasant and rural proletarian – perhaps the decisive aspect of the pair – is evident.

[14] The "peasant" variant was Robert Manners's study of Barranquitas, "Tabará: Subcultures of a Tobacco and Mixed Crops Municipality", in *ibid.*, pp. 93–170; the rural proletarian variant was Elena Padilla's study of Barceloneta, "Nocorá: the Subculture of Workers on a Government Owned Sugar Plantation", in *ibid.*, pp. 265–313.

[15] As Mintz implied, the peasant-proletarian dichotomy was the linchpin of a whole array of dichotomous pairings: "By and large, the difference between peasantry and proletariat was the difference between highland and lowland, between small and large, between other crops and sugar cane, and – some would argue – between white and black": Mintz, "Foreword" to Ramiro Guerra y Sánchez, *Sugar and Society in the Caribbean* (New Haven, 1964), p. xxxix. On the dichotomizing strategies of the *People of Puerto Rico* project, and their implications, see Lauria-Perricelli, "A Study in Historical and Critical Anthropology".

[16] Estimates of the Puerto Rico field labour force vary widely. In 1936, the Puerto Rico Reconstruction Administration arrived at a figure of 92,398, see Puerto Rico Reconstruction Administration, *Special Census* (1936). Mill workers were estimated at 8,482. Others offered a significantly higher figure for field labourers: 113,161, with mill workers estimated at 10,485: Arthur Gayer, Paul T. Homan and Earle K. James, *The Sugar Economy of*

believed to employ in season as many as 165,000 field labourers – more
than half the agricultural labour force, and a quarter of the total Puerto
Rican labour force.[17]

Much of the true significance of Puerto Rico as a research site at the
time was lost on US researchers: Puerto Rico was the most intensely
large-scale sugar producing territory in the Caribbean (if not the world)
in the twentieth century, the modern "Sugar Island" *par excellence.*
Cuba's production was much larger than Puerto Rico, but not in proportion to its size. And Puerto Rico's evolution, despite (or because?) of
its colonial condition, was more "self-contained" than elsewhere: in this
century, the densely-populated island was the only Caribbean sugar
producer without large labour migrations from elsewhere in the region;
nor were there major flows of working-class emigrants from Puerto Rico
until the 1940s.

Puerto Rican political traditions and images of cultural identity thicken
the significance of the "peasant"-"rural proletarian" dichotomy. Expropriation of the most important sugar latifundia in the 1930s–1940s is a
major historical icon of political discourse in Puerto Rico, the threshold
of economic and political modernization. Agrarian reform was cham-
pioned by the social-democratic Popular Democratic Party (PPD) in
concert with leading Washington New Dealers, and has been variously
linked to mass support by "peasants" (*jíbaros*)[18] or "proletarians"
(*obreros cañeros*).[19] The supposedly white, highland, subsistence-
producing *jíbaro* became the PPD's and the island's leading symbol of
cultural identity;[20] the supposedly darker-skinned, coastal, waged rural
proletarian did not.[21] Marxist-nationalist currents in Puerto Rico's "New
History" have but reversed things, and have enthroned the rural proletariat – supposedly betrayed in the 1940s by PPD reformism – as the
bearer of the "nation".[22] Little thought has gone into the possibility that

---

Puerto Rico (New York, 1938), p. 162. In Mexico, Sara Lara found it difficult to separate
the rural proletarians statistically – as conceptually – from smallholders: "[T]he principal
problem lies in the interpretation of the data, above all in the determination of the
agricultural proletariat": Lara, "La importancia de la comunidad campesina y las formas
de conciencia social de los jornaleros de Atencingo", in Luisa Paré and Ricardo Avila
(eds), *Ensayos sobre el problema cañero* (Mexico, DF, 1979), p. 135.

[17] Puerto Rico Minimum Wage Board, *La industria de azúcar de caña en Puerto Rico*
(San Juan, 1942), p. 18.

[18] The PPD's "agrarian radicalism [. . .] had won the PPD the votes of the *jíbaros*":
Raymond Carr, *Puerto Rico: A Colonial Experiment* (New York, 1985), p. 67.

[19] Mintz, "Cañamelar", pp. 397–399; idem, *Worker in the Cane*, pp. 193–203.

[20] "The emblem of the [PPD] became the jíbaros' straw hat, the pava. To the PPD, the
jíbaro, the subsistence farmer of the inland regions who was a loyal PPD voter, became
the symbol of Puerto Rican identity": Carr, *Puerto Rico*, p. 115.

[21] Juan Giusti-Cordero, "Puerto Rico entre los pueblos antillanos y latinoamericanos.
Algunos problemas de método", *Plural*, IV (1985), pp. 177–195.

[22] Angel Quintero Rivera and Gervasio García, *Desafío y solidaridad. Breve historia del
movimentio obrero puertorriqueño* (Río Piedras, 1982); Taller de Formación Política, *La*

these dichotomies are vastly overdrawn, or indeed that both groups were often *the same people*. Decades after the US anthropologists left the Puerto Rican "laboratory",[23] and years after rural social relations became (perhaps mercifully) less fashionable in world social science, the historical character of the sugar cane labour force continues to be a fundamental issue of Puerto Rican history, and one to which we continue to bring new questions.

Piñones: ecology and history, sixteenth–nineteenth centuries

Piñones, in the municipality of Loíza just east of San Juan, stretches over a 16-kilometre littoral of mangrove forest and lagoons, between the Atlantic Ocean and one of Puerto Rico's main sugar plains. Piñones has a secular history of black peasant-woodsmen-fishermen, going back to sixteenth-century maroons and free blacks.[24] Sugar centrals had been established near Piñones since the 1880s, and the *piñoneros* became deeply involved in sugar cane field labour in the twentieth century. However, Piñones gives no evidence of sweeping proletarianization. Rather, sugar plantation wage labour joined an already complex "peasant" array.

The ecology of Piñones is as heterogeneous, and as coherent, as its inhabitants' historical labour patterns. Piñones (40 square kilometres) compresses mangrove forest, coconut groves, lagoons and cropland at the point where the Loíza coastal plain meets the Atlantic Ocean. Piñones' coastline stretches from Puerto Rico's largest lagoon system to its largest river. The Luquillo mountain chain, only 10 kilometres away, catches moist trade winds and promotes rainfall; the Loíza plain is the wettest in the island.

Piñones' population in 1910 was 721, in 1920 it was 779, and 1,035 in 1936.[25] Earlier demographic information is meagre. The villages of Piñones stand on a 1,400-acre narrow and irregular "barrier island" between the forest and the surf, as narrow as 400 metres at some points and formed mostly of fertile sandy loams and alluvial soils. The Piñones mangrove forest is the largest coastal forest in Puerto Rico.[26] Until the

---

cuestión nacional: el Partido Nacionalista y el movimiento obrero puertorriqueño (Río Piedras, 1982).
[23] See Lapp, "The Rise and Fall of Puerto Rico as a Social Laboratory", pp. 169–199.
[24] Jalil Sued Badillo and Angel López Cantos, *Puerto Rico Negro* (Río Piedras, 1986), pp. 25–27.
[25] US Bureau of the Census, *Thirteenth Census* (1910), Population, Barrio Torrecilla Baja; *Fourteenth Census* (1920); Puerto Rico Reconstruction Administration, *Special Census*. In 1990, Piñones' population was 1,978: US Bureau of the Census, *U.S. Population Census* (1990).
[26] As much as 70 per cent of the original Piñones-Hoyo Mulas wetlands were drained in the late nineteenth-early twentieth century to form canefields and pastures.

late nineteenth-early twentieth century, the forest and the associated wetlands (*poyales*) stretched over 8,000 acres. Piñones' intricate ecology and its aqueous boundaries mirror its social complexity.

Piñones has been inhabited for at least a millenium. The forest afforded firewood, and its lagoons rich fishing; clams and land-crabs abounded. On the fertile Piñones "barrier island", the Taínos grew crops such as manioc, yams and maize.[27] Black settlement in Piñones probably began shortly after the Spanish conquest in 1508–1511. The prolific wilds of Piñones attracted Taíno and African maroons fleeing enslavement in the mines and haciendas of the Loíza plain;[28] free black settlers and hunters from adjacent Cangrejos and Loíza; and outlaws and fugitives.[29] The "enlightened" Fray Iñigo Abbad condemned freedmen that lived in forested coastal zones:

without means of subsistence, they settle in huts in the woods [*se arranchan*] where they live from fishing and theft, or trading contraband in pirogues without cognizance of either judge nor priest to observe their conduct; which prejudices might be avoided if they were given land where they could live from their labour.[30]

Yet they already *had* land, and much else, on which they lived off their labour. Piñones, like several other zones in Puerto Rico, was an outlaw black Cockaigne: an ecologically rich domain of autonomous peasants, who resisted the appropriation of their land and subordination of their daily life. To the colonial authorities, Piñones was a peasant "utopia" of the sort they did not care for. That Piñones lay along a major contraband route, when contraband was the principal form of overseas commerce in Puerto Rico, may be no coincidence either.

Eastern and western Piñones followed somewhat different trajectories. Eastern Piñones belonged to the Dominican order until 1838. Twenty or so slaves cultivated a small portion of the "Los Frailes" estate. The slaves had a fairly autonomous livelihood, especially as the Dominican order in Puerto Rico withered after 1800. In western Piñones, a wealthy and powerful creole *regidor*, Tomás Pizarro, "gradually took over land at his whim from the poor [*los pobres*]" in the 1790s and attempted to

---

[27] The earliest Arawak site in Puerto Rico is Hacienda Grande, just across the Río Grande from Piñones (*c*. AD 100). In Piñones itself, a preliminary, unpublished survey by the Institute of Puerto Rican Culture established 68 Arawak and pre-Arawak sites in Piñones and 57 additional sites in the cave-rich karst hills 3 km. south: Jaime Vélez, *A Study of the Piñones Special Planning Area* (San Juan, 1989).

[28] Sued Badillo, "El poblamiento etno-histórico del Valle de Loíza entre los siglos XVI-XIX", *Revista de Historia*, II (1986), pp. 24–50.

[29] Gilberto Aponte, *San Mateo de Cangrejos (comunidad cimarrona en Puerto Rico): notas para su historia* (San Juan, 1985), p. 55; Fray Iñigo Abbad y Lasierra, *Historia geográfica, civil y natural de la Isla de San Juan Bautista de Puerto Rico* (Río Piedras, 1959 [1788]), p. 153.

[30] *Ibid.*, p. 154.

force them into sharecropping.[31] The *piñoneros* preferred to move else-where in Piñones. This first-known mass eviction in Piñones had, in the long run, little consequence. Despite the claims of Pizarro and later titleholders, the hamlets (*caseríos*) of La Torre, at the west end, and Piñones Adentro, towards the middle, were formed in the late nineteenth century.

In 1838 the Crown seized Los Frailes in eastern Piñones. The colonial government found dozens of black and mulatto families "settled on their own authority" (*avecindados de su propia autoridad*):[32] 44 households occupied 362 *cuerdas*, with 124 of these under cultivation, mostly in manioc and maize, and had 208 head of livestock.[33] The government was unable to evict for another decade. The context was significant: slave revolts in the French islands and a harsher slave code in Puerto Rico in 1848, and in 1849 a new workbook (*libreta*) system for the island's free population.[34] This second eviction in Piñones, too, had little permanent effect. The best-documented genealogies of present-day Piñones families begin with the slaves and settlers of Los Frailes in the late eighteenth century.

In both eastern and western Piñones throughout the nineteenth century, the *piñoneros* continued to live off their fecund cropland, forest, lagoons and coastline, prompting furious denunciations by the colonial authorities as "usurpers", "intruders" and "prowlers".[35] Piñones was an annoying "backwoods of difficult vigilance" and "a den of acts prejudicial to morality, order and public safety".[36]

Agriculture and livestock, woodcutting and charcoalmaking, and fish-ing and marine gathering formed a complex "peasant" totality. Cassava was the island's breadstuff before the onset of massive US flour imports in the nineteenth century, and retained a market in San Juan among the lower classes; and charcoal remained the major cooking fuel until the early twentieth century.[37] The villagers also planted maize, yams,

[31] In the words of an aged *piñonero* interviewed by the colonial authorities in 1838. Archivo General de Puerto Rico, San Juan [hereafter AGPR]. Obras Públicas, Propiedad Pública, Box 32 [hereafter AGPR, OP, PP]. Antonio Hermoso to the Intendent, 1 September 1841; emphasis supplied.

[32] AGPR, OP, PP, Carolina, Boxes 32 and 120.

[33] AGPR, OP, PP, Box 120. "Relacion general de los habitantes qe residen en la Hacienda que fue de los Frailes Dominicos en Loíza [. . .]" (1848). The *cuerda*, the traditional Puerto Rican agrarian measure, equals 0.97 acres.

[34] See Fernando Picó, *Historia general de Puerto Rico* (Río Piedras, 1986), pp. 173–174; Sidney Mintz, *Caribbean Transformations* (Chicago, 1974), pp. 91–92.

[35] AGPR, OP, PP, Box 124, Loíza 1873–4, File 517, f. 71.

[36] AGPR OP, PP, Box 120, Exp. 1418, f. 78. Tribunal de Hacienda to Superintendent, 19 June 1850.

[37] "Charcoal burning involved cutting a large quantity of wood, which was then chopped into smaller pieces, tightly packed, covered with bush and dirt to reduce oxygen, and burned at a very low heat": Karen Fog Olwig, *Cultural Adaptation and Resistance on St. John. Three Centuries of Afro-Caribbean Life* (Gainesville, 1985), p. 109.

rice and melons; they grazed cattle, goats, pigs and sheep; and they gathered coconuts. Fishing in the riverine estuary, and above all in the lagoons, was an integral part of the "peasant" mode of life of the *piñoneros*.

At the same time, important slave haciendas developed hard by Piñones in the 1820s-1840s, on drained wetlands just south of Piñones Lagoon. Just across the Piñones Lagoon, the 100-slave, 1,000-acre Hacienda Machicote was established in the 1840s by the Marqués de Machicote, a leading pro-slavery figure. Immediately south and southeast of Machicote, numerous (albeit smaller) slave haciendas dominated the districts of Hoyo Mulas and Canóvanas.

The villages and the sugar centrals, 1890–1920

In the 1890s, the majority of the *piñoneros* lived in its eastern area, on the Los Frailes sea-shore. Settlement remained titleless and relatively dispersed.[38] Wealthy *sanjuaneros* purchased lots of Los Frailes land from the Crown treasury in the 1870s, but did not meet their payments, insisting that the Crown definitively oust the "prowlers". On two of those lots, a partially mechanized mill was established in 1876. The 400-acre plantation was the object of continuing incursions by "prowlers" (*merodeadores*) who cut down trees, made charcoal, took sugar cane and rustled cattle. In 1879 its manager lamented: "the damages to the property increase by the day".[39] The mill closed a year later. In 1890 the newly formed Central Buena Vista, operating out of Hoyo Mulas, purchased large lots in western Piñones, but only to exploit their wood (especially firewood for the mill). *Piñoneros* began to cut wood for the plantation on a task-work basis.[40]

In 1894, 61 *bohíos* and *ranchos* (thatch-palm cottages) were recorded in Piñones: of these, the largest number (30) was at La Arena, on the Los Frailes sea-shore; ten more were further south, at Hato Arriba. By 1910 there were almost double the number of households (121) and 721 inhabitants. By 1920, emigration began to have an effect, and Piñones' population increased much more slowly. Within Piñones itself there was also a marked shift west, towards San Juan: La Arena and adjacent

---

[38] Post-emancipation St John, again, was comparable: "[t]he descendants of the slaves made their living from small farming, fishing, and charcoal burning. They lived in their own settlements scattered about in the bush on small plots of land." Olwig, *Cultural Adaptation and Resistance*, p. 2.

[39] Barasoain & Cia. to the Crown Treasury, 6 February 1879. AGPR, OP, PP, Box 126, Loíza 1879–81, Leg. 35, Exp. 18, ff. 1, 9. Another landowner next to the same Real Hacienda lot denounced "the abuses both of cutting trees and making charcoal". AGPR, OP, PP, Box 126, Exp. 28. Administrador Central de Contribuciones y Rentas a la Intendencia, 13 November 1879.

[40] AGPR, OP, PP, Box 134, Antolín Romero to the Commander of the Department of Puerto Rico, 28 March 1900.

Monte Grande contracted, while Piñones Adentro and La Torre grew.[41]

Through these decades, the *piñoneros'* activities continued to express a "peasant-like" understanding of their ecology. Not unlike many scholars today, colonial officials in the nineteenth century defined the *piñonero* "squatters" merely as "landless". However, land tenure and labour patterns lead us to a more complex and historical portrayal. The *piñoneros'* smallholdings were undoubtedly important, and moreover much of the subsistence was obtained through a fairly spontaneous relationship to the zone's ecology. Woodcutting in the large Piñones forest and fishing in its lagoons shaped a deepened "peasant" (or just "human"?) sense of the Piñones ecology and of the world at large. And Puerto Rico courts have retroactively sanctioned the claim that the Piñones households were *not* squatters, having acquired legal title to their land through adverse possession at least by the early twentieth century.[42]

By going about their complex, resilient and autonomous ways, the *piñoneros* defied and defined the boundaries of "normality" in the adjacent capital of San Juan. This history marked both the peasant and the proletarian relations of the *piñoneros*, and perceptions of these relations by *piñoneros* and others, well into the twentieth century. It would be expected that the transformation of the *piñoneros'* "peasant" relations would be neither straightforward nor swift.

Indeed, decades after the US invasion in 1898, large-scale sugar production remained in the periphery of Piñones. In 1908, the Buena Vista holdings were absorbed by the Central Canóvanas, which was based in Canóvanas 6 kilometres away. It was the Central Canóvanas which most profoundly marked Piñones' history in this century. After long development out of a cluster of slave haciendas in barrio Canóvanas, the Central Canóvanas (founded 1881) straddled most of the Loíza coastal plain, including Piñones.

Central Canóvanas was founded by resident Spanish and US investors, but was soon taken over by a British firm, the Colonial Company, which owned sugar centrals in Guyana and Trinidad. In 1908, just as Central Canóvanas absorbed Buena Vista, Canóvanas was acquired by a Puerto Rican/Spanish corporation that included existing large landholders from the region, a further expression of the vitality of regional social relations.[43] By 1920, the Central Canóvanas encompassed canefields, large

[41] US Bureau of the Census, *Thirteenth Census* (1910), Population, Loíza, Barrio Torrecilla Baja; *Fourteenth Census* (1920).

[42] *Compañía de Fomento Industrial* vs. *Aníbal Quiñones Bulerín*, Civil Núm. 69–4980, Tribunal Superior, Sala de San Juan (1969); *PFZ Properties, Inc.* vs. *Demetria Escalera Osorio et al.*, Civil Núm. 88–1823, Tribunal Superior, Sala de Carolina (1988).

[43] Giusti-Cordero, "Hacia otro 98: el 'grupo español' en Puerto Rico, 1890–1940 (azúcar, banca y política)", *Boletín del Centro de Investigaciones Históricas*, 9 (1995–1996); idem, "En búsqueda de la nación concreta: 'el grupo español' en la industria azucarera de

areas of mangrove forest, *cocales*, pastures and cropland. The development of the Central Canóvanas expressed and transformed the region's historical ecology.

In the early twentieth century, Central Canóvanas was not among the very largest of sugar centrals in Puerto Rico; it invariably ranked fifth or sixth in importance. But Central Canóvanas had perhaps the most intensely "capitalist" canefield infrastructure on the island: the Central's drainage and rail networks were the largest and most complex in Puerto Rico. And as a significant sign in terms of social relations, Central Canóvanas remained in Spanish-creole hands until 1925. In that year, Canóvanas was absorbed by a US sugar corporation, the Fajardo Sugar Co. – the largest landholder in Puerto Rico. The Buena Vista, Loíza and Fajardo sugar central corporations successively owned most of the Piñones communities' cropland, pastures and *cocales* (some 1,200 acres); much of the Piñones mangrove forest; all the adjoining canefields south of the forest; the haystack hills to the south; but hardly the hundreds of *piñoneros* themselves.

In this historical context, the *piñoneros* were transformed from "peasants" into "peasant-proletarians", and perhaps ultimately into "proletarians", but all these moments are complex and contradictory in character, and are linked in hardly linear ways.

The *piñoneros* turn to the cane: seasons, and seasons within seasons

The earliest record of Piñones workers in the canefields dates from 1881.[44] From about 1910, most Piñones male adults worked in the fields of the former Machicote slave hacienda during harvest time (*zafra*). In the milieu of the canefields, the "dead time" (*tiempo muerto*) saw the labourers digging and cleaning drainage ditches, cane planting, weeding and cutting trees for new canefields. "The *zafra* tapered off beginning in July, and by September there was almost no work" (144).[45] From August to November, only the colonia's migrant labourers and *agregados* (tenant labourers) were hired. Then in November and December there was almost no work in the canefields: that was the heart of the dead time or the "winter" – "the *invierno*, as we called it" (160).

The passage of these "labour seasons" – "annual convulsions of class

Puerto Rico, 1890–1920", in Consuelo Naranjo *et al.*, *La Nación Soñada: Cuba, Puerto Rico y Filipinas ante el 98* (Madrid, 1996), pp. 211–224.
[44] AGPR, OP, PP, Box 127, "Expediente levantado por Alcalde de Loíza y el Comisario de Torrecillas [. . .]", 19 July 1881, f. 60. Two years later, a Real Hacienda list of squatters on a lot adjoining Virginia included two *intrusos* "who really and effectively do not possess goods of any kind, living solely from their labour as *braceros* [agricultural laborers]". Alcalde to Administración, 19 November 1883, f. 166.
[45] Numbers in brackets refer to page numbers in the author's transcript of taped interviews.

relations"[46] – pervaded the interaction of peasant and rural proletarian labour. This major dimension was not fully present in the "rural proletarians" and "peasants" of *The People of Puerto Rico*. *People* defined its "subcultures" in terms of *single* labour patterns corresponding to a given preponderant time and a single space. Mintz's study of the coastal "subculture" of Santa Isabel/"Cañamelar" left the different, complex spaces and times of the litoral in a penumbra. In Mintz's account, at those *times* when the sugar labourers were not "proletarian" they were simply formless, living in "dead time":[47] a time that almost did not exist, a history-less time. Similarly, Wolf's study of the "highland" peasantry disregarded the large seasonal flows of "highland" labourers to work on the coast, on a daily or weekly basis.[48] Thus Wolf did not contemplate the possibility that a labourer might, at different times of the year, straddle more than one "subculture";[49] or that Puerto Rico's various "subcultures" had profound historical connections. The *People* researchers did not contemplate that Puerto Rico cane labourers could have been "proletarian" and "peasant" at different times of the year, and in different spaces. In *People*, and despite suggestive intimations to the contrary, the seasons and time are presented as uniformly "Western": flat, linear and homogeneous, and without a specific history.

While not much more alert to the specificity of rural social times, Marx's distinction between labour time and production time adumbrated the complexity of agrarian production.[50] This distinction had "infinite" variations across and within branches of production, and importantly contributed to render the analysis of capital more historically concrete. Some of the strongest expressions of this distinction involve natural cycles, as in agriculture where there is a more extended labour time, and a marked difference between labour time and production time.[51] The perimeter of social relations beyond, though connected with large-scale agriculture, is absent from Marx's enquiry.

[46] Brian Pollitt, "Some Problems in Enumerating the 'Peasantry' in Pre-Revolutionary Cuba", *Journal of Peasant Studies*, IV (1977), pp. 167–168.

[47] For Mintz's account of "dead time" on the southern coast of Puerto, see *Worker in the Cane*, p. 22. A mill-centred concept of "dead time" also misconstrues the agrarian cycle of the sugar cane itself. For it is precisely during the "dead time" that cane grows most vigorously and is thus most alive: for the cane, it is the *harvest* that will mean death.

[48] Wolf, "San José", pp. 230–232.

[49] Wolf's account of the Ciales agrarian/religious calendar leaps from Three Kings Day to Holy Week, see *ibid.*, p. 200. This period (January-April) is the height of the sugar harvest on the adjacent coast; many *cialeños* probably migrated even for day-work, especially in the late 1940s when motor transport was widespread.

[50] Marx, *Capital*, vol. II (Mexico, DF, 1959), chs 12 and 13; esp. pp. 209, 213–216.

[51] *Ibid.*, pp. 209, 213. For some implications of production time vs. labour time, see Susan Archer Mann, *Agrarian Capitalism in Theory and Practice* (Chapel Hill, 1980); César Ayala, "La nueva plantación antillana (1898–1934), *Boletín del Centro de Investigaciones Históricas*, 8 (1994–1995), pp. 121–165.

Peasant rhythms defined "dead time" and impinged on the *zafra* itself. The coastal labourers' "peasant" calendar was actually a *peasant/ fisherman/woodsman* (and more) calendar,[52] which meshed with yet other calendars: first, the specific subtropical *natural-ecological* calendar of Puerto Rico; and second, the *religious-festive* calendar, which the coastal labourers observed, even if they were not frequent churchgoers; perhaps because it subsumed, as elsewhere, ancient *astronomical* calendars.[53]

In all, there were not one but at least *five* interwoven calendars and seasonal turns in the shaping of peasant-proletarian labour patterns in early twentieth-century Puerto Rico. It is in this matrix where we may search for regularities beneath seemingly "irregular" work rhythms.[54] The complex array of calendars and seasonal patterns, none of which is clock-like to begin with, generates much of the ambiguity and contradiction – the "practical logic" – that Pierre Bourdieu detected in rural calendars.[55]

A simple opposition between *zafra* and *tiempo muerto* assumes exactly what must be proven: that the social relations and attendant temporal rhythms of coastal peasant life had lost all vitality. In fact, the movement from *tiempo muerto* to *zafra*, considered generally, condensed within an annual cycle a century of the *piñoneros'* history. Living in "dead time" resonated with the "peasant" Piñones of the eighteenth–nineteenth centuries. There was dire material poverty in dead time, no doubt, but there was hardly much wealth during the *zafra*, or in rural social life generally throughout history; and material scarcity should not cloud the significant shift in social relations and historical meaning that the labourers traversed.

---

[52] Gervasio García writes of the agricultural labourers' "irregular rhythm", at odds with a "strict labor discipline": García, "Economía y trabajo en el Puerto Rico del siglo XIX", *Historia Mexicana*, XXXVIII (1989), p. 865. García argues that this "irregularity" was generated by the "intermittent and seasonal labor in the sugar plantations".

[53] In Puerto Rico, the most conspicuous natural seasons are associated with the religious calendar: the dry, warm Lent (*Cuaresma*) and the cool and rainy Christmas. The former is associated with the best fishing, and occurred in the midst of the sugar cane harvest; and there was alternation between both forms of labour even then. The rainier season at the end of the year made day-long work in the canefields relatively difficult; but the rains hardly forestalled the more intermittent rhythms of peasant production on the sandy, well-drained Piñones cropland, nor fishing in the lagoon. Indeed, rainy spells are excellent for crab-catching.

[54] On the superimposition of calendars in slave production in nineteenth-century Martinique, see Dale Tomich, *Slavery in the Circuit of Sugar. Martinique in the World Economy, 1830–1848* (Baltimore, 1990), pp. 230–233. "The temporal requirements of sugar production coincided imperfectly with the social relations of slavery": *ibid.*, p. 232.

[55] Pierre Bourdieu, *Le sens pratique* (Paris, 1980), pp. 23–26; idem, "The Attitude of the Algerian Peasant Toward Time", in Julian Pitt-Rivers, *Mediterranean Countrymen* (Paris, 1963), pp. 56–57. Bourdieu cautioned against confusing "logical models", oriented to economy of observation and coherence, with the real principles of the practices: Bourdieu, *Le sens pratique*, p. 25. "Peasant" and "rural proletarian", of course, are themselves "logical models".

Peasant *and* proletarian

The Central Canóvanas owned or contracted most of the Loíza region's canefields during 1920–1950; the Central's canefields blanketed the coastal plain and climbed hundreds of feet on the foothills just south. In diverse ways – by purchasing higher-yield land, draining *poyales*, obtaining lower property tax assessments, making exacting contracts with *colonos* that left the Central almost risk-free, extending the Central's railway system, pushing the Central's supply zone further into the hill country, and so forth – the Central administration steered regional economic activities and social relations to its advantage.

Yet the ecological and social patterns of the Loíza region did not easily yield. Though in straitened conditions, the *piñoneros* continued to labour in the land and aquatic ecologies of their zone. Their peasant dimensions remained substantial. In the 1910, 1920 and 1936 censuses, a majority of the Piñones male working population did not return cane labour as their primary occupation.[56] Between 1910 and 1936 the absolute number of cane labourers remained about the same (around 80) while their proportion declined with respect to the total number of persons informing occupations: 39 per cent in 1910, 44 per cent in 1920, and 30 per cent in 1936. In 1910, 39 per cent were employed in other agricultural wage labour; 50 per cent were employed in coconut labour in 1920; and in 1936, 38 per cent were engaged in charcoalmaking.

Smallholding continued to be significant in Piñones in the early twentieth century, with the same array of crops as in the mid-nineteenth century. The 1910 US Census listed 721 inhabitants living in 121 households, and 43 *fincas* ("farms"), which corresponds to a third of the households.[57] Hogs, goats, cattle, and even sheep were common. "Here everyone has had goats and pigs" (36). Piñones agriculture built partially on Arawak and African patterns, growing the same crops as Taínos on the same sandy soils cultivated by the Taínos for centuries. Mounds (*montones*) were used for cultivating manioc in *conucos* into the late nineteenth century;[58] and manioc plantings were always distinguished from the rest of the field (*tala*). A complex array of highly productive crops was also grown.[59] In fishing, *trasmayos* of parallel Arawak, African

---

[56] On the perils of census categories identifying "primary occupations", see Brian Pollitt, *Agrarian Reform and the "Agricultural Proletariat" in Cuba, 1958–66: Some Notes* (Glasgow, 1979), p. 4.
[57] US Bureau of the Census, *Thirteenth Census* (1910); Social and Population Schedules, Loíza, Barrio Torrecilla Baja.
[58] Jaime Vélez, Personal Communication (1995). Vélez, an archaeologist, has detected traces of mound formation in the old core of Piñones settlement in La Arena.
[59] Francisco Moscoso, *Tribu y clases en el Caribe antiguo* (San Pedro de Macorís, 1986), pp. 420–428. On Arawak *conuco* agriculture, see David Watts, *The West Indies: Patterns of Development, Culture and Environmental Change Since 1492* (Cambridge, 1986), pp. 53–61.

and European origin were used, as well as hand-fishing. It is hard to find any labour technique of specifically and uniquely African origin.[60] However, the deep practical understanding of the coastal ecology, and indeed the very disposition to settle and remain in this not wholly hospitable ecology (given its insect pests and malaria) does suggest African legacies. In any case, the question of cultural origins in the world of labour remains little-studied in Puerto Rico.

The Piñones forest was an important source of firewood, charcoal and *madera negra*. *Madera negra* is the aged wood of trees fallen and buried centuries ago in the deep muck of the forest floor. In the midst of the forest penumbra, large trunks had to be painstakingly pulled out; then the labourers had to cut the nearly fossilized, stonelike wood, then take it to the nearest canal on wagons running on portable rail planks furnished by the Central (223). For a single large trunk, the process might take a week. Work on *madera negra*, while nominally (and perhaps spatially) "peasant" labour, had striking connections with the canefields. The tough, termite-immune *madera negra* was chiefly in demand by the sugar plantations themselves, for fence-posts and especially railway cross-ties. Its extraction was gruelling, more so than all other canefield tasks, and workers often preferred the open space and sociability of the canefield.

Coconut labour was also an important form of "peasant" labour in Piñones where, again, vital "proletarian" dimensions quickly surface. Piñones was at the centre of a 4,000-acre plus coconut belt that stretched from the Río Espíritu Santo in Río Grande (just east of Loíza) to Toa Baja west of San Juan. Piñones' *cocales* extended over 1,300 acres. The Loíza coconut belt – a geographer called it the "coconut fringe" or the "coconut-garden zone" – was the largest in Puerto Rico, and centred the island's coconut industry.[61] While coconut palms were hardly alien to Piñones in the nineteenth century, the large coconut groves of Piñones originated in the late 1890s. By the 1920s, fully-grown *cocales* stretched across Piñones, in land leased to coconut growers. The Piñones villagers were employed in husking the coconuts prior to shipment, on a piece-work basis. An arduous pace of 1–2,000 coconuts a day had to be maintained in order to earn $1–$2, jabbing each coconut on to a man-grove spike – a hazardous task.

A complex and seasonally-variable array of occupations existed in Piñones whereby most male adults and some women incorporated sea-sonal sugar cane labour.

What people did here was to work in the *montes*, make charcoal, all those things [. . .] Here everyone made charcoal, and when there was no charcoal,

---

[60] See Eugenio Fernández Méndez, "Los corrales de pesca indígenas de Puerto Rico", *Revista del Instituto de Cultura Puertoriqueña*, IX (1960), pp. 9–13.
[61] Margaret Uttley, "Land Utilization in the Canóvanas Sugar District" (Ph.D., University of Chicago, 1937), p. 65.

firewood, and when there was no firewood the *madera*, and when there was neither firewood nor *madera*, they worked in the cane (238).

However, cane labour was not uniformly a last alternative: cane paid relatively well and was a welcome change from the damp and dark work waist-high in the mangrove muck; it also did not require time-consuming trips to the San Juan market to sell charcoal or produce.[62] Coconut shelling was more autonomous than cane labour, but was strenous and could be dangerous. The question of choice between activities was complex, and often ran in unpredictable directions. Of course, important social constraints existed on these choices: for instance, alternatives such as cultivating substantially more land within Piñones were virtually closed given customary patterns of land tenure there, and strictures against depriving neighbours and kin of land customarily held.[63]

The peasant and the rural proletarian dimensions of the *piñoneros* were not discrete; peasant and proletarian dimensions were conspicuous throughout. The *piñoneros* carried out their autonomous peasant activities in spaces they regarded as their own, through labour they paced and whose product they appropriated, working individually or in small groups. Rural proletarian social relations comprised agricultural labour for a wage, under supervision, and in co-ordination with large numbers of other labourers, both those physically present in the canefields and in the distant sugar mill. Strong physical exertion not solely paced by the labourer and repetitive movement were also major characteristics of rural proletarian social relations. Since the tangents between peasant and proletarian relations were so significant, I choose to approach rural proletarian *dimensions* rather than to identify a "social type" of rural proletarians or distinct rural proletarian "roles".

Peasant labour in Piñones underwent deep transformations after 1900. Village activities and social relations retained autonomy but in the 1930s were eroded in their market conditions (charcoal burning) or in their ecology (fishing, hunting, crab catching). Piñones' ecology was literally shrinking as adjacent wetlands were further drained, and population growth and falling prices for firewood and charcoal led to the cutting of much of the mangrove forest. Various nominally peasant activities now had accentuated proletarian dimensions, due to the pace and intensity of work that was demanded: chiefly coconut husking and *madera negra*. This may help explain why the *piñoneros* often preferred to work in

---

[62] I have not detected among the old *piñoneros* a suspicion of wage payment, much less a sense that it was demoniacal or charged with mystical power, such as Taussig found in *The Devil and Commodity Fetishism*. Of course, until the 1940s they rarely saw a cash wage, as they were paid in scrip redeemable at the Central store or in other nearby stores.

[63] See Taussig, "Peasant Economics and the Development of Capitalist Agriculture in the Cauca Valley, Colombia", *Latin American Perspectives*, V (1978); idem, "Rural Proletarianization".

the canefields. "Peasant" labour was increasingly becoming difficult, time-consuming, exhausting and "proletarian" [. . .] even as "proletarian" labour was itself shrinking. The peasant dimensions of *piñoneros* did not remain aloof from broader transformations, and it would be a serious mistake to view their production activities as part of a changeless "tradition".

Peasants in the cane?

Perhaps most surprisingly, canefield labour was itself markedly "peasantlike" even into the mid-twentieth century. In the canefields near Piñones an array of tasks spanned age-groups and gender in a "peasant" spectrum, from tasks such as taking lunch to the canefields, weeding and fertilizing – where women and children participated[64] – to the generally male heart of the cane harvest process: cane cutting and loading.

Planting was carried out by brigades whose members were often linked by kinship and residence. Some children and adult labourers carried the seed, others sowed it, and still others did the actual planting. Planters drove the seed (a cutting from a mature stalk) into the ground with special picks. Sometimes whole lengths of cane were planted in furrows and covered with loose earth.[65] Fertilizing (*regar abono*) began after the first weeding and replanting. Like the digging and maintenance of drainage ditches, and like planting, this was fully manual labour. Two applications of fertilizer were made. After the first weeding of the cane, some 400 lbs per acre of fertilizer were applied. A second application was made four to six weeks later. The labourers cast the fertilizer on either side while walking down the furrows (*sangrías*) between banks.[66] In newly planted Canóvanas fields as much as 3–4 tons of crushed lime was applied to correct acidity and improve texture.[67] Brigades combined different types of cultivation work as they moved from field to field.

In canefield labour, the Piñones labourers consistently avoided the most "proletarian", most individualized and most perilous canefield task: cane cutting. This task is often erroneously equated with the totality of canefield labour.[68] Cane *loading* was much preferred. Indeed, loading

[64] While boys from Piñones were active in canefield tasks such as fertilizing, it seems that Piñones women rarely worked in the canefields in any capacity; the women's connection to the canefields was cooking lunch and taking it to their spouses. A number of women from nearby Carolina did work regularly in those tasks.
[65] *Gilmore's Puerto Rico Sugar Manual* (New Orleans, 1931), p. 98.
[66] Uttley, "Land Utilization in the Canóvanas Sugar District", p. 97; German Kali Works [F.S. Earle], *The Cultivation of Sugar Cane in the West Indies* (Havana, 1926), p. 32.
[67] *Ibid.*, p. 33.
[68] See, for example, Eric Wolf, *Peasant Wars of the Twentieth Century* (New York, 1969), p. 257. In their attitude toward canefield labour, the *piñoneros* resembled Mintz's main

equalled cane cutting in its strategic location at the heart of the harvest process. Cane loading paid slightly better than cutting, probably because of the skill and speed involved; a day's work could be delayed by the cane tumbling from improperly loaded carts as these moved on rails. Though less dangerous than cane cutting, loading was probably more strenuous: it included the lifting and heaving of 315-lb. iron rail planks for the portable rail track. Over this track passed the small wagons to be loaded with cane. No oxcarts were used in the often wet and sluggish fields of the Central Canóvanas. "It was harder work than cutting cane; the *llenadores* had to both fill the wagons and carry the rail planks" (158). And loading, unlike cutting, directly involved teamwork: all loading was done in pairs of two, one loading from each side of a cart.

Of course, the rhythm and pace of work in planting and fertilizing may not have been wholly peasantlike, and one might well argue that this was decisive. But there is a difference in physical rigour between these tasks and cutting and loading cane. Moreover, there are other "peasant" dimensions that are relevant to *all* phases of canefield labour, including those that seem least peasantlike. We know that field labour was extremely labour-intensive and relied heavily on manual labour, in sharp contrast to the factory phase of production.

On the whole, it appears to me that the manufacturer of sugar in Puerto Rico is in advance of the cultivation. No pains are spared to erect the best machinery and to get the best results from cane delivered to the mills. As a rule, all operations are under the supervision of experts, and modern sugar making has reached a high state of perfection. *But the fields have been neglected.*[69]

Manuel Moreno Fraginals has concluded that even into the twentieth century cane cultivation remained technologically in the slave epoch.[70] However, Moreno Fraginals remained silent on the social relations of production – and more specifically of *labour* – in the post-emancipation canefields. For his part, in his ethnographic view of canefield labour, Mintz focused systematically on the similarities with urban-industrial labour at the expense of affinities that are at least as strong with regard to peasant labour, to the point of dismissing visibly peasant dimensions as conjunctural anomalies.

In fact, peasant social relations traversed various canefield labour processes (especially planting and weeding). These tasks demanded spe-cialized skills and dexterity (as in machete-cutting) that were common

informant *Taso* Zayas, the "worker in the cane". Zayas cut cane only once during his decades in the cane, and quit by mid-morning: Mintz, *Worker in the Cane*, p. 202.
[69] US Tarriff Commission, 1926, p. 259; emphasis added.
[70] Manuel Moreno Fraginals, "Plantaciones en el Caribe: Cuba-Puerto Rico-Santo Do-mingo (1860–1940)", in idem, *La historia como arma* (Barcelona, 1983), pp. 56–117.

among Puerto Rican peasants. Instead of "deskilling", in terms of "peasant" skills canefield labour was more like "superskilling". These skills were a matter of pride for the labourers, especially in the socialized milieu of the canefields and the "animal spirits" that socialized labour stimulated.[71] Skill pride facilitated a smooth flow of co-operation with a minimum of supervision, and allowed the workers a sense of personal and group identity in the canefields.

Field labour in the cane was invariably organized in *labour gangs*. The labour gangs were formed in part through village ties of kinship and friendship; continuous face-to-face relations with foremen, as distinct from overseers; and "peasant" work implements that often belonged to the labourers (machetes, hoes, shovels, etc.). The gangs were not supervised directly by the (white) overseer, who spent his days on horseback making the rounds of the plantation, but by an (almost always black) foreman from Piñones or Carolina. Labour gangs thrust us into the vast and little-analysed field of simple co-operation on a quite massive scale (see below). Francisco Scarano has rightly noted that "the daily interaction between workers, foremen, overseers and managers" in Puerto Rican canefields remains quite under-researched.[72]

As an integral part of labour-gang organization, until the 1940s canefield work was paid by the task (*ajuste*) rather than in time-wages. *Thus there was no "true" wage labour.* Mintz overstated the case when he wrote of "the emergence of a 'genuine' rural proletariat" in the 1940s.[73] In the labour gangs, delegation of supervision was no unforeseen windfall. The Puerto Rico Labour Bureau concluded in 1913: "The principal objective of [the *ajuste*] system, it appears, was to avoid the annoyance of watching over the men who contract".[74] Moreover, in the Loíza littoral as elsewhere task-work was remunerated by *non-cash* means such as scrip (*vales*) that nourished debt relations. Cash is a seemingly secondary attribute of the wage-form that, in fact, is surprisingly important in terms of the social relations and social context that it presupposes.[75]

<hr/>

[71] Walter Rodney wrote that in Guyana field hands took pride "in their proficiency with cutlass, shovel, and fork": *A History of the Guyanese Working People*, p. 161. See also Mintz, "Cañamelar", p. 357; Juan Martínez Alier, "'Tierra o trabajo': notas sobre el campesinado y la reforma agraria, 1959–60", in Juan and Verena Martínez Alier, *Cuba: economía y sociedad* (Madrid, 1972), p. 174. The phrase "animal spirits" comes from Marx on simple co-operation; see below.
[72] Francisco Scarano, "Las huellas esquivas de la memoria: antropología e historia en *Taso, trabajador de la caña*". Preliminary study to *Taso, trabajador de la caña* (Río Piedras, 1988), pp. 36, 40, the Spanish translation of Mintz's *Worker in the Cane*.
[73] Sidney Mintz, "Was the Plantation Slave a Proletarian?", *Review*, II (1978), p. 85.
[74] Puerto Rico Labor Bureau, *Report* (1913), p. 34.
[75] García, "Economía y trabajo", pp. 858–859. I appreciate Gervasio García's comments on this score. It is significant, in terms of theories of capitalists' role in capitalist development, that the transformation into cash time-wages was accomplished in Puerto Rico after 1938 only through widespread labour agitation and aggressive interventions by the Puerto

Both scrip payment and endebtment have a long history in Puerto Rico, in and out of sugar production.[76] The last major chapter of these forms of payment of labour in Puerto Rico – which have not, however, disappeared[77] – extended into the 1940s in the space of the canefields. Also relevant is the pattern of wages paid for *each day's* labour (though on a weekly basis), which gave the *jornaleros* (literally, "day-labourers") greater leeway in terms of the days worked per week.

Too often historical research on Puerto Rico's cane labourers has conflated all "wage" labour into time-wages, in a quest for an early, full-scale proletarianization.[78] It is hard to argue for a "conceptual" rural proletarian status on the basis of labour gangs, task-payment, non-cash wages and endebtment, and where the forms of supervision, sociability and autonomy are still "face to face" *within* and *between* the labour gangs. In "Cañamelar", Mintz registered many of these specificities, but missed their historical, customary (and indeed "universal") character. Remarkably, Mintz labelled the old rural patterns, featuring labour recruiters and gang foremen,[79] as *temporary measures initiated by the US sugar corporations.* "Until the corporation had worked out its own estimates on labour performance, it left the jobs of recruiting, bossing and arranging pay of workers with labour recruiters."[80] And in Mintz's account, the social practices of the recruiters became merely "unscrupulous[81]."

By and large, it is probably true that peasant labour involved greater skills and more accumulated local knowledge than proletarian labour. But in other ways, proletarian labour *was more highly developed and complex* than peasant labour.[82] Labour processes in the canefields expressed a more socialized and historically more developed organization that co-ordinated and integrated the labour of the *piñoneros* and

Rico government (and, indirectly, of at least segments of the US government), and *against* the wishes of many or most cane employers.

[76] Significantly, task-work was also the norm in Piñones peasant labour such as wood-cutting, while piece-work governed coconut husking.

[77] Task-work remains especially important in the construction industry, especially in smaller projects.

[78] The question of task-work raises many issues that extend deep into plantation slavery. See Tomich, *Slavery in the Circuit of Sugar*, pp. 245–248; Philip Morgan, "Work and Culture: The Task System and the World of Low Country Blacks, 1700–1880", *William & Mary Quarterly*, XXXIX (1982), pp. 563–599; idem, "Task and Gang Systems: The Organization of Labor on New World Plantations", in Stephen Inness (ed.), *Work and Labour in Early America* (Chapel Hill, 1988), pp. 157–219.

[79] On the labour gangs of freedmen shortly after emancipation, see Andrés Ramos Mattei, "El liberto en el régimen de trabajo azucarero en Puerto Rico, 1870–1880", in Ramos Mattei (ed.), *Azúcar y esclavitud* (Río Piedras, 1982).

[80] Mintz, "Cañamelar", p. 349.

[81] *Ibid.*

[82] Of course, this has large political implications; see Raymond Williams, *The Country and the City* (New York, 1973).

other *loiceños* in field and factory, to a degree unthinkable in peasant labour.[83]

Thus my final point with respect to the peasant dimensions of canefield labour concerns *simple co-operation*: the integrated, co-operative, and often largely manual labour processes conceptualized by Marx in *Capital*. This angle has been largely overlooked by students of sugar canefield labour, or of rural labour generally.[84] Co-ordination between cane cutting, carrying and loading made for an astonishing development of simple co-operation in the canefields. The urgency of deploying vast amounts of labour at a given time is part and parcel of the relationship between "production time" and "labour time" in sugar cane agriculture.[85]

Marx valued the complexity and productive power of *rural* simple co-operation more than most of his students have noticed.[86] His comments on "rural idiocy" and peasants as "potatoes" in more journalistic texts have overshadowed his perspectives on simple co-operation in agriculture. Marx criticized Aristotle's assumption that sociability was necessarily *urban*, and proposed a *rural* polis of simple co-operation. Co-operation multiplied the energies of the workers by begetting "a rivalry and a stimulation of the 'animal spirits' ".[87] And remarkably, Marx even writes that co-operation (not the expropriation of smallholders?!) was "the starting-point [that] coincides with the birth of capital".[88] He envisaged as a pre-eminent terrain for simple co-operation "that kind of large-scale agriculture which corresponds to the period of manufactures", where substantial numbers of workers laboured in integrated labour processes, with or without tools.[89]

Simple co-operation has always been, and continues to be, the predominant form in those branches of production in which capital operates on a large scale, but the division of labour and machinery plays only an insignificant part.[90]

---

[83] "Less than thirty-five hours from standing cane to sugar in the sack is the aim at Central Canóvanas. Within twenty-four hours from the swing of the machete in the field, the cane is delivered to the unloader at the mill. In eight to ten hours from the time the cane reaches the revolving knives, sugar pours into the bag". Uttley, "Land Utilization in the Canóvanas Sugar District", p. 155.

[84] But see David H. Morgan, "The Place of Harvesters in Nineteenth-century Village Life", in Raphael Samuel, *Village Life and Labour* (London, 1975), pp. 27–72, and others in that collection; idem, *Harvesters and Harvesting: A Study of the Rural Proletariat* (London, 1982).

[85] Thus there are "critical moments [. . .] determined by the nature of the labour process, during which certain definite results must be obtained": Karl Marx, *Capital*, I (New York, 1976), p. 445. In a "combined working day", shortness of time is compensated for by the large mass of labour thrown into the field of production at the decisive moment: *ibid.*

[86] *Ibid.*, ch. 13.

[87] *Ibid.*, p. 443. This was already present in the second form of co-operation, as Marx stressed.

[88] *Ibid.*, p. 453. This viewpoint meshed with Marx's "heroic" sense of the rural proletariat as a world-historical class, and clashed with the historical account that Marx offers of the "gypsy" labour gangs in England. But then that "tension" runs throughout Marx's writings on the rural proletariat. Giusti-Cordero, "Labour, Ecology and History", ch. 2.

[89] Marx, *Capital*, I, p. 444.

[90] *Ibid.*, p. 454. See also pp. 441–442 on two other forms of co-operation.

Sugar plantation field labour in the Caribbean certainly fits this description. Sugar labour, indeed, is an excellent example of how simple co-operation involves peasant and proletarian dimensions. The complex peasant-proletarian patterns of Puerto Rico's canefields probably obtained through the collapse of large-scale sugar production in the 1960s. True, the generalization of time-wages at the beginning of that decade appears to mark the arrival of a rural proletariat in Puerto Rico's canefields. Yet in Piñones as elsewhere, if anything, there may have been a process of *de*proletarianization after 1940: (1) technological advances expanded "dead time", at a quickening pace;[91] (2) the colonial state expropriated tens of thousands of acres of corporate sugar cane lands, and a new state sugar corporation became the largest employer of sugar cane field labourers; (3) a fraction of the land expropriated by the Authority was distributed in allotments (*parcelas*) to landless labourers; (4) Puerto Rico's sugar production contracted as the US federal tariff system opened its doors more widely to foreign sugars, and US and world sugar prices declined; and (5) very significantly, a massive emigration gushed to Puerto Rican cities and to the US.[92]

Rural proletarianization, in so far as it came about in Puerto Rico after 1940, may have been less a sign of the maturity of the "American Sugar Kingdom" in the hispanophone Caribbean, as is suggested in Mintz and others, than a sign of impending demise and transformation.

Tropical discourse

In recent decades, the question of the social and historical character of large-scale plantation wage labour has been relatively neglected by world social science, particularly with respect to sugar-central production. This may be due to the brilliant ethnography of Sidney Mintz's original research, as well as its congenial mix of Marxist and Weberian approaches.[93]

---

[91] Already in the 1930s, Gayer and associates found that there was a "trend toward successively greater drops in employment during the slack months, particularly in field labour": Gayer *et al.*, *The Sugar Economy of Puerto Rico*, p. 180; Puerto Rico Minimum Wage Board, *La industria de azúcar*, pp. 76, 180; see also Mintz, *Worker in the Cane*, p. 272.

[92] *Ibid.*, p. 273. Total migration from Puerto Rico to the US shot up from 151,000 in 1940–1949 to 430,000 in 1950–1959, the greatest increase ever both in absolute and relative amounts. José L. Vázquez Calzada, *La población de Puerto Rico y su trayectoria histórica* (Río Piedras, 1978), p. 277.

[93] In the field of agrarian history, and particularly regarding agrarian capitalism, Marx and Weber are in any case quite close. In his study of East Elbian agriculture, Weber considers "the transformation from the estate economy into a capitalistic economy on the basis of the underlying organization of labor": Martin Riesebrodt, "From Patriarchalism to Capitalism: The Theoretical Context of Max Weber's Agrarian Studies (1892–3)", in Kenneth Tribe (ed.), *Reading Weber* (London, 1989), p. 140. Riesebrodt adds: "In his analysis of the proletarianization process [Weber] also underlines the same elements as Marx": *ibid.*

In Puerto Rico, the authority of Mintz's perspective on Puerto Rican social history has been especially strong. Mintz and *The People of Puerto Rico* as a whole "have exerted decisive influences in the historical literature [of Puerto Rico] of recent years";[94] Mintz's work has been the source of "many of our ideas on the trajectory of sugar in our milieu".[95] "Cañamelar" and Mintz's related writings were pillars of "capital importance" of the "New History" (*la Nueva Historia*).[96] Interest in Puerto Rico paralleled attention to *The People of Puerto Rico*, and particularly in the work of Mintz and Wolf, on the part of Anglo-American "dependency studies" and then "peasant studies".

In the early 1970s, Angel Quintero Rivera's work on the Puerto Rican rural proletariat followed the main lines of Mintz's argument, and it was through Quintero's work that Mintz's influence has been especially strong in Puerto Rico.[97] Quintero Rivera laid a cornerstone of the "New History" with his analysis of the sugar cane rural proletariat (*proletariado cañero*).[98] While differences exist between the two authors – for instance, Quintero Rivera stressed broad political and ideological dimensions – there are also strong continuities. In both Mintz and Quintero, capitalist social relations governed after 1898 (though Mintz posited a longer "transition"); and historical agency pertained basically to the US sugar corporations. Little is said of autochthonous agrarian social relations and their problematic mesh with the new order of things. Mintz and Quintero Rivera stripped the bourgeoisie and the rural working class of their complexity; the many "peasant" dimensions of the sugar labourers, and indeed the "proletarian" dimensions of their peasant patterns, were

---

[94] Scarano, "Las huellas esquivas de la memoria", p. 37.

[95] Scarano, "El colonato azucarero en Puerto Rico, 1873–1934: problemas para su estudio", *Historia y Sociedad*, III (1990), p. 155.

[96] Scarano, "Las huellas esquivas de la memoria", p. 13. Gordon Lewis's masterly *Puerto Rico: Freedom and Power in the Caribbean* (New York, 1963) further strengthened the authority of Mintz's analysis in Puerto Rico. Lewis argued that in the twentieth century Puerto Rican rural workers became propertyless and wage-earning workers "in the classical sense", especially in the island's "locus classicus of economic change", the sugar industry: *Freedom and Power*, pp. 89, 95.

[97] For example, Quintero Rivera, "El capitalismo y el proletariado rural", *Revista de Ciencias Sociales*, XIX (1974), pp. 61–103; Quintero Rivera and García, *Breve historia*.

[98] On several important issues, Quintero Rivera pushed Mintz's already bold conclusions even further. Three "new historians" offered dissenting voices: Gervasio García called attention to the strong "precapitalist" features of the Puerto Rican rural labour force, and political economy as a whole, into the twentieth century; the argument around "irregular labour discipline", discussed above, is part of that analysis: García, "Economía y trabajo". Andrés Ramos Mattei stressed the significance of sugar-central production prior to 1898, and thus raised vital questions about the real meanings of US penetration: Ramos Mattei, *La sociedad del azúcar en Puerto Rico: 1870–1910* (San Juan, 1988). And Fernando Picó has demonstrated the resilience of smallholders and the durability of black circum-cane labourer communities: *Amargo café: los pequeños y mediados caficultores de Utuado a fines del siglo XIX* (Río Piedras/Huracán, 1979); idem, *Vivir en Caimito* (Río Piedras, 1979).

almost deliberately obscured (as were the mercantile and financial dimensions of the agrarian bourgeoisie).[99]

In Mintz's and Quintero's reading, the US sugar centrals became "the bourgeoisie" and the sugar workers (representing the rest of the nation) became the "proletariat". Despite its radical and class strains, such a perspective happens to mesh easily with old currents of hispanophone Caribbean nationalism; in a sense, both Quintero Rivera and Mintz are heirs of Fernando Ortiz and Ramiro Guerra y Sánchez.[100] Thus native social classes come into view only as victims of massive US capital – although Mintz and Quintero make rural proletarians, rather than the *colonos* and *guajiros* (analogous to *jíbaros*), the heroic victims.[101]

Especially in Quintero's account, proletarians (rural, invariably led by urban artisans-cum-proletarians) are made to be the bearers of the nation. Thus Quintero Rivera collapsed the national question into working-class politics: the rise of the rural proletariat was, to Quintero Rivera and to many of the "New Historians", the strongest evidence that cultural-nationalist interpretations of Puerto Rican history and the symbology of the *jíbaro* missed the acute class conflicts of early twentieth-century Puerto Rico.

Quintero Rivera held in tension the national and class dimensions of his analysis. Subsequent work basically forked off in one or another direction: towards a narrow class reading (José Luis González), perhaps close to Mintz, or towards a narrow nationalist interpretation (Taller de Formación Política, a research collective). In *País de cuatro pisos*,[102] González invoked Quintero's research to dismiss Puerto Rican nationalist politics in the 1930s as Fascist, and situated the peasant *jíbaro* as a banner of that current. González located the nation rather in the black and mulatto coastal population, presumably with special force among rural proletarians. The Taller exalted nationalism and especially Pedro Albizu Campos, claiming that he converged with the sugar workers – once again viewed as "classic" rural proletarians – in the 1930s. Both "forks" after Quintero are a departure from hispanophone Caribbean nationalism, but neither goes beyond being mirror reversals-in-continuity of it.

The question of the rural proletariat is evidently entwined with the controversy between national vs. class politics in Puerto Rico. However, subsequent discussion turned on a putative Puerto Rican "national bourgeoisie", while the agricultural proletariat remained a murky presence assumed, and at times asserted, but never subjected to critical scrutiny.

---

[99] See Giusti-Cordero, "En búsqueda de la nación concreta"; idem, "Hacia otro 98: el 'grupo español' en Puerto Rico".
[100] Fernando Ortiz, *Cuban Counterpoint* (New York, 1947); see Mintz, "Foreword" to Guerra y Sánchez, *Sugar and Society in the Caribbean*.
[101] Martínez Alier, *Cuba: economía y sociedad*.
[102] José Luis González, *El país de cuatro pisos* (Río Piedras, 1980).

Indeed, the most prominent themes in recent years have moved even further away from agrarian social relations: the social and political character of the Puerto Rican nationalism, the *hispanismo* of the intellectual elite, the ideology of its riveting leader Albizu Campos.[103] In the background of these debates lay more practical and messy issues concerning the direction ("workerist" vs. more national) and political alliances of the complex Puerto Rican independence-socialist movement in the 1970s-1980s, which happened to be the matrix of most "new historians".

The counterpoint in Puerto Rico between the categories of peasant and rural proletariat, as typically defined, is suggestive. To a large extent, this dichotomy has defined discussions of Puerto Rican cultural and social history, and national identity, over most of this century. In Puerto Rico, as elsewhere, anthropological argument has been the stuff of cultural discussion and political folklore. But the opposite is also true, perhaps rarely with such force as in Puerto Rico, for The *People of Puerto Rico* project canonized both the categories of rural proletarian and peasant in world anthropology as part and parcel of its detonation of Puerto Rican national identity. *People* researcher Robert Manners was perhaps especially forthright: in his analysis, he stated, Puerto Rico

has been seen in reality as a number of interrelated subcultures with certain basic similarities running throughout, but with many differences owing not only to the pattern of earning a living but the way in which each person is related to the means of earning a living. On the basis of this investigation, we have been forced [!] to reject any assumption that the cultural particulars found among the people in any one region – especially the particulars involved directly and indirectly in the relationship of people to the land – will be just like those found in other regions of the island. *We see even less reason for any assumptions of a homogeneous national character for the people of Puerto Rico.*[104]

Thus Puerto Rico's vernacular discussions of class and nation in the 1920s-1940s acquired unusually broad, if often implicit, ramifications, while subsequent Puerto Rican discussions were significantly shaped by the vast and authoritative field of world anthropology and social science.

The peasant-rural proletarian dichotomy at the heart of the Steward project was at least partially a political project of the PPD and allied metropolitan interests. For the PPD privileged the *jíbaro* peasant with

---

[103] Quintero Rivera, "Historia de unas clases sin historia. Comentarios críticos al *País de cuatro pisos*" (San Juan, 1983); Taller de Formación Política, *La cuestión nacional*; Luis Angel Ferrao, "Nacionalismo, élite intelectual e hispanismo en el Puerto Rico de los años treinta", in Silvia Alvarez-Curbelo and María Elena Rodríguez Castro (eds), *Del nacionalismo al populismo: cultura y política en Puerto Rico* (Río Piedras, 1993), pp. 37–60; Luis Ferrao, *Pedro Albizu Campos y el nacionalismo puertorriqueño* (Río Piedras, 1990); Taller de Formación Política, *Pedro Albizu Campos: conservador, fascista o revolucionario* (Río Piedras, 1991); Juan Manuel Carrión et al., *La nación puertorriqueña: ensayos en torno a Pedro Albizu Campos* (Río Piedras, 1993).
[104] Manners, "Tabará", pp. 168–169 (emphasis added).

its left hand even as with its right hand it split both the CGT (*Confederación General de Trabajadores*), energized by newly powerful sugar worker unions in 1945, and the independence movement. The CGT was aligned with the CIO in the US and had a sizeable Communist and pro-independence presence. Mintz disingenuously attributed the division of the CGT unions to "internal dissension", and found an "identity of interests" between the PPD and the (now deeply PPD-manipulated) CGT into the 1948 elections,[105] a moment of decisive political conflict in Puerto Rico. The torpedoing of the *Congreso pro Independencia* (by both the PPD and the US government) receives a similarly cavalier treatment in *People*, which describes pro-independence forces as being in the main "bitterly anti-American".[106]

The *jíbaro* privileged by the PPD, which was indeed a specific version of the *jíbaro*, informed the reading made by *The People of Puerto Rico* of Puerto Rico's rural population. The PPD *jíbaro* resonates in *People* both affirmatively – as in Wolf's research – and negatively in Mintz's account of the rural proletariat. Both Wolf and Mintz constructed (*and* "saw") the rural proletariat largely in contrast to the *jíbaro* peasant, and both underpinned (and "naturalized") the *jíbaro*/rural proletarian social dichotomy with a further, spatial dichotomy between highland and lowland.

And both Wolf and Mintz not incidentally affirmed the class rather than class *and* national content of Puerto Rico's decisive political conflicts of the 1940s. In the broader context of the Steward project, Mintz and Wolf generated an ideological, colonialist interpretation of Puerto Rican history that neither of these important anthropologists has ever reassessed.

Later, in the "New History", the rural proletariat and the *jíbaro*[107] were again held in tension as dichotomy. Perhaps trapped by the dichotomy, Quintero attempted a strategy that was almost doomed from the start: to instil the class construct of the rural proletariat with a national content.[108] Quintero's attempt remained unpersuasive: his writings on the working-class *patria* find only urban artisan-intellectuals; and, on the whole, these were linked to sugar workers tenuously at best.

I have argued here that we need to go beyond dichotomies or counterpoints between peasants and rural proletarians.[109] The relationship was

[105] Mintz, "Cañamelar", p. 397. For a contrasting interpretation of the CGT split, see Quintero Rivera and García, *Desafío y solidaridad*, pp. 124–125.
[106] *Ibid.*, p. 82; but see Francisco Scarano, *Puerto Rico: cinco siglos de historia* (San Juan, 1993), pp. 722–726.
[107] Perhaps not trivially, the term "rural proletariat" is usually phrased as plural, while "*jíbaro*" appears as the singular.
[108] Quintero Rivera, "Puerto Rican National Development: Class & Nation in a Colonial Context", *Marxist Perspectives*, IX (1980), pp. 10–31.
[109] For a pathbreaking analysis of the "peasant" and "proletarian" dimensions of slave labour, see Tomich, *Slavery in the Circuit of Sugar*, pp. 261–262. Tomich qualifies Mintz's concept of "proto-peasant" not by arguing, as some have done, for the formation of an

rather one between peasant and proletarian dimensions pervading both
the nominally "peasant" and "rural proletarian" milieux. In other words,
the "factory in the field" of classic description in Mintz's "Cañamelar"
was indeed a factory *in* the field: the sugar mill. Yet that hardly exhausted
the characterization of the "field". And in this perspective, another
metaphor that Mintz employed, the "land-and-factory combine",
becomes a land-and-factory *and village* combine, or perhaps more con-
cretely a land-and-factory-*and labour* combine, with "labour" itself
having quite complex meanings.[110]

Culturally and otherwise, universal rural proletarianization and wholesale destruction of peasant subsistence – assuming that swift suppression
of peasant practices and outlooks is possible – was not necessarily in
the interest even of the sugar centrals corporations, or for that matter any
other capitalist enterprise. Under full proletarianization, the reproduction
costs of the labourer would fall below that of the wages, or the labourer
would reproduce his or her labour only partially. Productivity would
plummet amidst disease, in the end imperilling the existence of the
labourer population itself. On the other hand, the very skills that plantation labour required are in many ways *peasant* skills, honed at least
partly in peasant milieux.

In Piñones, an old black lowland population of "squatter"/peasant-
woodsmen-fishermen communities entered the sugar-central era with
a strong, and already complex, heterogeneous "peasant" background,
notwithstanding the physical proximity of the mills. The pre-plantation
history of a labourer population needs to be weighed seriously, especially
where the labourer populations predate large-scale plantation development in a particular region – as was the case in the hispanophone
Caribbean.

In the Piñones villages, an array of labour patterns defined the *piñoneros* as peasants, and far more than that: they farmed cropland, but
also grazed cattle, fished and caught crabs, cut wood and made charcoal,
extracted *madera negra*, felled and shelled coconuts, etc., in a variety
of arrangements some of which were laced with proletarian dimensions.

Proletarian labour processes such as cutting and loading were intertwined in the canefields with more "peasant" processes such as planting
and fertilizing. Following the ambiguous rhythms of natural and socially-
developed seasons, and of seasons within seasons, the Piñones labourers
moved actively between forms of peasant labour, peasant and proletarian
spaces, and undertook work in the canefields much as they did within

---

independent peasantry, but "by examining the historical interrelation between the various
types of laboring activities performed by the slave population". At the same time, Tomich
locates the "focal point" of the development of the slaves' autonomous production and
marketing activities in "the struggle between master and slave over the conditions of labor
and of social and material life within slavery": *ibid.*, p. 261.
[110] See Warman, "El problema del proletariado agrícola".

labour processes. This takes us beyond received images of a uniformly proletarianized lowland black population.

Upon the onset of sugar-central production in the early twentieth century, the labourers of Piñones, like many of Puerto Rico's field labourers generally, did not become merely landless, waged rural proletarians devoted overwhelmingly to sugar cane labour. Peasant activities may have been "subsidiary" in terms of cash income, but not so in terms of their importance for subsistence, or for the social autonomy of the labourers.

Mintz ultimately recognized as much in "Cañamelar", in a crucial passage near the end of the study whose full meaning we may now appreciate and which anticipated Mintz's more historical sense of the peasant-plantation relationship in later work. Mintz had elsewhere recognized the existence of non-cane activities among rural proletarians of "Cañamelar", but relegated them to "subsidiary economic activities". Now, in reference to persistent "folk arts and skills" – or is it *"peasant arts and skills"*? – those activities appear as far more than "subsidiary".[111]

One of the remarkable features of the life of the rural proletariat is its curious blending of the patterns we think of as customarily urban, such as landlessness, wage-earning, food-buying, etc., with those associated with rural life. The values of folk arts and skills come to have special meaning in such a context, particularly since life is as dependent in many ways on successful subsidiary economic activities as it is on the main wage-earning activity (Mintz offers examples). These random examples demonstrate that the rural proletarian subculture has not been stripped bare of its earlier material culture and technology by the imposition of the land-and-factory combine system. In many areas of life, new material items – including foods, fabrics, containers and shoes – have partly supplanted more traditional ones which were home-made rather than purchased. But the innumerable items of culture which make life possible, which help to shape it and to give it depth and meaning, have by no means been completely eradicated. *Life in Barrio Poyal is not urban life nor is it rural: it consists of a mixture of the features of both urban and rural in special ways and in a special historical setting.*[112]

If rural proletarians combined, according to these strategic comments, *rural and urban* material life, might not they also combine *peasant and proletarian*, as a "mixture of the features of both [. . .] in special ways and in a special historical setting"?[113] Mintz almost palpably drew back from the implications of his findings. Even the terms "rural proletarian" and "peasant" do not appear in a straightforward manner in this com-

---

[111] Of course, the cultural significance of those activities was a concern that Mintz the anthropologist could not elude and which in any case could not be measured only quantitatively.

[112] Mintz, "Cañamelar", p. 401; emphasis added.

[113] *Ibid*; emphasis added.

mentary: peasant is coded as "folk" and as "the earlier material culture and technology", while "rural proletarian" appears as the "urban".

We need to move beyond perspectives on Puerto Rico, as elsewhere, that render social history in fragmented ways and tend to promote undemocratic political objectives. Such is the case of the dichotomous concepts of "peasant" and "rural proletariat", which had their origins in anthropological research in Puerto Rico. Exploring concepts brings us closer to social reality, if our concepts become as fluid as the reality that they (we) explore.

Coal and Colonialism: Production Relations in an Indian Coalfield, c. 1895–1947[*]

DILIP SIMEON

Introduction

The year 1995 marked the centenary of the exploitation of a 400 square-kilometre tract in the Indian province of Bihar known as the Jharia coalfield. From 1895, when rail lines entered the region, until the end of the World War I, coal output in India increased tenfold and the size of the mines' workforce fivefold. By 1907 Jharia was yielding half of India's output. One of its oldest mines was Khas Jharia, which worked a 260-feet deep source. Thirty-four years after it opened, its surface had merged with the outskirts of Jharia township and restrictions were imposed on the dimensions of its galleries. Despite these, Khas Jharia's pillars collapsed on 8 November 1930 causing an 18-feet deep subsidence and widespread destruction.[1] This incident was the proximate cause of an underground fire which rages to this day.

Emissions and subsidences at Khas Jharia continued, despite efforts by the Mines Department and the railways to douse the seams. In 1933 the flaming crevasses alarmed local residents, many of whom deserted their houses.[2] The Bihar earthquake of 1934 enhanced air circulation in the mine,[3] and by 1938 an observer's first impressions of Jharia town were of fissures belching colourful flames.[4] The disaster was the most

[*] This paper contains certain material from a paper presented to the Davis Center seminar at Princeton University in January 1995, and from my book, *The Politics of Labour Under Late Colonialism: Workers, Trade Unions and the State in Chota Nagpur, 1928–1939* (Delhi, 1995). In the following essay, the *Report of the Labour Enquiry Commission* (1896), will be referred to as *RLEC*; the *Treharne-Rees Report* (1919), as *Rees*; the *Report of the Coalfields Committee* (1920), as *Foley*; the *Report of the Coal Mining Committee* (1937, L.B. Burrows), as *CMC*; the *Report of the Indian Coalfield's Committee* (1946, Mahindra), as *ICC*; the *Report on an Enquiry into Conditions of Labour in the Coal Mining Industry in India* (1946, S.R. Deshpande), as *Deshpande*; the *Transactions of the Mining and Geological Institute of India*, as *TMGI*; the Tata Steel Archives as TSA, and the *Annual Report of the Chief Inspector of Mines in India* as *ARCIM*. All file references are from the Bihar State Archives, except those suffixed NAI, which are from the National Archives of India. *CEHI* denotes *The Cambridge Economic History of India* (1983); GOI, the Government of India; RCL, the Royal Commission on Labour (1931); COI, the Census of India and *BLEC*, the *Report of the Bihar Labour Enquiry Committee* (1940).

[1] *ARCIM* (1930), p. 34.
[2] *Searchlight*, 13 January 1933: "Fire in Jharia Collieries – An Alarming Situation – Danger to Jharia Town", Report, 9 January 1933.
[3] *TSA*. See the article "Fire at Jharia", *TISCO Review* (March 1934), p. 145.
[4] Mukutdhari Singh, *Bhuli Bisri Kariyan* (Patna, 1978), vol. 2, p. 17.

International Review of Social History 41 (1996), pp. 83–108

notorious example of a general malaise: by 1936, 42 of the 133 collieries in the area were on fire.[5]

These phenomena were the more dramatic ramifications of production relations in the coal industry. Like its other features, they may best be comprehended through a contextual analysis of institutional forms. Such an analysis would have a bearing on matters such as mines safety, the organization of natural resources, and the emergence of an *Adivasi* (tribal) political estate. It would also add substance to the ongoing debates about the colonial economy, which have tended to revolve around concepts such as "deindustrialization" and "economic progress". I believe that such economies become more accessible to historical research when considered as alloys of novel and customary relationships – an approach which entails a study of specific enterprises, their strategic functions and the social and technical aspects of production. This paper will focus upon the forms of wage labour and patterns of employment peculiar to Jharia. It will examine how these relate to the social reproduction of the workforce, and suggest the place of this enterprise in colonial history. The remarks concerning forms of capital and landed property are intended to support the argument about the fusion of the social-institutional and the material-technical aspects of production.

The historical specificity of production relations

Writing about the sale and purchase of labour power, Marx suggested that the scale of the workers' "so-called necessary requirements", and the manner of their satisfaction depended upon the "level of civilization" of a country, and the "habits and expectations" of its class of free labourers. He continued: "In contrast [. . .] with the case of other commodities, the determination of the value of labour power contains a historical and moral element".[6] This "element" presumably included conditions which engendered specific types of enterprise and production relations, and must, therefore, have affected the entire circulation process of capital. These remarks, combined with the view that the constant factor of colonial economies was "the search for and control of cheap labor [. . .]", and that, " 'feudalism' in labor relations may be considered a function of the development of the colonial economy in its entirety [. . .]",[7] provide a provocative approach to our study of Indian coal mining.

An examination of the ways in which pre-capitalist social forms affected the character of colonial capitalism has other theoretical implications.

[5] *Searchlight*, 24 January 1936.
[6] Karl Marx, *Capital* (London, 1976), vol. 1, p. 275.
[7] Rodolfo Stavenhagen, "Seven Fallacies About Latin America", in J. Petras and M. Zeitlin (ed.), *Latin America: Reform or Revolution?* (New York, 1968), p. 17.

For example, the logical outline of *Das Kapital* leaves out the notion of state-structure from the account of the self-augmentation of value and the money form of capital – thus passing over the matter of the formalization of the money commodity. However, the reproduction process of capital requires the existence of formal boundaries describing "communities of money", so to speak, which constitute the limits of its valid circulation, and which thereby pull into the argument the history of the state and the materials of culture and tradition – the "historical and moral element", once again.

The analytical value of the concept of "the relations of production" is enhanced when these are situated in the history of given societies. Money, fixed and variable capital, production price, profit and rent, are abstractions which in Marx's scheme are infused with a meaning derived from the labour theory of value. Their social representatives appear in our context as managing agents, *zamindars* (landlords), company lessees and piece-rated low-caste and tribal miners. The agencies functioned as primordial banks, the *zamindars* as rentiers. The outlay on variable capital included commissions paid to certain villagers in the hinterland who used kinship networks to recruit labour. The Railway Board's control of the selling price of coal derived from its position as the principal consumer and transporter and its ownership of captive collieries. The system's informal mode of regulation[8] developed out of a pre-industrial social context which affected recruitment, remuneration and managerial strategies. (It needs to be considered that the type of workforce available in a given situation engenders a certain form of capital and conduces to specific forms of employment.) The colonial economic regime was represented by a legal structure which accommodated to this mode of regulation by way of inertia and laxity of enforcement. The ethnographic stereotypes current among the managers and technocrats were part of the mode of regulation and helped perpetuate it.

The era of steam

By the second quarter of the nineteenth century, the Indian economy was being transformed into an exporter of indigo, tea and opium and

---

[8] This term enables us to develop a fresh approach towards the issue of the "colonial mode of production". In Lipietz's use of the twin concept of the "regime of accumulation and the mode of regulation", the "regime" is defined as "the stabilization [. . .] of the allocation of the net product between consumption and accumulation", a process which "implies some correspondence between the transformation of both the conditions of production and the conditions of the reproduction of wage-earners [. . .] (and) some form of linkage between capitalism and other modes of production". He defines the "mode of regulation" as the "materialization" of such regimes, "taking the form of norms, habits, laws, regulating networks [. . .] that ensure the unity of the process, i.e. the approximate consistency of individual behaviours with the schema of reproduction". The

an importer of textiles. The steam engine appeared in mints, baling presses, tugs and riverine trade. By the late 1830s steam vessels were operating on the Ganga, and a decade later plying coastal routes. Steam-driven gunboats also played crucial roles as imperial weapons in Burma and China.[9] As coal rapidly acquired significance for purposes of commerce and conquest, the exploitation of the "Bengal coalfield" at Raniganj began in 1814. Rail construction began to be promoted by businessmen interested in selling textiles and importing cotton, and by shipping companies which needed coal supplies at Indian ports.[10]

From 1855 onwards the extension of rail lines to the coalfields led to a surge in output. In the aftermath of the 1857 revolt, railway investment accelerated, with the Government of India (GOI) underwriting profits. Partly for famine management, but mainly for military reasons, it authorized the laying of tracks to strategic points.[11] One such was the Jharia field, adjacent to Raniganj, which had been surveyed in 1866 and 1887, but seriously developed only after the East Indian Railway's (EIR's) technical survey of 1890. Extraction there was heralded by track extensions in 1894–1895. In six years, Jharia's output rose from 1,500 to 2 million tons, after which it became the most productive field in the country.[12]

The forms of capital which developed Jharia were an outgrowth of the agency houses, which had invested the fortunes of English gentlemen

---

"mode" is seen as a "body of interiorized rules and social processes": see Alain Lipietz, "New Tendencies in the International Division of Labour: Regimes of Accumulation and Modes of Regulation", in A.J. Scott and M. Storper (eds), *Production. Work, Territory: The Geographical Anatomy of Industrial Capitalism* (Boston, 1986).

[9] See D.R. Headrick, *The Tools of Empire: Technology and European Imperialism in the Nineteenth Century* (New York, 1981), ch. 1. Also see R.S. Rungta, *The Rise of Business Corporations in India 1851–1900* (Cambridge, 1970), ch. 1; and M.D. Morris in *CEHI*, pp. 563–564. In 1840, there were five private and nine government-owned steam boats on the Ganga: Blair Kling, *Partner in Empire: Dwarkanath Tagore and the Age of Enterprise in Eastern India* (Berkeley, 1976), p. 99.

[10] In "The Pattern of Railway Development in India", Daniel Thorner stressed that the great railway networks were built in order to intermesh the economies of Britain and India: *The Far Eastern Quarterly*, 14(2) (1955), pp. 201, 203. In *Investment in Empire: British Railway and Steam Shipping Enterprise in India 1825–1849* (Philadelphia, 1950), p. 23, Thorner noted: "the East Indian Railway [. . .] began as little more than an extension of the Peninsular & Oriental Steam Navigation Company [. . .] The struggle for governmental aid to steam shipping was, in many respects, simply a dress rehearsal of the later and greater campaign for the introduction of railways into India."

[11] Thorner, "Railway Development", pp. 204–209; and J.M. Hurd, in *CEHI*, p. 742. "Defence needs and fear of Russia thus eventually triumphed over economy and financial considerations", wrote W.J. Macpherson, in "Investment in Indian Railways", *Economic History Review*, 8(2) (1955), p. 186. "The Government wanted railways for social, economic and perhaps mainly military reasons."

[12] *CMC*, pp. 9–10. Bihar was part of the province of Bengal until 1912.

early in the nineteenth century.[13] After their collapse in the 1830s, the so-called managing agencies began controlling joint stock associations by proxy, a practice initiated by the trader and landowner Dwarkanath Tagore, who in 1836 entered into a partnership over a steam tug association after purchasing India's then largest coal mine. The coal was consumed mainly by the steam boats of the public company.[14] In mid-century, as the locus of financial decision-making shifted to London, Indian trade came under the interlocking control of the agencies and English cartels such as the Peninsular & Orient's Calcutta Conference and the Indian Jute Mills Association. From 1890 to 1920 the number of coal companies in Bengal and Bihar increased from 6 to 227.[15] In 1911, seven managing agents controlled 55 per cent of the jute, 61 per cent of the tea and 46 per cent of the coal companies.[16] Annual all-India coal production increased from 4.7 million tons during 1896–1900, to 11.5 m. tons in 1906–1910, 19.3 m. tons in 1916–1920, and 23.8 m. tons in 1930.[17]

On behalf of the managed firm, the agents would take charge of buildings, machinery purchases, staff, operations, and marketing, as well as the leading part in finance. Remuneration took the form of a commission on production or profits. The "poundage" system, with commissions based on the weight of the product, was popular in the nineteenth century, and was supplemented in the twentieth by a percentage of the profits, generally ranging from 7.5 to 12.5 per cent. Commissions were over and above dividends paid to the agents and others – the agent could make a "poundage" even when the firm was making a loss. Some promoters would divide their commissions with other furnishers of capital. Managing agents could manage over a hundred companies at the same time – in jute, tea, coal, ships, flour mills, and so on. Their special function came to consist in supervision. Directed by their financial branches and focusing on immediate rather than future gain, they trans-

[13] See Rungta, *Business Corporations*, ch. 1; S.K. Basu, *The Managing Agency System in Prospect and Retrospect* (Calcutta, 1958), ch. 1; and Rajat Ray (ed.), *Entrepreneurship and Industry in India* (Delhi, 1994) pp. 19–24, 30.
[14] B. Kling, "The Origins of the Managing Agency System", in Ray, *Entrepreneurship*. See also Kling, *Partner in Empire*, chs 5 and 6. Tagore's first mine was abandoned to an underground fire caused by de-pillaring and spontaneous combustion: p. 96.
[15] Henner Papendieck, "British Managing Agencies in the Indian Coalfield", in D. Rothermund and D.C. Wadhwa, *Zamindars, Mines, and Peasants* (New Delhi, 1978), p. 184. From 1890 till 1918, Indian coal production increased tenfold, capital invested in coal twelvefold, and the size of the workforce fivefold (p. 175). Also see A.K. Bagchi, *Private Investment in India* (Delhi, 1972), pp. 163–164, 176–179; and Ray, *Entrepreneurship*, pp. 30–36, 47.
[16] Bagchi, *Private Investment*, p. 176. They were Andrew Yule, Bird, Shaw Wallace, Williamson Magor, Octavius Steel, Begg Dunlop and Duncan Bros.
[17] A.B. Ghosh, *Coal Industry in India* (Delhi, 1978), pp. 278–280.

ferred profits from one company to another and sold cheap fuel to their other concerns.[18] The calculation of the net profits of coal companies before deductions for depreciation and reserves rendered this form of management detrimental to the collieries.[19]

Well before World War I, coal had become the empire's major source of energy. By 1927, metallurgy consumed 24.2 per cent of output and jute and textile mills 8.2 per cent between them. Railways took a third (a proportion that remained broadly stable till 1947), increasing their demand from under a million tons in 1893 to 7.5 m. tons in 1936.[20] By charging relatively low freight rates for long-haul bulk goods to and from the interior and the great port towns, railway companies rendered internal trade more expensive than foreign.[21] Their freight wars and zonal boundaries prevented network integration and the EIR used its monopoly to charge high rates for coal deliveries to Calcutta.[22] Until 1914 this tendency combined with the impact of the Suez Canal and low freight-rates on India-bound shipping (from Britain) to render British and South African coal cheaper in western and southern India.[23] The war enabled Indian coal to capture the home market.

The development of Jharia boosted Indian entrepreneurs' investments in mining. From 1900 to 1947 their share of output grew from one-fifth to one-third in a process marked by tremendous fluctuations. Half the collieries of the inter-war period were Indian companies whose share in

---

[18] D.H. Buchanan, *The Development of Capitalistic Enterprise in India* (New York, 1934), pp. 166–171; and *CMC*, p. 28. In certain areas in Jharia, more pits were sunk and more machinery installed than necessary. "Sometime this was due to the fact that although the coal was near the surface, the advisors had interest in the sale of mining equipment": Buchanan, *Development of Capitalistic Enterprise*, p. 261.

[19] Papendieck, "British Managing Agencies", pp. 190–192. There were marked and arbitrary differences between coal prices quoted for independent and associated buyers, pp. 204–212.

[20] *RCL*, vol. 4, part 1, p. 242; and B.R. Seth, *Labour in the Indian Coal Industry* (Bombay, 1940), p. 8. The 1946 report estimated railway consumption at 6.3 m. tons in 1920, 7.0 in 1928, and 7.4 in 1935: *ICC*, p. 298.

[21] Hurd, *CEHI*, p. 752. See also *CEHI*, pp. 752–758; and Thorner, "Railway Development", p. 208.

[22] The agents claimed that coal contributed more to tonnage hauled than to profits earned. Given its freight structure, the EIR was making a concession to coal. See *CMC*, pp. 91–92.

[23] Hurd, *CEHI*, pp. 752–758. The EIR's share of track in 1897 was 9 per cent, but it garnered 23 per cent of total railway earnings. The popularity of foreign coal was also due to unreliable grading of Indian coal. In 1925 a Grading Board began standardizing grades exported from Calcutta: *CMC*, pp. 73–77. The "raw" nature of Indian exports generated a surplus of cargo space on return voyages from Britain, which carried less bulky manufactured goods. This was made available for British coal, and helped lower transport costs. See C.N. Vakil and S.K. Muranjan, *Currency and Prices in India* (Bombay, 1927), pp. 234–236.

production was about 5 per cent.[24] They mined low grade coal from labour-intensive shallow mines, were quickly opened and wound up, and competed ferociously. Combining in the Indian Mining Federation (IMF) in 1913, they prospered in the post-war boom, mining over a third of output. In the mid-1920s slump their output share underwent a 10 per cent decline. Internecine strife bred the Indian Colliery Owners' Association (ICOA) in 1934. The two bodies often asked for state-regulated prices, but such a course conflicted with the cost-cutting interest of the Railway Board.[25] By 1928, British-controlled coal companies, which had combined in the Indian Mining Association (IMA) in 1892, accounted for 60 per cent of output.[26] In 1944 this had risen to 70.6 per cent, with the railways' captive collieries accounting for another 11.5 per cent.[27] A system had emerged in which geo-strategic and economic elements had blended together. If the British Indian Army was "the iron fist in the velvet glove of Victorian expansionism"[28] its mobility hinged around the labours of Indian coal miners.

The demography of employment

Some 125,000 persons were engaged in Jharia during the 1920s and 1930s.[29] Their employment patterns reveal relationships between grades, skills and identity. In a manifestation of an industrial system adapting to the cultural demography of its hinterland, the workforce was mainly "low" caste, female and tribal. Supervisory and clerical jobs were held by upper-caste males. In the 1920s, nearly three-fourths of the workforce was from Manbhum and districts contiguous to it, and almost half (47.5 per cent) from Manbhum alone.[30] Most immigrants came from Hazaribagh, and the two nearest non-contiguous districts of Gaya and

[24] C.P. Simmons, "Indigenous Enterprise in the Indian Coal Mining Industry, *c.* 1835–1939", *Indian Economic and Social History Review* [hereafter *IESHR*], 13(2) (1976), p. 204.
[25] In an address to the IMF in 1929, A.L. Ojha spoke of "a merger and combination of isolated small undertakings", and suggested an Indian version of the German Federal Economic Council, "for a better adjustment of our [. . .] rapidly changing economic life": *Searchlight*, 3 March 1929; and Simmons, "Indigenous Enterprise", pp. 200–215.
[26] *RCL*, vol. 4, part 1, p. 242.
[27] *ICC*, p. 116.
[28] David Washbrook, "South Asia, The World System, and World Capitalism", *The Journal of Asian Studies*, 49(3) (1990), p. 481. Also see J. Gallagher and R. Robinson, "The Imperialism of Free Trade", in idem, *The Decline, Revival and Fall of the British Empire* (Cambridge, 1982).
[29] *COI*, 1921, vol. 7, part 1, ch. 12; *BLEC*, vol. 1, p. 17, and vol. 4, part C, p. 199. Managements may have deflated the figures out of a desire to renege on housing responsibilities.
[30] *RCL*, vol. 4, part 1, pp. 3, 4. Contiguity implied Bengal as well, although in this case it refers mainly to Hazaribagh and Santhal Parganas.

Monghyr.[31] Thousands walked in to work from Hazaribagh, and the two other districts were easily accessible by rail. Many trekked in even from the non-contiguous districts.[32]

Of the twenty-six "most numerous castes" in Jharia,[33] "aboriginals" and "semi-aboriginals" comprised 48.8 per cent; "depressed classes" 20.2 per cent; and the intermediate peasant and artisan castes 22 per cent. Larger Adivasi groups such as the *Hos, Mundas, Oraons, Bhumij*, etc., were noticeable by their absence, the only exception being the *Santhals*. Only four categories (comprising 8.8 per cent) were of "high" status – *Brahmins, Rajputs, Pathans* and *Kayasths*. The largest single castes were *Santhals* (13.3 per cent), *Bhuiyas* (11.8 per cent), *Bauris* (11.7 per cent) and *Chamars* (9.4 per cent). The first three caste-clusters constituted 91 per cent of the workforce as a whole, and 94 per cent of the actual coal cutters, themselves a quarter of the workforce. Less than 2 per cent of the miners were "upper caste", but a fifth of them were women, as were nearly half the number of coolies who loaded and carried coal above and below ground. (Women workers were generally known as *rezas*.) The number of upper-caste coolies was negligible. Among other skilled occupations the pattern changed slightly. Seventy-one per cent of the winding and hauling enginemen and firemen belonged to the first two groups; i.e. aboriginals, semi-aboriginals and depressed classes. Upper castes dominated supervisory grades, with 78 per cent of the overmen and more than 50 per cent of the contractors. Tribals and depressed classes were less than 1 per cent of the overmen but 11 per cent of the contractors, this figure being dominated by *Bauris* and *Kurmis*. In the late 1930s Jharia's hinterland remained its main recruitment area, with 84.2 per cent recruited from Bihar (excluding Orissa). However, Manbhum's share declined by more than half in two decades – a phenomenon linked to the declining proportion of Adivasis and women. *Santhals* were down to 6.7 per cent, and *Bauris* to 5.2 per cent. Other aboriginal groups formed less than 2 per cent of the mining population.[34] The groups which had dominated the mines at the turn of the century were replaced by immigrants from Bilaspur, Chhatisgarh and up-country.[35] However, this decline was tempered by the link between ethnicity and mechanization – in

---

[31] *COI*, 1921, vol. 7, part 1, p. 106.

[32] *BLEC*, vol. 3 C, p. 204.

[33] These adjectival terms and phrases are used in Subsidiary Table 12, in *COI*, 1921, vol. 7(1), ch. 12, which is the source for the following data. The proportions are based on the number (73,241) of "actual workers". *Bauris* were considered a semi-aboriginal caste in Manbhum and an untouchable caste in Bengal and Orissa. *Kurmis* were an "aboriginal" tribe in Chotanagpur, but an intermediate peasant caste in Gangetic Bihar.

[34] *BLEC*, vol. 2 A-B, pp. 307–311.

[35] *Searchlight*, 27 March 1936. Prof. S.R. Bose's lecture on Jharia in Patna College.

1946 it was observed that manual coal cutters were mainly *Santhals* and *Bauris*.[36]

Women formed 37.5 per cent of the workforce in 1920. This fell to 25.4 per cent in 1929, the year that the central government ordered the gradual exclusion of female labour from underground work (90 years after their British counterparts). It declined further to 13.8 per cent in 1935 and 11.5 per cent in 1938. This trend was linked to the mechanization of loading, hauling and screening and the eclipse of Adivasi family labour – *rezas* were predominantly tribal.[37] Another set of statistics on coal mining for all of British India tells us that the number of women workers for every ten males was 5.6 in 1915, 6.1 in 1920, 4.8 in 1925, 2.7 in 1930 and 1.6 in 1935, rising to 3.6 in 1944, the year after the ban on female labour underground was lifted temporarily.[38]

Given that such a large proportion of the mining population was drawn from Jharia's immediate vicinity, the social conditions prevailing in the region acquire especial relevance. Mohapatra's study of the crisis in Chota Nagpur agriculture between 1880 and 1920 examines migration to the coalfields. The price of rice increased 150 per cent in a period during which the area suffered five famines and an influenza epidemic. Yet its population grew faster than the provincial or national rate. This was related to an expansion of arable lands under an agrarian regime vulnerable to climate and irrigation. Many households were at the mercy of fluctuating crop yields.[39] Seventy-five per cent of the population was indebted, and Hazaribagh and Manbhum were monocrop zones, whose peasants were seasonally unemployed. The hut in the village and the colliery lines became adjuncts of a household in which the rural location of the one effected savings on infrastructure for capital in the other. This arrangement depressed wages, because of the tendency to evaluate earnings in terms of the minimum required to keep the village household functioning. In the case of landless families this simply meant keeping a migrant alive in the coalfields. Erratic labour supply suited small collieries which opened and shut down abruptly. Miners defrayed the cost of their own reproduction, since capitalists undertook minimal responsibilities for settling labour. The history of Indian coal seems to bear out Washbrook's argument that "by increasing the competition of labour for land and subsistence", the pressures of social necessity under colonialism "increased the dominance of capital and enabled it [. . .] to cast off more and more of its responsibilities for the social reproduction of the labour force".[40]

[36] *Deshpande*, p. 21.
[37] *RCL*, Report, p. 127; Seth, *Labour in the Indian Coal Industry*, pp. 153 and 140–141; and Radhakamal Mukerjee, *The Indian Working Class* (Bombay, 1951), p. 82.
[38] *Deshpande*, pp. 18–19.
[39] P.P. Mohapatra, "Coolies and Colliers: A Study of the Agrarian Context of Labour Migration from Chota Nagpur, 1880–1920", *Studies in History*, 1(2) (1985).
[40] See D.A. Washbrook, "Progress and Problems: South Asian Economic and Social History c. 1720–1860", *Modern Asian Studies*, 22(1) (1988), p. 87.

The sub-infeudated control of labour

The relationship between capital and wage labour was straddled by a nexus of intermediaries. Companies recruited a segment of their work-force directly – this so-called *sarkari* recruitment was the one miners preferred. However, immediate control over labour until the 1930s was exercised by *raising-contractors*, engaged for the entire process ranging from hiring (*sardari* recruitment) to the cutting and loading of coal. The owners would supply the machinery and administrative structure and pay the contractors a commission on raisings. The system had its origins in the early history of Jharia, when persons with local landed interests contracted to influence villagers to mine coal. In 1929–1930 raising-contractors accounted for about 70 per cent of Jharia's output. Mine managers legally responsible for safety, housing and compliance with mining regulations, very often had no control over the safety men, let alone the distribution of work, the payment of wages and the number of miners going down the shafts. Contractors' labour contributed about half of output till the 1930s, when financial stringency led to a decline in the system, already under criticism (in official reports) for undermining the responsibility of managements. On the eve of World War II raising-contractors still accounted for a quarter of the coal extracted in Jharia and Raniganj, but their largest employers were the railway collieries at Bokaro and Giridih, where they controlled nearly 30,000 workers.[41]

In some cases large-scale recruitment was done by labour-contractors – this was a variant of the raising-contractor system. The work-rhythms for both *sarkari* and *sardari* labourers were the same, although the potential for extortion was diminished in the former. Both systems relied on the gang-*sardars* (gang-masters) who advanced food and money to "their relatives, acquaintances and co-villagers and employ(ed) them in surface or underground work [. . .]". Gang-*sardars* were the last link in the managerial chain. Workers themselves, they led groups 15 to 40 strong around the coalfields, supervising work and wage-receipts for a commission. Patriarchs of their gangs, they arranged for loans, adjudicated petty disputes and mediated with larger vested interests.[42]

The term "sub-infeudation" relates to the plethora of intermediate revenue collectors generated by the agrarian Settlement of 1793 which had granted perpetual ownership to the *zamindars* of Bengal. Under its regime, seven landed estates had emerged in the Dhanbad subdivision where Jharia lay. One of the cesses the estate-owners exacted from new lessees was called *salami*, which combined obeisance with extortion, and became a lucrative source of rentier income with the opening up of the

[41] *Deshpande*, pp. 33–35; and *BLEC*, vol. 1, pp. 188–190.
[42] From the evidence of W.C. Bannerjee, representing the Indian Mining Association, in *Rees*, p. 62. Also see *Rees*, pp. 78, 88; Seth, *Labour in the Indian Coal Industry*, p. 45; and *RCL*, vol. 4(1), p. 221.

collieries.[43] In 1880 the GOI recognized the landlords' title to mineral rights, anticipating that they would supervise extraction. However, an investigation in 1920 found that protective provisions were absent or not enforced, and suggested regulated leasing. Using customary authority to levy a toll upon variable capital, certain landlords also received a fee "per head of miners taken away from their villages". The Burrows Report (1937) remarked that the *zamindars* had left the future to "look after itself". Their demands for fresh *salami* payments for the secondary operation called "depillaring" fostered reckless extractions in first workings; and their greed for the initial gratuity payments led to the subdivision of estates into numerous irregularly shaped leases, which tied up much coal under boundaries and exacerbated malpractices such as the opening of multiple shafts to save on underground roads and the avoidance of conservation. (Jharia had a number of shallow workings with little or no machinery, which were susceptible to market fluctuations.) The Mahindra Report (1946) noted that the "small dimensions and fantastic shapes" of coal leases were also the consequence of the Revenue Department's estate boundaries, and recommended the abolition of private property in mineral rights in the *zamindari* areas.[44]

Landed property thus affected the mining industry as an enabling factor and a parasite. As a discrete interest it exacted a levy both from fixed and (sometimes) variable capital. As an institutional category embedded in colonial society, it entered the very structure of enterprise: certain collieries possessed service tenancies stemming from their status as estate-owners. The Bengal Coal Company held 130,000 acres in 1920, and the East Indian Railway leased lands to miners who were liable to work for 230 days a year. There were other instances of collieries using a rentier position to recruit labour.[45] During World War II (see section on *Coal and the state* below, p. 105), the GOI took a more interventionist approach towards the regulation of labour supply.

Miners' lives were characterized by a ceaseless mobility. Evidence rendered to the Royal Commission on Labour (1931) stressed their "primarily agricultural" nature, and the connection between labour supply and agrarian seasons. Even established collieries which had stabilized half to three-quarters of their workforces experienced seasonal absenteeism in April, July and winter.[46] Estimates of the proportion of miners settled in Jharia varied from 15 per cent to 25 per cent. "Recruited", or seasonal workers comprised 50 to 75 per cent; and

[43] See D.C. Wadhwa, "Zamindaris at Work (1793–1956)" and idem, "Zamindars and their Land", in Rothermund and Wadhwa, *Zamindars, Mines, and Peasants*, pp. 86–92 and 93–130.
[44] *Foley*, p. 3; *Rees*, p. 101; *CMC*, pp. 31, 69–71; and *ICC*, pp. 134, 273–274.
[45] C.P. Simmons, "Recruiting and Organising", *IESHR*, 13(4) (1976), pp. 465, 471–481; *RCL*, vols 4(1), p. 221, and 4(2), p. 143.
[46] *RCL*, vol. 4, part 1, pp. 16–17.

"local" or *dehati* workers, 5 to 10 per cent of the workforce.[47] The *dehatis* trekked in from villages within a 15-mile radius. Seasonal recruits lived in colliery lines or in makeshift huts. Until the eve of World War II, an unstable workforce was the norm. Indian magnates complained most about this: "The recruited labourers [. . .] retire wholesale for two seasons. It is estimated that withdrawal is responsible for the loss of about 33 per cent of what might have been their aggregate annual wages otherwise", wrote the secretary of the Indian Mining Federation, D.D. Thacker, forwarding its suggestion that the Santal Parganas and Chota Nagpur be reserved "as the exclusive area of recruitment for the coal industry".[48] Although the industry did pay for some of its social costs by means of levies which financed the Water Board, the Board of Health, road maintenance and security, this bare infrastructural contribution was grudgingly given, and not commensurate with the cost of stabilizing the workforce. The Royal Commission on Labour, 1931 (RCL) noted that the rural connection provided social and old-age security. A prominent manager endorsed this view. The "link with the village" acted as a sanatorium for the sick, he said, adding that *"if we (had) a full supply of labour settled in the collieries, there would always be an overproduction [. . .] it would be a heavy burden on the industry* at a time like the present one, if the labour did not have homes in the villages to which to go" (emphasis added).[49]

Life and recreation in the coalbelt

It was not surprising that miners did not treat the coalbelt as a stable place of residence. Even the officials considered the company-built miners' quarters, known as *dhowras*, "mere apologies for homes", their surroundings "generally filthy" and their "whole appearance [. . .] most forbidding".[50] They were ill-ventilated, unsanitary and built back to back. Piped water in some collieries had put an end to annual epidemics of cholera and smallpox, but leprosy persisted. There were no baths or latrines, and the pit water used for bathing and washing was reported "unwholesome and filthy".[51] Clean water supply amounted to one tap for 60 to 80 houses. Insecurity obliged some workers to carry their belongings to work in baskets, and others to share lodgings between two families. Children and babies would either be left in the care of

---

[47] *RCL*, vol. 4, part 1, pp. 182, 207, 212. Also see Seth, *Labour in the Indian Coal Industry*, p. 56. The 1946 enquiry put the percentage of "permanently settled labour" in Jharia at "25 to 45". The broad range of these figures highlights the difficulty of determining the size of the stable segment.

[48] *RCL*, vol. 4, part 1, p. 212.

[49] *TMGI*, vol. 27(2) (1933), pp. 96, 107.

[50] *Deshpande*, pp. 32, 88.

[51] *BLEC*, vol. 1, p. 195.

co-tenants, or taken along and kept opiated.[52] By-laws of the Jharia Mines Board of Health laying down a maximum of two adults and two children per room were ignored, with five to ten persons in occupation. Illnesses or childbirth would result in miserable domestic circumstances.[53] Subject to land subsidences, *dhowras* would often have to be vacated, and were known to have buried their residents. Colliery workers tended to live in clusters according to caste and place of origin. The *Santhals* preferred not to use the *dhowras* at all.[54] According to a budget enquiry conducted in 1938, the average mining family consisted of four persons. Most adult males, 40 per cent of adult females and 2.3 per cent of the children were working members of their families, with tribal workers contributing the highest percentage of working females.[55] Nearly three-quarters of total expenditure was on food. The average miner's diet in Jharia yielded 2,674 calories, as compared with the proposed calorific intake for Indian workers of 3,000 calories.[56] The percentage of adult males who were literate was 13.4.[57] The survey did not investigate female literacy and reported a prejudice against female education. Eighteen per cent of the boys and 3 per cent of the girls of school age actually attended school. Colliery schools were supposedly free, but teachers charged fees such as 2 annas per week which deterred poorer miners.[58] Forty-four per cent of the families were indebted to *sardars*, contractors, shopkeepers, clerks and usurers; among the worst debts being contractors' advances. Stores owned by the latter charged exorbitant prices from which miners would be pressurized to buy essential items. Hard-pressed miners would stealthily migrate. Less than a fifth of the families sent money home.[59]

Until the late 1920s there were no child welfare centres, maternity allowances, nor women doctors available for working mothers, who

[52] Seth, *Labour in the Indian Coal Industry*, pp. 164, 168, 176–178.

[53] *Ibid.*, p. 172.

[54] See Ranjan Kumar Ghosh, "A Study of the Labour Movement in Jharia Coalfield 1900–1977" (unpublished thesis, Calcutta University, 1992), chs 1.15 and 1.14.

[55] *BLEC*, vol. 2 A-B, p. 331. Nearly 60 per cent of the tribal and 72 per cent of Oriya (also mostly tribal) women present worked in the collieries. The statistics should be taken as indicators – the Family Budget Enquiry questioned 1,030 families.

[56] *BLEC*, vol. 2 A-B, pp. 353–357; Mukerjee, *Indian Working Class*, pp. 223–229. The Bengal jute worker consumed 2,752 calories, while the Bengal jail diet yielded 3,508 calories.

[57] *BLEC*, vol. 2 A-B. pp. 319–320. 68.6 per cent of the Lohars and Barhis, 59 per cent of the upper castes such as Brahmins, Rajputs, Kayasthas and Chhatris, and 43 per cent of the Muslims were literate. Literacy rates were the lowest among the tribals and lower castes.

[58] *ARCIM* (1929), quoted in Margaret Read, *Indian Peasant Uprooted* (London, 1931), p. 127.

[59] *Searchlight*, 27 March 1936, Prof. Bose's lecture. The BLEC reported peons and shopkeepers arranging with mines clerks to collect usurious dues at source, *BLEC*, vol. 1, p. 160; Also see vol. 2 A-B, pp. 344–352, 370, 442–443; and vol. 3 C, p. 229.

would be attended by *dais* in late pregnancy. These traditional midwives
would be paid a few rupees and ate with the family.[60] In 1937 there
were eleven certified midwives for the whole belt. The main development
was the operation of ten maternity and child welfare centres in the area,
although in 1938 only a fifth of the collieries were paying out maternity
allowances (one or two annas a day). Most women workers returned to
their villages for childbirth. Mortality rates among women were 6 to 7
per cent higher than their proportion in the population of the settlement,
and infant mortality 7 per cent higher, during 1934–1936, than the rate
for the province as a whole.[61]

Gambling, cock-fighting and participating in festivals were the main
forms of recreation. The last was not very prominent, as many miners
preferred to celebrate the major festivals in their villages.[62] Given their
"drab and mechanical existence", remarked an official report, "under
the present circumstances, the only relaxation (the miners) can look
forward to, and which [. . .] can make them forget the coal mine is
the grog shop".[63] Whereas in South Africa the mine owners made the
initial investments in liquor manufacture,[64] in Jharia it was the administration which legalized outstills in 1932 to encourage localized production.
This cheapened liquor by up to 75 per cent, and increased revenues
through the auctioning and licensing of outstills and grog shops. From
1929 to 1933 the number of outlets in the Dhanbad area went up from
20 to 121, effecting a twelvefold increase in consumption.[65] Men and
women drank heavily after being paid at weekends, and were absent
on Mondays and sometimes on Tuesdays as well. In 1931 the observer
Margaret Read emphasized "the harm done, particularly to the aboriginal
population by the sale of spirits".[66] By the mid-1930s owners were
complaining about the "drink evil". In 1939 the Bihar Labour Enquiry
Committee reported:

On any Sunday evening, one could encounter [. . .] groups of miners intoxicated
with drink tumbling down the road [. . .] most confessed to us that they could
not give up [. . .] but they would not mind and would rather be happy if the
drink were stopped altogether [. . .] We note, with satisfaction, that the

[60] *RCL*, vol. 4, part 2, pp. 111, 134, 138 and 150.
[61] Seth, *Labour in the Indian Coal Industry*, pp. 190 and 198.
[62] See Ghosh, "A Study of the Labour Movement", pp. 76–77.
[63] *Deshpande*, p. 86.
[64] See Charles van Onselen, "Randlords and Rotgut" in idem, *Studies in the Social and
Economic History of the Witwatersrand 1886–1914*, vol. 1 (Johannesburg, 1982).
[65] There had been a 56 per cent decline in excise revenue between 1923 and 1932. With
the new system, revenues increased and liquor consumption rose from 30,924 gallons in
1931 to 376,000 gallons in 1933: Seth, *Labour in the Indian Coal Industry*, pp. 243–245.
[66] Read, in *Indian Peasant Uprooted*, pp. 119–120. The RCL also provided figures to
illustrate "the extent of the present evil".

Government has introduced prohibition in Jharia from the 1st of April 1939
[. . .][67]

The proportion of budgets spent on drink increased from 13 per cent
to 20 per cent between 1929 and 1934, affecting entire families. The
trend was linked to child prostitution, absenteeism, malnutrition, a high
rate of minor accidents and declining productivity. In 1940 there was
little evidence that prohibition (which lasted only one year) had curbed
drunkenness or illicit distillation.[68] Two-thirds of the families surveyed
in 1938 reported the consumption of liquor, which cost them 16 per
cent of their monthly incomes. Ninety-four per cent of the families
consumed tobacco. Other inebriants included *handia* (rice beer), toddy,
opium, *ganja* and *bhang* (hemp derivatives).[69]

The social knowledge of the managers was a mixture of racial prejudice, ideas about the mean status of work in the mines, and apparently
altruistic judgements about its civilizing effects. Their stereotypes generally reinforced the structures of employment. A mine manager in 1894
was in no doubt that *"Bauris are dirty and have no moral courage"*
and that *"Santhals are brave but stupid".*[70] A 1913 article on labour
begins with the assertion that "There are probably no other coalfields
in the world where the habits, peculiarities and superstitions of the
labour force have more to be studied than in ours", and is full of terms
such as "semi-savage" and "low-class Hindu gipsy tribe". It explains
the *Santhals'* aversion to living in the *dhowras* by way of an anecdote
in which the miners interpreted the deaths of two of their mates as the
work of devils residing under the floors of their quarters. These were
dug up and exorcisms performed on the orders of the manager. The
author praises his pragmatism for falling in "with the superstition of the
men" to prevent the migration of the gang. He went on,

It is chiefly on account of this and other superstitions that the above races do
not prefer to live in barrack-like houses with pucca floors, though as time goes

[67] *BLEC*, vol. 1, pp. 196–197.
[68] Seth, *Labour in the Indian Coal Industry*, pp. 244, 248, 251.
[69] *BLEC*, vol. 1, p. 196; and vol. 2 A-B, p. 366. Muslim families consumed little liquor,
but showed the highest expenditure on tobacco. *Manjhis, Dusadhs* and *Bauris* were
reported to be "the most regular drunkards". Mukutdhari Singh asserted that one-fourth
of miners' incomes was spent on liquor: *BLEC*, vol. 4 C, p. 271. The RCL estimated
expenses of a million rupees on drink and drugs in the Dhanbad colliery area in 1928:
RCL, Report, p. 121. Lower prices led to 1.2 million rupees being spent on liquor in
1934: J.E. Copeland, *Enquiry into the Outstill System in Bihar and Orissa*, quoted in
Seth, *Labour in the Indian Coal Industry*, p. 244. Till 1940 there was little evidence that
prohibition, introduced in 1939, and which lasted a year, had curbed drunkenness or illicit
distillation: *ibid.*, p. 251.
[70] Communication from Walter Saise, E.I.R. Colliery Manager, Giridih, in *Report of the
Inspector of Mines in India for the Year Ending the 30th June 1894* (Calcutta, 1894),
pp. 51–53.

on and the younger generation gets more civilised, the present objection will probably pass away.[71]

An Indian manager in 1918 suggested the recruitment of convicts, "which would fetch a very good income for the Government, (whilst) [. . .] improving their morality and [. . .] decreasing crime".[72] The author of a housing plan stated that it was the "labourers' insanitary habits" and trips to their villages which brought about the unsavoury state of housing. His scheme kept "the different castes separate from one another" and, in accord with the observation that "Santhals and Koras (have) an aversion to living in a line of attached huts", his diagram included discrete dwellings in the "Santhal Dhowrah", in contrast to the unbroken line of *dhowrahs* for the *Bauries*, *Kahars* and *Gopes*.[73] The 1894 manager endorsed hereditary immobility:

A child of 8 years is fit to work [. . .] little girls and little boys should go into the mines early and become accustomed to carrying coals [. . .] it is questionable whether children should be educated [. . .] they would not, afterwards work as coal-cutters, but try to get other work [. . .] those who can read and write will never cut coal; on the other hand, they take a most important attitude, and demand respect from everybody [. . .][74]

The work process and its remuneration

Coal mining has distinctive characteristics. Mines are wasting assets and best worked to exhaustion, since stoppages increase physical risks. The recession of workfaces requires regular maintenance, as do water pumping and timbering. The chemistry and friability of the coal, and the presence of gas and dust need to be monitored constantly, as high moisture and volatility are conducive to oxidation and spontaneous combustion. The physiognomy of the seams determine mining strategies – Jharia's were shallow, inclined, gassy and congested with eighteen proximate seams, some of them 60 to 80 feet thick. Thick seams require "pillar and stall" extraction, galleries being forced into them, with pillars interspersed to be removed later. In the 1930s, Jharia's pillars were contributing more coal than its galleries, but unsystematic techniques had led to the formation of excessively tall pillars, more liable to heating and collapse.[75] Buchanan, whose researches were conducted in the late 1920s, found this matter significant enough to merit detailed comment.

---

[71] E.C. Agabeg, "Labour in Bengal Coal Industry", *TMGI*, 8 (1915), pp. 25, 27, 29, 33, 35–38.

[72] Evidence of D.N. Das, General Manager of Bannerjee & Co., in *Rees*, p. 78.

[73] J.H. Evans, "Housing of Labour and Sanitation at Mines in India" *TMGI*, 12 (1918), pp. 79–89, with attached plates.

[74] Communication from Walter Saise in *Report of the Inspector of Mines in India* (1894), pp. 51–53.

[75] *CMC*, pp. 12–20, 35–49.

At one place in Jharia, he notes, there are 105 feet of coal in five seams within the first 402 feet of ground. Although thick seams are popular with miners, in India they are too thick, for the great height of the props required to support the roof makes the removal of all the coal impossible. Hydraulic stowing was possible, he said, but rarely used. When the pillars are removed, the surface settles, and about a third of the coal is lost.

The great weight on these pillars, as well as the character of the coal, frequently results in crumbling and falls dangerous to the miners. It also leads to spontaneous combustion and fires become so serious as to endanger entire areas. In some fields the cave-ins are suggestive of great canyons and the escape of smoke and steam through crevices is so like smouldering volcanoes and so dangerous that not only is mining impossible but there is great danger to life and property in the neighbourhood. These dangers become intensified as the mines are worked to greater depths.[76]

The main occupations were cutting, loading, bailing water and tramming. Most coal was manually cut – in 1944 there were only 210 mechanical cutters in 75 of the 910 mines in India. Some mines used pneumatic drills. Until the 1920s many small mines were using manually operated gins and capstans. Atmospheric conditions were not regulated and ventilation depended mainly upon the arrangement of galleries, leading to extreme temperatures. None of the collieries provided the required drinking water and sanitation. Many miners drank water from the seams and defaecation underground caused hook-worm infections through bruises in bare feet. First aid kits were sadly lacking.[77]

Only 6 per cent of Jharia's mines were electrified. Movement between workfaces, which could number up to seventy and be located as much as two miles away from each other, was rendered difficult with many sectors in darkness. There were 28,835 safety lamps in use in Jharia in 1942 (an increase of over 20,000 since 1929), but illumination was in the main dependent upon naked kerosene lamps known as *kuppis* or *mugbathis*, 90 per cent of whose illumination was absorbed by the surroundings. About a quarter of all miners suffered from forms of nystagmus, a disease caused by deficient lighting and resulting in photophobia, eyeball oscillation, vertigo, depression and headaches. The activity known as "holing" (undercutting coal by lying supine and concentrating upwards), put a particular strain on the elevator muscles of the eyes. Sometimes the change-over to electric lighting aggravated latent

[76] Buchanan, *The Development of Capitalistic Enterprise in India*, p. 260.
[77] Ghosh, *Coal Industry*, pp. 148, 152–154; Seth, *Labour in the Indian Coal Industry*, p. 30; *Deshpande*, pp. 41–45; R. Das Gupta, *Labour and Working Class in Eastern India* (Calcutta, 1994), p. 194; and Read, *Indian Peasant Uprooted*, p. 123. The lack of stretchers could aggravate bone injuries. The problem was made worse by the absence of pit telephones.

cases of the disease but even the bulbs used supplied less than one candle-power.[78]

For many years collieries depended upon piece-rated family labour, with women and children performing auxiliary tasks. Most women worked with male relatives. In specific jobs they were called *kamins*, a term signifying the performance of service. Gangs usually broke up into pairs, the hewers, or *malkattas* cutting the coal, and *kamins* walking long distances with baskets on their heads to load it. In 1921 some 40 per cent of the workforce were classed as "skilled", and included miners, mechanics, enginemen, firemen, carpenters and bricklayers.[79] Other categories included "coolies" working on haulage; maintenance apprentices (*khalasis*); masons, drillers and shot-firers, blacksmiths, boilermen, lamp-boys, carters and carriers, ash-cleaning *kamins*, shale-pickers, store-keepers, switch-men, power-house men, processors of coke, and horse-boys. A day's work by a miner and loader produced 2.6 to 3 tubs. Some supervisors earned bonuses on output exceeding standard-load multiplied by the number of tubs filled – a blatant incentive to cheat.[80] Clerical graft combined with tub shortages to breed atomization and the intensification of labour. If the miners cut coal without tubs on hand, they risked losing it. Deductions included fines for stones in the coal, for sleeping or coming late and the cost of explosives. A third of earnings could be lost this way,[81] and they could also be affected by the overstaffing of gangs to absorb excessive labour supply. Wage-rates varied up to 50 per cent in adjacent collieries depending on the nature of the seams. Ventilation, tub-availability, hardness and gallery dimensions affected miner's attitudes towards the wages offered.[82]

Piece-rates were ubiquitous, and combined with mediate forms of supervision to enable cheap extraction. Workers could be dismissed, wages reduced and uncertain labour supply dealt with by maintaining reserves of raised coal.[83] When the RCL recommended a minimum

---

[78] *Deshpande*, pp. 43–44; Appendix IX.

[79] *COI*, 1921, vol. 7, part 1, p. 272.

[80] *RCL*, vol. 4, part 1, pp. 58–59, 206 and 216. The standard tub size was 30 cubic feet, but collieries used sizes from 27 to 40 cubic feet. Thirteen hundredweight of coal was the standard load, but this varied, giving clerks scope for under-assessment: Seth, *Labour in the Indian Coal Industry*, pp. 116–117; *BLEC*, vol. 4 C, pp. 253–255. The RCL recommended weighment and tub-uniformity (Report, p. 123), but in 1939 none of the managements was using weighing machines. For their part, the miners resisted innovations such as double-headed picks and tin lamps, and thought of weighing machines "as an invention of the evil one": Seth, *Labour in the Indian Coal Industry*, p. 9.

[81] *Ibid.*, chs 5 and 7; pp. 79, 112; *RCL*, Report, p. 121; and *BLEC*, vol. 4 C, p. 246.

[82] Seth, *Labour in the Indian Coal Industry*, pp. 61–67. The RCL singled out the railways' collieries in Giridih for unhealthy working conditions: *RCL*, Report, pp. 115, 134.

[83] Even when the raising contractor system began to decline, in the mid-1930s, recruiting and gang *sirdars* remained, along with the piece-rates.

tub-credit, owners protested that it was the piece system alone that obtained "any useful effort from the aborigine miner".[84] The rail companies also opposed the idea, drawing support from the Inspector of Mines and the Railway Board who cited the existence of raising-contractors as an impediment to the scheme. The GOI rejected the recommendation in 1933.[85] However, miners' unrest in the late 1930s and a labour shortage during the war highlighted the need for a stable workforce. The Report of 1946 suggested that "a fair wage to labour (should) form the starting point for price fixation".[86]

Twelve-hour shifts were permitted in mining until 1935. Certain gangs worked for twenty-four hours with breaks underground – a pattern which suited those who trekked in from nearby villages.[87] Some managers and engineers favoured mechanization, training and stabilizing the workforce, regular shifts, time and motion studies and a stricter work regime; while others were satisfied with the "idiosyncrasies" of "the Indian miner", suggesting that the proposal for regular hours "savour(ed) of slave-driving".[88] In the late 1930s, the nine-hour limit on shifts was scarcely enforced, while actual hours worked fell short of the limit of fifty-four hours per week underground, indicating that many miners worked long spurts within short weeks. The 1946 enquiry spoke of "flagrant" violations of the Mines Act with respect to hours of work, citing instances of miners working second shifts on the same day under assumed names. It also reported that wages continued to be paid on Sundays despite the RCL's opposition to the practice. Apart from this, loaders were often forced to overload tubs by the *munshis* and *sardars* who profited from the excess. Pay-clerks would make payments in round figures on the ground of shortages of change.[89] Gang-*sardars* bribed clerks for suitable seams, contractors bribed executives and owners paid *salami* to

[84] *RCL*, Report, p. 122; and "Memorandum submitted by the Indian Mining Association in connection with the recommendations of the RCL in India": File M-1265 (14), 1933, Dept of Industries & Labour, NAI. The Memorandum continued: "The Indian coal miner is, generally speaking, an aborigene, whose ethical concepts – or want thereof – would not give him understanding to the need of an honest effort in return for a provided wage".

[85] Comment dated 20 May 1932 by the Chief Inspector of Mines in File M-1265 (14), 1933, Dept of I&L, NAI; and Order by A.G. Clow, dated 1 November 1933, in File M-1265 (14), 1933, Dept of I&L, NAI. On 17 August 1933, the new Inspector admitted that wages could be "deplorably low", but opined that statutory raises would lead to closures, and an increase in unemployment – a strange argument, given the notoriously unstable patterns of employment.

[86] *ICC*, p. 268.

[87] *TMGI*, 11 (1917), pp. 130–131; *Foley*, p. 13; Seth, *Labour in the Indian Coal Industry*, p. 15.

[88] "Discussion on Glen George's Paper on Development of Deep Coal Mining in Bengal", in *TMGI*, 11 (1917), pp. 115, 120, 130–132.

[89] *Deshpande*, pp. 109, 60.

the *zamindars*. This endemic graft signified the nexus within which the colonial system obtained its fuel. Managements did not notice the "want of ethical concepts" among their supervisory staff.

Women workers bore the brunt of the consequences of the coal slump and mechanization (see section on *The demography of employment* above, p. 89). Their impoverishment impinged upon living conditions in the coalbelt, and their exclusion from underground work in October 1937 had an adverse effect. Competition intensified amongst them for surface jobs. Family incomes went down by about 40 per cent due to this factor as well as to a decline in wage-rates. Significantly, some managers considered their withdrawal a convenient means of curbing over-production.[90] Women ceased accompanying their menfolk to the coalfields, and there was greater seasonal migration. Observers commented upon the increase in prostitution. One positive effect appeared to be the decline in the opiating of children.[91]

The need to improve conditions was noted by the RCL,[92] but the industry remained conservative. In a discussion at the Mining Institute in 1932,[93] the Commission's recommendations were rejected by managers. Arguments were aired about earnings being a function of the miners' volition,[94] their unreasonable attitudes regarding tubs, the sums they spent on drink and their unwillingness to work for longer than four or five days a week, "the obvious reason being that the extra wages were not required". Low stamina and efficiency were deemed part of the "hereditary characters" of the Indian miners. The two Indian participants and the Inspector of Mines, R.R. Simpson, insisted that low wages and inadequate diets were responsible for deteriorating health and an incapacity to work harder. "From the remarks made by certain speakers", added Simpson, "it would seem that in their opinion, the lower the wages of the miner, the happier he will be."[95]

Despite the slow development of their unions, the miners were not passive. The Mines Board of Health was created in 1914 after desertions

---

[90] See Seth, *Labour in the Indian Coal Industry*, pp. 150, 146–165; and J. Thomas's remarks in the discussion of R.R. Simpson's paper, "The Social Conditions of Miners in India", in *TMGI*, 27(2) (1933), p. 124.

[91] *Searchlight*, 27 March 1936. Prof. Bose's lecture.

[92] *RCL*, Report, p. 119.

[93] Simpson, "The Social Conditions of Miners" and discussion, *TMGI*, 27(2) (1933), pp. 89–139.

[94] In their evidences before the RCL, owners often argued that miners were content with the earnings of a short week and that better wages would exacerbate drinking and indebtedness: "the wages of miners are controlled by the miners themselves [. . .] when wages were increased [. . .] (they) [. . .] put in less work". See *RCL*, vol. 4, part 1, pp. 217, 247, 233, 254–255. The Indian Mine Managers Association, however, stated: "wages paid have no relation to the profits earned", and that improved conditions would increase output. Also see *BLEC*, vol. 4 C, p. 273; and vol. 3 B, book 3, p. 59.

[95] Simpson, "The Social Conditions of Miners", *TMGI*, 27(2) (1933), p. 138.

in the wake of deaths due to cholera.[96] Miners were known to leave empty spaces in the bottoms of their tubs and cheat on advance food allowances by taking these from more than one contractor.[97] They also used officially provided opportunities to express grievance: "I am amazed at the amount of work I have done already, how can I do more?" remarked a miner to the RCL,[98] whose visit to the East Indian Railways' mines at Giridih became the occasion for protest actions by 2,000 miners, who took initiatives in striking, picketing and mobilizing sympathy strikes.[99]

Complaints by English managers about "labour" provide the historian with a point of reflection. In their view, it was the psycho-ethnic character of Indian miners and their apparent economic *autonomy* which resulted in low earnings. This may be gleaned from comments such as: *"the ethical standard of aborigines and semi-savages is hardly compatible with the principle of a minimum wage"* (emphasis added); "As commodity prices fall, the miner is content to earn less"; "the Indian miner and his family can live according to custom on ten hours of effective man-hours per week [. . .] In England [. . .] 40 hours is barely sufficient [. . .]"; "The Indian miner (is) able to support himself for long periods [. . .] from the bountiful resources of the country, thereby still further reducing his effective man-hours in the mines"; "Mine owners in England are protected by law against absenteeism and malingering, but in India, owners are absolutely at the mercy of the labour", etc.[100]

What may we make of these remarks? In Jharia, for the greater part of our period, coal was won through family labour working on piece-rates, and through congeries of small-scale activities. Extraction proceeded in reverse tandem with agrarian seasons, and on a weekly basis the workday was influenced by the variegated preferences of the labour force.[101] These methods signified the emergence of an industry which

[96] *RCL*, vols 4(2), p. 179; and 4(1), p. 234; Mukerjee, *Indian Working Class*, p. 26; Seth, *Labour in the Indian Coal Industry*, pp. 53–56.
[97] *BLEC*, vol. 3 B, book 3, pp. 246, 250 and 282.
[98] Miner Sakaram, speaking for himself, Kamrai and Jarimiyan, to the RCL, on 25 January 1930: *RCL*, vol. 4, part 2, p. 170.
[99] The summer of 1932 saw some 4,000 miners of Tata's colliery in Jamadoba strike against cuts in wage-rates. For more information about these movements see D. Simeon, *The Politics of Labour Under Late Colonialism: Workers, Trade Unions and the State in Chota Nagpur, 1928–1939* (New Delhi, 1995), ch. 4.5, and ch. 6, section 2.
[100] *TMGI*, 27(2) (1933), pp. 122–126.
[101] Referring to migrations to Bombay in the mid-nineteenth century, Jan Breman remarks that the phenomenon "was probably more a result of the seasonality of the urban economy than of the rural". In Jharia, however, the characteristics of the workforce and the industry complemented each other. Despite their complaints about the irregularity of labour, the "instability" of the workforce suited the capitalists, even though their interests varied with the scale and location of the operation, the degree of mechanization, and the radius of recruitment: Breman, *Labour Migration and Rural Transformation in Colonial Asia* (Amsterdam, 1990), p. 9.

did not need to adhere to the Western calendar or to clock time. What the managers perceived as the lack of total control over labour was an aspect of the colonial mode of regulation – it was compensated for by an aggregate mechanism adequate for the needs of the system as a whole. The persistence of irregular working days, when seen in conjunction with the overall "instability" of labour supply, expressed the normalization of a regulatory practice. In Thompson's words, "attention to time in labour depends [. . .] upon the need for the synchronisation of labour". The prevalence of small-scale work processes, without an intricate sub-division of jobs, did not demand such synchronization.[102]

Contingent accidents

The industry reacted to the global coal depression of the 1920s by production increases, wage cuts and infrastructural savings. (Internal fragmentation prevented trade combinations.) Between 1926 and 1935, output in nine major companies rose by 80 per cent, whereas depreciation costs, raising costs and wages fell by 66 per cent, 46 per cent, and 45 per cent respectively.[103] Safety became an urgent subject and the contents of contemporary debates highlight the connection between the institutional and technological aspects of mining. A Subsidence Committee (1929–1935) warned that if sand-stowing and the control of gallery height and initial extraction were not enforced, collapses and spontaneous combustion were inevitable. The Coal Mining Committee noticed risks "which would not have been possible with less ignorant labour", estimating "avoidable waste' in the two coalfields at 50 per cent.[104] The 1930s saw a dramatic growth in casualties and accidents in mines run by the railways and agencies.

At a seminar in 1929 the Chief Inspector of Mines argued that immediate conservation measures were necessary to forestall the "inevitable" loss of half of Jharia's coal.[105] Seminarists asked why state railways did not implement his suggestions, and insisted that small average property sizes in Jharia and the low selling price of its coal made sand-stowing too expensive. The railways' collieries had "enhanced the wastage of coal by lowering the selling price", making "cheap mining indispensable to profit earning".[106] In 1930 the Indian Mine Managers' Association asked the GOI to enforce sand-stowing to forestall subsidences and

[102] E.P. Thompson, "Time, Work-Discipline and Industrial Capitalism", in idem, *Customs in Common* (London, 1991), p. 370.
[103] Ghosh, *Coal Industry*, pp. 63–67; *CMC*, p. 26; *ICC*, pp. 20–21, 118.
[104] *CMC*, pp. 27, 35–41.
[105] R.R. Simpson, "The Future of the Jharia Coalfield"; and "Discussion on Mr Simpson's Paper", in *TMGI*, 24 (1930), pp. 110–114, 114–146 and 226–257.
[106] J.E. Phelps's comments on Simpson's paper, in *ibid.*, p. 140.

fires.[107] Such proposals had previously been abandoned on account of financial hurdles and the problems of imposing standard cesses. In this instance, opposition from the industry was also cited.[108] An official noted that "the present low selling price of coal is ascribed partly to competition with Railway-owned collieries [. . .] producers apparently consider that if the Govt. wish to conserve their supplies [. . .] it is for the Govt. to pay [. . .]" Estimating that freight rebates alone would cost the railways a four million rupee annual reduction in earnings, he ruled out subsidized conservation, "especially during present financial stringency", drawing comfort from the fact that high grade coal reserves in India were calculated as sufficient for over a century.[109]

With the government unwilling to effect any drastic reforms in a system which provided cheap fuel to its transport network, and coal magnates with not much to worry about by way of strict state supervision, the logic of the colonial mode of regulation developed unhindered, and with disastrous consequences. The decade 1930–1940 witnessed 8,981 serious and fatal accidents in coal mines, an increase of 66 per cent over the previous decade. The number of miners either fatally or seriously injured was 9,710, compared with 5,846 during 1920–1930.[110] An explosion in Poidih colliery in the adjacent Asansol field in 1936 killed 210 persons:

A loud report was heard on the surface [. . .] the cage which had been at the bottom of the shaft [. . .] had been blown [. . .] into the headgear, a distance of over 700 feet [. . .] the bonnets of three safety lamps which had probably been those used at the bottom of the shafts were also found on the surface [. . .][111]

That these events were not simple accidents was indicated in the currency of the term "slaughter mining" to describe business strategies then in vogue. But when the experts spoke of "slaughter", they were referring to what was happening to the coal seams, rather than to those who worked them.

Coal and the state

During World War II, it has been said, the GOI became "a large scale interventionist machine".[112] With regard to coal an interventionist stance

[107] File M 76 (19), 1931, Dept of I&L, NAI. Letter from J. Dholakia, Association President, dated 19 September 1930.
[108] File M 76 (19), 1931, Dept of I&L, NAI. Notes dated 23 January 1931 and 7 March 1931.
[109] File M 76 (19), 1931, Dept of I&L, NAI. Comments by the Chief Inspector of Mines, dated 1 April 1931, and by (signature illegible), dated 10 October 1931.
[110] See Ghosh, *Coal Industry*, p. 162. These figures are for mines all over India.
[111] *ARCIM* (1936), p. 23.
[112] D. Rothermund, "Problems of India's Arrested Economic Development Under British Rule", in Clive Dewey (ed.), *Arrested Development in India: The Historical Dimension*

had appeared in official texts soon after the end of World War I. Thus, in 1920 the Foley Committee asked the state "to step in and prevent the dissipation of the country's resources".[113] The Burrows Report of 1937 criticized the notion of an "'economic man' actuated by self-interest", drew attention to the "world-wide trend away from the competitive ideal towards formulas of public control", and lauded Germany and France for state regulation of coal mining.[114] Nevertheless, it required the shock waves of national upheaval and international conflict to shake the GOI out of its apathy. In 1937, nationalist provincial ministries emerged across India. The following year saw an upsurge of labour movements. In Jharia lightning strikes erupted over demands relating to harassment, graft, working and living conditions, and benefits. Interests crystallized on both sides of the class divide. Indian coal magnates consolidated with British managing agents. In the mining settlements Congressman Abdul Bari's extreme speeches roused the working population as never before, and the left-wing slogans heard at miners' meetings alarmed the adminstration. *Rezas* were active at pickets and in some strikes there were instances of water-pumping being sabotaged. These movements achieved the recognition of miners' unions such as the Chota Nagpur Mazdur Sangh.[115]

The outbreak of war enhanced the importance of coal as a strategic commodity. The period 1937–1942 witnessed increasing demand and better prices, and from 1939 onwards the provincial government began interventions to settle ongoing conflicts in the industry. Employers were cajoled to concede a war allowance, and a cess collected towards a welfare fund. Even the long-expressed wish of the miners to see an end to the system of mediated recruitment began to be fulfilled (although not by design) – by 1946, over 60 per cent of the workers of Jharia were being recruited directly, signalling the decline of contractorship.[116] These changes demonstrated official concern to ensure the continuity of coal supply. Thus the effects of inadequate plant replacement during the 1930s and a wartime wagon-shortage, coupled with the movement of workers into better-paid ordnance jobs, led to a 4 m.-ton shortfall in coal production during 1942–1943. Thereupon women were permitted underground again (1943), and the government launched the Coal Con-

(New Delhi, 1988), p. 8. From 1930 onwards, in an effort to widen the market for inferior grade coals, the Indian Soft Coke Cess Committee began refuting the prejudice against food cooked on soft coke. Citing the Bengal Smoke Nuisance Commission and the Ahmedabad Committee on Smoke Nuisance it propagandized against dung cakes and wood by highlighting their polluting effects in urban areas (*ICC*, pp. 47–48).
[113] *Foley*, pp. 5–6.
[114] *CMC*, pp. 96, 102.
[115] For miners' movements in the 1920s and 1930s, see Ghosh, "A Study of the Labour Movement", and chs 4.5, 6 section 2, 8.8, 8.11 and 9.11 of my *Politics of Labour*.
[116] *Searchlight*, 5, 9, 13 and 20 December 1939; Mukerjee, *Indian Working Class*, p. 26; and *ICC*, pp. 251–253.

trol Scheme (1944) and the Young Plan, under which miners were given an attendance bonus in cash along with a grain ration. The newly established Raniganj Coalfields Central Recruiting Organisation and the Directorate of Unskilled Labour Supply began contracting workers and housing them in dormitories fenced with barbed wire. These schemes were meant to fulfil the objects of the Labour Recruitment Control Order of 1944, to regulate recruitment in designated areas "to ensure that there is ample supply of labour for collieries". The Defence of India Rules (1942) empowered government to enforce adjudication and prohibit strikes. Between 1942 and 1945, the GOI issued seven Ordinances pertaining to coal mining. Jharia reached its highest production level of 16.59 m. tons in 1945.[117]

State intervention in labour-management relations was quite visible when there was an impelling motive. But the GOI began to investigate the basic disorganization of the industry[118] only on the eve of the transfer of power. Thus far, policy had been dictated by the necessity of fuelling transport, facilitating the operations of the agencies and allowing *zamindars* to exact ground-rent regardless of the consequences. Commercially relevant recommendations were implemented, but on structural matters state policy "continued to be one of laissez-faire", and the industry encouraged this stance.[119] The Burrows Committee had been appointed in the aftermath of the accidents of 1936. Its insistence on sand-stowing, coupled with the unrest of 1938, had pushed government towards implementing limited safety measures in November 1939. But on wages, working conditions, coal conservation and land leasing the Burrows recommendations, along with those of other commissioned enquiries, were ignored. Thus in 1940 the BLEC criticized agency management, asked for an investigation into the railways' role in price fixation and, after citing state subsidies of coal exports in Britain, asked the GOI to discard its "faith in laissez-faire".[120] The Mahindra Report of 1946 asked for a National Coal Commission, citing the Tennessee Valley Authority, the British Coal Commission and the nationalization of British coal. It is a measure of the stamina of colonial production relations that these

[117] See B.M. Prasad, *Second World War and Indian Industry 1939–45* (Delhi, 1992), pp. 71–74, 257–259; M. Kumaramangalam, *Coal Industry in India: Nationalisation and Tasks Ahead* (New Delhi, 1973), pp. 47, 72–73; Simmons, "Recruiting and Organising", p. 457; *Deshpande*, pp. 55–56; Hans Raj, *Executive Legislation in Colonial India 1939–1947* (Delhi, 1989), pp. 40, 94–96, 121; and *ICC*, pp. 20–21. For the text of the GOI's Labour Recruitment Control Order of 1944, see *Deshpande*, Appendix VII.
[118] Coal distillation yielded coke, tar, naphthalene, combustible fuels, benzene and toulene, an ingredient of TNT. Yet in 1945, only 18.25 per cent of the coal consumed was being processed into coke, gas, tar, ammonia and light oils – the remainder being burnt as fuel. The production of road tar in India was a bare 50,000 tons per annum (*ICC*, pp. 227–231).
[119] *ICC*, p. 20.
[120] *BLEC*, vol. 1, pp. 205–206.

voices were only paid heed to a quarter of a century later, when Indian coal companies were nationalized in 1972–1973.

In 1995, a week before the 125th anniversary of Gandhi's birth, headlines about Jharia appeared once more in Indian newspapers: "75 feared killed in Dhanbad mines disaster"; "Figures speak of failing safety norms"; and "Mine tragedy man-mady".[121] In 1994, the press had reported the death of fifty-five miners. All these stories spoke of managerial negligence – after the latest case, arrest warrants were issued for colliery executives. In the 1994 "accident", miner Mukhi Dusadh had tucked a note under his wrist-watch: "It is now 10 pm. Though we are trying to save ourselves, I do not see any chance of escaping the clutches of death which is closing in on us".[122] The fate of the miners of Jharia is a reminder of the deadly ramifications of modernity's appetite for fossil fuels. Did the relations of production in the coalfields of Bihar reach unprecedented levels of ossification in colonial times? An answer may be read in Mukhi's message for posterity and in the flames of the still-extant Jharia underground fire.

[121] *Indian Express*, 28 and 29 September 1995; and *The Hindustan Times*, 1 October 1995.
[122] *The Times of India*, 28 January 1994.

"Capital Spectacles in British Frames": Capital, Empire and Indian Indentured Migration to the British Caribbean*

MADHAVI KALE

They came in ships.

From across the seas, they came.
Britain, colonising India, transporting her chains

from Chota Nagpur and the Ganges Plain.

Westwards came the Whitby,
The Hesperus,
The Island-bound Fatel Rozack.

Wooden missions of imperialist design.

Mahadai Das, "They Came in Ships"[1]

As "They Came in Ships" by the Guyanese poet Mahadai Das suggests, scholarship on indentured immigration is not an exclusively academic concern in Caribbean countries with sizeable Indian populations. An international conference on Indian diaspora held recently at the University of the West Indies, Trinidad and Tobago, was not only covered by national news media, but also attended by Trinidadians (almost exclusively of Indian descent) unattached to the university, some of whom also contributed papers, helped to organize and run it.[2] In Guyana and Trinidad and Tobago, contestations over national identities are grounded in and self-consciously refer to a shared historical archive. This includes conventional, written material such as colonial administration records, newspapers, travelogues, and memoirs that reflect the concerns of privileged observers: government officials, reporters and editors, missionaries,

* Research for this project was supported by dissertation fellowships from the Mellon Foundation and Social Science Research Council-South Asia programme, and by a faculty research grant from Bryn Mawr College. Many thanks to Rob Gregg, Shahid Amin and Antoinette Burton for reading and commenting on earlier drafts of this article.

[1] Mahadai Das, "They Came in Ships", in David Dabydeen and Brinsley Samaroo (eds), *India in the Caribbean* (London, 1987), pp. 288–289.
[2] ISER-NCIC Conference on Challenge and Change: The Indian Diaspora in its Historical and Contemporary Contexts, University of the West Indies, St Augustine, Trinidad and Tobago, 11–18 August 1995.

110   *Madhavi Kale*

labour activists, historians, anthropologists. It also includes memories and accounts of personal and group experiences by others in these societies, transmitted orally or through other popular media, and they all simultaneously and unevenly undermine as well as authorize each other.[3]

Two issues continue to frame debate on the history and politics of Indian immigration and cultural diversity in the English-speaking Caribbean. One, on which the first part of this article focuses, concerns interpretation of emancipation and its aftermath. Was Trinidad's sugar industry threatened by emancipation and "saved" by indentured immigration (from India, but also – on a smaller scale – from Sierra Leone, China and elsewhere)? Or did the introduction of indentured labourers from overseas undermine Afro-Trinidadian labourers' prospects in the post-emancipation period? The second, related set of questions articulates with the first and with emergent imperial discourses on race, class, gender and nation. In the context of post-emancipation Trinidad, this involved crystallization of a cultural register calibrated to the needs of an increasingly monopolistic sugar industry and an empire predicated on naturalizing and reproducing hierarchies of race, class, gender and nation along which ethnically-constituted populations in the colony were continuously, contradictorily evaluated.[4] Were Indian indentured migrants the outcasts of colonial Indian society, "the sweepings of bazaars" as some contemporaries claimed? Or were they "respectable" folk – pushed out of traditional villages by deteriorating economic or (particularly in the case of women migrants) social conditions, and either trapped or drawn by often unscrupulous recruiters into taking the enormous risk of emigrating to improve their lives and prospects? Were they, like Afro-Trinidadian working people, also victims and unwilling instruments of British imperialism? Or were they cannily complicit in the reassertion of a racially-inflected plantation economy in the post-

[3] Rhoda Reddock, "Contestations over National Culture in Trinidad and Tobago: Considerations of Ethnicity, Class, Race and Gender", paper presented at Bryn Mawr/Haverford/Swarthmore Colleges series on Colonialism and the Disciplines, 29 February 1996; D.V. Trotman, "The Image of Indians in Calypso: Trinidad 1946–86", in Frank Birbalsingh (ed), *Indenture and Exile. The Indo-Caribbean Experience* (Toronto, 1989), pp. 176–190; Jeremy Poynting, "East Indian Women in the Caribbean: Experience and Voice", in Dabydeen and Samaroo, *India in the Caribbean*, pp. 231–263; Monica Schuler, *"Alas, Alas, Kongo": A Social History of Indentured African Immigration into Jamaica, 1841–1865* (Baltimore, 1980); Shahid Amin, *Event, Metaphor, Memory: Chauri Chaura, 1922–1992* (Berkeley, 1995).
[4] Madhavi Kale, "Projecting Identities: Empire and Indentured Labor Migration from India to Trinidad and British Guiana, 1836–1885", in Peter van der Veer (ed.), *Nation and Migration: The Politics of Space in the South Asian Diaspora* (Philadelphia, 1995), pp. 73–92; idem, "Casting Labor in the Imperial Mold", paper presented at Conference on Challenge and Change, University of the West Indies, St Augustine, Trinidad and Tobago, 13 August 1995.

emancipation period?[5] The second section of the article focuses on the literature on recruitment of indentured migrants in India: where, how and by whom migrants were recruited, the conditions prevailing at the time, and who was recruited.

In considering these two topics, this article questions the causal link established by contemporaries and further elaborated by historians and others between post-emancipation labour shortage on British Caribbean sugar plantations on the one hand, and patterns of labour recruitment in colonial India for those same plantations on the other. Indeed, I present these topics in an effort to uncouple these two narratives, and reconsider the imperial narrative train in which they have served as engine and caboose. Seventy-odd years of Indian indentured migration overseas, and more than a century and a half of struggle by migrants and their descendents both exceed the narratives that have been proposed to contain them. Indian indentured migration is not reducible to Caribbean (or Fijian, South African, and so on) "labour shortage", and formation of distinctive communities among migrants and their descendants is not reducible to tradition, great or little.

Genesis

Commissioners came,
capital spectacles in British frames
consulting managers about costs of immigration.

                    Mahadai Das, "They Came In Ships"

Sugar planters in the British Caribbean had long complained that the labour available to them was inadequate, numerically or otherwise. After abolition of the slave trade, they explored the possibility of importing labourers from India and China to both augment and control the labour of slaves.[6] The Act of Abolition, passed in 1833 by the reformed Parliament elected in 1832, reflected planters' and West India merchant-creditors' success in shielding their investments from hostile abolitionist sentiment. The Act provided that slave-owners be compensated for the loss of their human property through a combination of financial award (a sum of £20 million was approved for the purpose) and deferral of adult slaves' full emancipation for six years. It also provided that compensation be paid in London, rather than in the colonies, which

[5] See Aisha Khan, "Purity, Piety, and Power: Culture and Identity among Hindus and Muslims in Trinidad" (Ph.D., City University of New York, 1995), pp. 71–74.
[6] UK (HC) 1810–11, II, no. 409, "Report of the Select Committee Appointed to Consider the Practicability and Expediency of Supplying our West India Colonies with Free Labourers from the East"; B.W. Higman, "The Chinese in Trinidad, 1806–1838", *Caribbean Studies*, 12, 3 (1972), pp. 21–44.

enabled merchant-creditors, who often held power-of-attorney for their clients, to recuperate some or all of the loans they had made to planters over the years. During this period former slaves were to continue to work as "apprentices" for their former masters for six days of the week in exchange for continued provision of customary allowances (food, clothing, housing). Apprenticeship was skipped entirely in some affected colonies, and ended early (summer 1838) elsewhere, subverted by the actions and interactions of both apprentices and planters.[7]

In December 1839, 773 "Clergy, Planters, Merchants, and other Inhabitants" of British Guiana signed a petition imploring the Queen and her ministers to give them the means to recuperate from a debilitating labour shortage precipitated by emancipation the previous year. Extolling the colony's enormous untapped natural resources and enormous economic potential, they warned that prevailing conditions were "not only pregnant with ruin to the landed interest of this colony, but prejudicial to the moral condition of the labourers themselves, as idleness tends to increase, and is almost universally the originator and companion of crime". They proposed that they be allowed to recruit plantation labourers from among "the vast population of India". Such a scheme would save investments already made in the colony's sugar industry, "open a field for the employment of a large additional amount of capital" in the colony's still-unexploited territories, "prevent the demoralization" of freedpeople, and finally, give undercompensated Indian labourers the opportunity to sell their labour "where the fertility of the soil, and demand for their labour, will ensure them comfortable, even abundant subsistence".[8]

In a letter written to Colonial Secretary John Russell at the same time, the London West India Merchants' Association made the same case. They elaborated on the framework of labour shortage, British Guiana's potential for investment and profit, social crisis and imperial *noblesse oblige*. The Merchants' Association argued that estates in the colony were suffering from an absolute decline in the number of labourers available to them after emancipation, "many of the emancipated labourers having, since the 1st of August 1838, betaken themselves to petty trading, and other employments in preference to the cultivation of the soil, most of the women having altogether withdrawn, and the

---

[7] Kathleen Mary Butler, *The Economics of Emancipation: Jamaica and Barbados, 1823–1843* (Chapel Hill, 1995). UK (HC) 1836, no. 560, "Report of the Select Committee on Negro Apprenticeship in the Colonies"; UK (HL) 1839, VII, no. 1, Glenelg to Nicolay (Governor of Mauritius), 20 January 1836; W.K. Marshall, "The Termination of Apprenticeship in Barbados and the Windward Islands: An Essay in Colonial Administration and Politics", *Journal of Caribbean History*, II (May 1971), pp. 1–45; Hilary Beckles, *Black Rebellion in Barbados: The Struggle against Slavery, 1627–1838* (Bridgetown, 1984).

[8] UK (HC) 1840, encl. in no. 23, Light to Russell, 23 December 1839, Petition to the Queen from British Guiana, 21 December 1839.

children affording scarcely any assistance".[9] They warned that wages currently being offered in the colony were so high that many good workers would "gradually become independent, purchase land, and cultivate provisions for their own account, and consequently withdraw themselves from the cultivation of exportable produce". The Merchants' Association complained that not only were emancipated men and women unreliable labourers, but they were also, in their capacity as parents, unreliable in reproducing labour. They lamented that, "unfortunately for themselves", emancipated youth were not being "trained up by their parents to industrious habits, and consequently, no assistance [could] be expected from them in the cultivation of produce at a future period".[10]

Like their counterparts in British Guiana, the Merchants' Association urged the government to allow interested employers in British Caribbean colonies to recruit workers from Africa and Asia, "those densely populated countries whose inhabitants, from climate and other circumstances, are best adapted for tropical labour". Such a scheme would be mutually beneficial to the Caribbean colonies and India, where "hundreds of thousands of the natives [. . .] were starved to death in 1838, in various parts of that over-populated country, which is well known to be afflicted with a frightful dearth at times". They concluded:

it would, therefore, be an act of humanity, on the part of the British Government, to give the inhabitants of those regions access to a country capable of affording profitable employment to industrious labourers for ages to come, and where such dreadful calamities as that just adverted to are utterly unknown; a country where they would also have the means of obtaining religious instruction.[11]

Labour migration would address the shortage of labour in the British Caribbean, underemployment in India, and the not unrelated problems of immorality and heathenism at both ends of the empire.

For the most part, historians of emancipation and its aftermath have either modified this sugar and slavery line, or ignored it, focusing instead on the needs and logic of "plantation economy".[12] However, research (sometimes that of these very historians) suggests that there was not as much consensus among colonial planters, freedpeople and officials or among metropolitan abolitionists, entrepreneurs and bureaucrats as the

---

[9] UK (HC) 1840, encl. 1, West India Association to Russell, 17 December 1839, in Russell to Light, 2 February 1840.

[10] *Ibid.*

[11] *Ibid.*

[12] See, for example, William A. Green, *British Slave Emancipation: The Sugar Colonies and the Great Experiment 1830–1865* (New York, 1975); Eric Foner, *Nothing But Freedom: Emancipation and its Legacy* (Baton Rouge, 1983); Thomas Holt, *The Problem of Freedom: Race, Labor, and Politics in Jamaica and Britain, 1832–1938* (Baltimore, 1992); Malcolm Cross and Gad Heuman (eds), *Labour in the Caribbean; From Emancipation to Independence* (London, 1988).

standard narrative implies. For example, several historians have noted the progressive consolidation of Trinidad's sugar industry after emancipation. According to historian Donald Wood, in 1838 there were 206 sugar plantations in Trinidad. Of these, two-thirds were owned by resident proprietors. In 1866 there were 142 estates in the colony. In 1872 the Colonial Company set up the usine St Madeleine, one of the largest central sugar processing plants in the world, followed by two others, in Northern Plain and in Naparimas, thereby effectively eliminating the production by open-vat methods of inferior Muscovado sugar, and accelerating the expansion of cane cultivation by smallholders on the peripheries of the sugar estates, and the consolidation of industry. In 1896 there were only 52 sugar plantations in Trinidad, and in 1936 that number had dwindled to 32. By 1959 "the sugar industry was in the hands of five companies".[13] In other words, after emancipation, the plantation system developed in such a way as to progressively disempower a large group of small-scale producers (a group that might have been expanded to include the freed population), and consolidate the power and prestige of some plantation owners controlled increasingly by metropolitan capital. In addition, historian Kusha Haraksingh has argued that, far from fleeing the sugar estates in revulsion after emancipation, in Trinidad freedpeople were often pushed off, evicted by rationalizing plantation owners eager to eliminate from their workforces those deemed least productive – women, the elderly, children, the infirm – and to shift some of the costs of reproducing their labour to the labourers and their families.[14]

Official records indicate that, while Colonial Office personnel eventually accepted claims of labour shortage, and helped develop policies predicated on post-emancipation labour shortage in the British Caribbean, they were not always persuaded by planters' representations of their plight. Rather, constellations of other variables and agendas intersected to make both labour shortage and indentured immigration respectable in the 1840s. For example, in a letter to Governor Light of British Guiana, Colonial Secretary John Russell rejected allegations that emancipated creoles had become lawless and degenerate after emancipation, as suggested in a petition from British Guiana lobbying for both government-subsidized immigration, and the reopening of India and Africa for labour recruitment. Russell observed:

None of the most inveterate opponents of our recent measures of emancipation allege that the negros have turned robbers, or plunderers, or blood-thirsty

[13] Donald Wood, *Trinidad in Transition: The Years After Slavery* (London, 1986), pp. 36, 295; Bridget Brereton, *Race Relations in Colonial Trinidad, 1870–1900* (Cambridge, 1979), p. 49.
[14] Douglas Hall, "Flight from the Estates Reconsidered: The British West Indies, 1838–42", *Journal of Caribbean History*, 10 and 11 (1978), pp. 7–24; Kusha Haraksingh, "Control

insurgents. What appears from their statement is, that they have become shop-keepers, and petty traders, and hucksters, and small freeholders; a blessed change, which providence has enabled us all to accomplish.[15]

Far from sharing petitioners' alarm at this turn of events, Russell argued that they indicated that the Act of Abolition had already gone a long way towards fulfilling Britain's civilizing mission. However, he also noted that the moral victory had come at some cost. "It is important, but still a secondary question," he wrote, "to consider how we can maintain the natural prosperity of our West India colonies, promote the cultivation of products for which the climate is adapted, and keep up, if not increase, the consumption of British manufactures." Russell observed that if these objectives were to be achieved through continued cultivation and export of sugar, then the imperial government ought to help facilitate private colonial efforts to pursue and expand these established economic activities. In short, he proposed that Parliament ought to give "encouragement to a large emigration of labourers into Guiana, Trinidad, and other colonies, with a view to introduce a large population" so that the ratio of land to labour would approximate that of more densely populated Caribbean colonies like Barbardos.

Other research raises questions about the conviction, evident both in primary data and historical interpretations, that women were particularly averse to field labour specifically and wage labour generally. Taken together, the work of Lucille Mathurin, Barry Higman, Hilary Beckles, Marietta Morrissey and other Caribbean historians indicates that since the end of the slave-trade early in the nineteenth century, women had formed increasingly significant proportions of field "gangs" on some plantations in some of the British Caribbean colonies, with no noticeable diminution in the amount of sugar such estates produced.[16] In 1836–1837, the Liverpool merchant John Gladstone, along with a few other British Guiana plantation owners in London, had tried to import Indian indentured labourers for his British Guiana estates. In presenting their case to the Colonial Office, Gladstone had professed himself willing to hire as many Indian women for his plantations as men – provided they worked in the fields as enslaved women had done, and for lower wages.[17]

If after emancipation, employers offered freedwomen lower wages than

and Resistance Among Indian Workers: A Study of Labour on the Sugar Plantations of Trinidad, 1875–1917", in Dabydeen and Samaroo, *India in the Caribbean*, pp. 61–62.

[15] UK (HC) 1840, XXXIV, no. 121, Russell to Light, 15 February 1840.

[16] Lucille Mathurin, *The Rebel Woman in the British West Indies during Slavery* (Kingston, Jamaica, 1975); Barry W. Higman, *Slave Populations of the British Caribbean 1807–1834* (Baltimore, 1984); Marietta Morrissey, *Slave Women in the New World: Gender Stratification in the Caribbean* (Lawrence, KS, 1989); Hilary McD. Beckles, *Natural Rebels: A Social History of Enslaved Black Women in Barbados* (New Brunswick, 1989).

[17] UK (HC) 1838 (232), encl. no. 1, in Gladstone to Glenelg, 22 February 1838; Gladstone to Gillanders, Arbuthnot and Co., 4 January 1836.

men (as Gladstone had proposed in the case of indentured Indian women) freedwomen may have rejected these conditions, taking up foodcrop cultivation and sales instead – and thus planters may indeed have lost a significant proportion of their pre-emancipation labour force. Whatever its motivations, women's absence from plantation waged labour forces dovetailed with colonial Baptist missionaries' and metropolitan abolitionists' aspirations for emancipation and freed Afro-Caribbean people. In the years before abolition, anti-slavery activists had condemned colonial slavery for what they saw as its perversion of gender roles: specifically, of conjugal and parental rights and responsibilities among slave-owners and enslaved alike. As the journal of the British and Foreign Anti-Slavery Society (BFASS) and other such publications indicates, the veterans of abolitionism hoped to see this situation rectified in bustling post-emancipation villages of cottagers, wives and mothers at home, husbands and fathers at work in the fields and workshops. To the extent that abolitionists and their fellow-bourgeois subscribed to a "separate spheres" gender ideology (the Society's refusal to accept the credentials of four American delegates to their World Anti-Slavery Convention in 1840 because they were women suggests that they did so), wage-earning women field labourers jarred with this vision. Most metropolitan reformers of colonial labour conditions did not question, indeed applauded the propriety of freedwomen's declining participation in field labour. Like Russell, they interpreted this as a promising sign of progress among black men and women "degraded" by slavery.[18]

Further, at abolition, British Guiana and Trinidad (along with British Honduras) were distinguished among British colonies in the Caribbean for having more enslaved men than enslaved women: ratios of between 110–112 men per 100 women (in British Honduras, the ratio was 162.5:100).[19] However significant women's removal from plantation labour may have been in other colonies, in these two it may have been less important than contemporaries asserted or assumed. Historian Hilary Beckles has suggested that, "In general, the data suggest that the more developed the colony as a plantation system, the greater the tendency for the normalization of sex ratios, moving from a male predominance under frontier condi-

---

[18] See, for example, *The Anti-Slavery Reporter*, published by the British and Foreign Anti-Slavery Society from 1840 on; Howard Temperley, *British Antislavery 1833–1870* (Columbia, SC, 1972), pp. 87–90; Clare Midgley, "Anti-Slavery and Feminism in 19th-Century Britain", *Gender and History*, 5, 3 (Autumn 1993), pp. 343–362; Catherine Hall, "Competing Masculinities: Thomas Carlyle, John Stuart Mill and the Case of Governor Eyre", in idem, *White, Male and Middle Class. Explorations in Feminism and History* (London, 1992), pp. 255–295; idem, " 'From Greenland's Icy Mountains [. . .] to Afric's Golden Sand': Ethnicity, Race and Nation in Mid-19th-Century England", *Gender and History* (special issue on Gender, Nationalities, and National Identities), 5, 2 (Summer 1993), pp. 212–230.
[19] Higman, *Slave Populations*, p. 116.

tions, to female predominance with maturity."[20] In the "frontier" contexts of Trinidad and British Guiana in the 1830s, where land would have to be cleared and reclaimed, dikes and canals built and dug before cane cultivation could proceed, employers may have preferred male labourers over women, thus giving added incentive to employers and speculators to seek male labourers wherever they could get them, and push women out of the waged plantation workforce.

"Labour shortage" was the idiom in which some British Caribbean sugar planters, along with a coterie of metropolitan creditors and entrepreneurs with investments throughout the British empire represented their unhappiness with conditions under which they both produced and sold sugar. For even as the British Caribbean sugar producers were losing the privileges over labour they had enjoyed under slavery, they were also losing their protected status in the home sugar market. In 1825 Mauritius-grown muscavodo (a low grade of sugar) was admitted into Britain at rates previously reserved for British West Indian sugar. In 1836 the rate was extended to sugar produced in India. By the time of emancipation, it was clear that the abolition of duties that protected British colonial sugar – against even the cheaper and higher quality sugar produced by slave labour in Cuba and Brazil – was imminent.

What the labour shortage argument in fact points to is an attempt to mould sugar production in Trinidad and British Guiana into vertically and horizontally-integrated industries. The motive, for some colonial planters and metropolitan entrepreneurial capitalists, was the relative abundance in the two colonies of still-unexploited land suitable for large-scale sugar cultivation. That this was understood as investment potential was reflected in the fact that higher prices were paid for slaves in these two colonies between 1822 and 1830 than in any other, and established in the significantly higher rates of compensation paid by the British government to slave-owners there, than to those in any other. The average compensation awarded former slave-owners in Honduras, British Guiana and Trinidad was over £50 per slave. The next highest average compensation was paid to former owners of slaves at the Cape of Good Hope and Mauritius (£34 11s 7d and £31 10s 6d, respectively). In the British Caribbean, those who had owned slaves in the smaller islands of St Vincent, Grenada and St Lucia, received the next highest average compensations: approximately £25–£27, or just over half the average amount awarded former owners of slaves in Trinidad and British Guiana. The average compensation paid for slaves in Barbados, Tobago, Jamaica and Dominica, was between £19 and £21.[21]

As Eric Williams noted, "Trinidad's economic potential in comparison with that of the exhausted soil of the older islands made the slave in

---

[20] Beckles, *Natural Rebels*, pp. 18–19; Higman, *Slave Populations*, pp. 58–63.
[21] Butler, *Economics of Emancipation*, Appendix, Table A.1., p. 143.

Trinidad an infinitely more valuable piece of property than the slave in any other West Indian colony except British Guiana." He added that a labour shortage would result from the intention to expand sugar production. He wrote:

The presence of a mere 17,439 slaves in Trinidad and a mere 69,579 in British Guiana changed the whole course of history of these two colonies after emancipation. The labour problem led to the introduction of an entirely new population in Trinidad, *which converted* the island from a society of small farmers into a typical plantation economy.[22] (emphasis added)

The ability of some plantation owners in Trinidad and British Guiana to use their imperial connections to propagate the notion that freedpeople would or did handicap colonial development helped to establish these two as leading British Caribbean sugar producers throughout the nineteenth century.[23]

Not all landowners in the two colonies were as enthusiastic about indentured immigration as those in British Guiana who signed the 1839 petition, or members of the West India Merchants' Association in London. Indentured labour was only affordable on fairly large estates, which could provide the housing and medical facilities required by imperial government and colonial regulations. Historian Bridget Brereton has argued that in Trinidad, French creole planters were displaced as sugar producers by better-capitalized, British-based or -backed owners during the 1840s and 1870s as a consequence of reductions in protective sugar duties. Cocoa cultivators in Trinidad (among whom numbered French creoles who had abandoned sugar production to the better-capitalized British-owned estates, as well as Afro-Trinidadians and, as the century progressed, Indo-Trinidadians) were unenthusiastic about indentured immigration. Free or unindentured workers and smallholders in Trinidad complained that indentured immigration depressed their wages. They, like some historians, pointed out that even during depressions in the sugar industry, Trinidad and British Guiana continued to requisition and get substantial numbers of Indian indentured migrants, who were required to do more work per task than in the past, thereby contributing to deteriorating conditions for all.[24]

Two other factors that contributed to naturalizing labour shortage in Trinidad and British Guiana after emancipation were the imperial government's fluctuating and malleable commitment to free trade, and

[22] Eric Williams, *Capitalism and Slavery* (London, 1987; first pub. 1964), p. 86.

[23] Higman's analysis of data from approximately 1832 modifies Williams's position, but not dramatically: *Slave Populations*, pp. 102–103.

[24] UK (HC) 1910, XXVII, "Committee on Emigration from India to the Crown Colonies and Protectorates", part 2, Minutes of Evidence; Brereton, *Race Relations*, pp. 49, 179; Wood, *Trinidad in Transition*, pp. 107–159; K.O. Laurence, *A Question of Labour: Indentured Immigration into Trinidad and British Guiana 1875–1917* (London, 1994), p. 11.

working-class activism – most notably Chartism – in the 1830s and 1840s. The protective sugar duties were attacked as privileges subsidized by high prices paid by British consumers, working-class, middle-class and aristocratic alike. British Caribbean sugar investors successfully argued that the only way for free trade and free labour to triumph in world sugar markets was for British Caribbean sugar producers to import, with imperial assistance, adequate labour from other parts of the British empire. Even some factions within the British and Foreign Anti-Slavery Society came around to the view that indentured immigration into the British Caribbean, specifically from India, was an acceptable price to pay towards the goal of eliminating slavery throughout the world. By 1842, BFASS was torn by conflicting opinions on the sugar duties, elimination of which the central committee in London joined planters and sugar merchants in opposing. In 1844 Thomas Spencer, W.T. Blair and G.W. Anstie sent a circular letter to other BFASS members, urging them to repudiate the resolution in favour of continued protection of British colonial sugars pushed through the 1843 Anti-Slavery Convention by the London Committee. "Who are the men who object to our receiving slave-grown sugar?" they asked. "Not the poor, but a small, very small minority of the more comfortable or richer classes", they responded, adding:

Our own colonies produce enough to supply those who can pay the high price they charge for their sugar, and these, consequently, get enough; but the poor go without, to satisfy the scruples of those who, under any circumstances, know nothing of scarcity. We feel constrained to put it to the latter, whether their conscientious scruples ought to impose sacrifices upon their poorer countrymen, who do not partake of their scruples?[25]

It was not coincidental that Indian indentured migration, under the auspices of Parliament, the Colonial and India Offices, colonial and Indian governments, was approved by Act of Parliament in 1844, and the Act providing for elimination of preferential sugar tariffs – as well as that striking down the Corn Laws – was passed in 1846.

The continuing resiliency of the "labour shortage" model of post-emancipation labour conditions can in part be traced to its fit with the assumptions, methods and agendas of social history as they developed in the 1960s and 1970s. If in claiming that they were short of labour nineteenth-century planters represented freedpeople as negatively as they could – as shiftless, lazy, unreliable, heedless, happy-go-lucky and the rest of it – social historians have reread such representations as evidence of freedpeople's resistance to capitalism, planters and their vision of virtue, and as alternative interpretations of the meanings of freedom.

[25] "The Sugar Question", *The Anti-Slavery Reporter*, 5, 7 (3 April 1844), p. 50; Temperley, *British Antislavery*, pp. 111–136; George J. Schuette, "The London West India Committee, 1838–1854: An Imperial Pressure Group in Action" (Ph.D., Duke University, 1975), p. 85.

Such rereadings of the primary evidence are not unconvincing. Neither are they unproblematical. They are not only predicated on, but also reproduce assumptions about gender, labour and history that naturalize some aspects of patriarchal authority (the plantation-dominated, sugar-producing, post-emancipation colonial economies, for example) and romanticize others (the idealized bourgeois family), even if they don't necessarily endorse them. With some notable exceptions (Kusha Harak-singh and Rhoda Reddock, for example), the literature on Indian inden-tured migration to the British Caribbean builds on this scholarship on abolition, emancipation and their aftermath, and for the most part proceeds from the assumption that freedpeople's – and especially freedwomen's – reluctance to continue to work on sugar plantations after 1838 made importation of labour from overseas necessary.[26] They have not adequately considered either the extent to which ever-emergent imperial discourses on labour, race and gender informed the myriad policies designed and implemented by colonial, imperial and Indian officials for the protection and regulation of Indian indentured migrants; or by extension, the extent to which these large and small acts of empire helped shape the distinctive communities and cultures emergent among Indian migrants and their descendants in the British Caribbean.

Making a colonial labour shortage was a complicated business. It involved mobilization of a battery of discursive resources, as well as transformative interventions in material conditions (colonial legislation and commodification of customary allowances, employer collusion regarding wages and task sizes, strikes by workers). It also involved the emergence of a new, post-emancipation hierarchy of labour imagined in an imperial framework, and based on the presumed cultural affinity and shared history of metropolitan and Caribbean imperial subjects, black and white, and on the absolute alien-ness of other imperial subjects. There was nothing inevitable about Indian indentured migration to the British Caribbean. If Trinidad, British Guiana and to a much lesser extent Jamaica had not been imagined and represented as they were, there would have been no call for Indian indentured immigration. If the price of sugar had not been made such a pressing issue in the early 1840s, British legislators, bureaucrats, and reformers of domestic and colonial labour conditions might not have been persuaded by the labour shortage thesis. If the shortage had not been cast in terms of freed-people's racial and social inadequacies, Indian indentured migrants and their descendants might not have been cast the ways they were either. The migration and its representations were scripted in a particular moment of convergences. The rest of the paper turns to consider contem-porary discourses on community and culture in colonial India, and how

---

[26] Hugh Tinker, *A New System of Slavery: The Export of Indian Labourers Overseas, 1830–1920* (New York, 1974).

they were articulated with those on Caribbean labour shortage to produce a historical narrative that further reified the former and naturalized the latter.

Exodus

Some came with dreams of milk-and-honey riches
fleeing famine and death:
dancing girls,
Rajput soldiers, determined, tall,
escaping penalty of pride.
Stolen wives, afraid and despondent,
crossing black waters,
Brahmin, Chammar, alike,
hearts brimful of hope.

Mahadai Das, "They Came in Ships"

In 1839, the report on immigration into British Guiana published in the Parliamentary Papers included tables listing the names of each of the Indian indentured migrants brought to the colony by Gladstone and his associates, along with their sex, ages, religions, the estates to which they had been assigned, their occupations on the estates and their wages and allowances. Reports compiled by the Office of the Protector of Emigrants in Calcutta (1871–1910) and Madras listed the emigrants' destinations, the districts in which they were born, those in which they were recruited, their sex, age and caste. In the British Caribbean, to be Indian was to be, first, a sugar worker. This relational identity situated Indians within, often uncomfortably, the history of Caribbean slavery, sugar and British capitalism. Secondarily, to be Indian was to be a migrant, an alien from a space made known and accessible through mediation of British industry and enterprise. In India, to be a labourer invoked other geographic and relational identities, also made known through British industry and enterprise, and sometimes situating labourers within other narratives of bondage.[27] The difference between these sets of data suggests the parameters in which administrators in British Caribbean colonies and British India operated, the values and identities they assigned migrants, and the categories and conditions to which they attached importance. They also indicate the discursive frameworks – overlapping but not coterminous – which migrants themselves had to negotiate, and in which they had to operate.

Between 1845 and 1917 approximately 450,000 Indian indentured migrants left for the British Caribbean, the majority going (in steeply descending order) to British Guiana, Trinidad and Jamaica. Of these,

---

[27] Gyan Prakash, *Bonded Histories: Genealogies of Labor Servitude in Colonial India* (New York, 1990), and "Introduction", in Gyan Prakash (ed.), *The World of Rural Labourer in Colonial India* (Delhi, 1992).

the great majority embarked from Calcutta, as British Caribbean
employers came to prefer indentured workers recruited in northern India
to those recruited in the southern peninsular region and embarked from
Madras. After 1862 Trinidad and British Guiana closed their recruiting
agencies in Madras, and recruitment for these colonies in the latter
region almost ceased. Thanks to a combination of high levels (historically
and throughout the indenture period) of seasonal and long-term migration, Indian government policies restricting recruitment by overseas colonial employers to certain areas, and competition from a shifting constella-
tion of recruiters for Assam tea plantations and other industries in the
subcontinent, most of those who left for Trinidad and British Guiana
from Calcutta were recruited in the following districts in the eastern
part of the United Provinces and Bihar: Basti, Azamgarh, Ghazipur,
Gonda, Fyzabad, Allahabad, Gorakhpur, Jaunpur, Lucknow, Shahabad;
Baraich, Partabgarh, Rae Bareli, Sultanpur, Benares, Bara Banki,
Kanpur, and Patna. K.O. Laurence has estimated that of the nearly
271,900 recruit registrations recorded in the Calcutta emigration department records, nearly 198,000 were registered in the first ten districts
above, and nearly 56,500 in Kanpur, Benares and Patna.[28] Further, the
majority of those registered were born in the same districts, although
there was also considerable registration of recruits born in Bengal, the
Central Provinces, and elsewhere in India. Indentured migrants to the
British Caribbean appear to have been drawn from a representative
cross-section of these regions' populations, various castes being represented in the migration in proportions commensurate with those of the
recruiting regions in general. Families appear not to have emigrated
together.

   In 1838 the Master Pilot at Calcutta testified that, to his mind, the
migrants who boarded the British Guiana-bound *Whitby*, "were generally
composed of ignorant creatures from the interior, kidnapped or cajoled
away for the benefit of a set of crimps who laugh at humanity for the
sake of profit".[29] Some twenty years later, Jane Swinton, widow of the
captain of the *Salsette*, which had transported migrants to Trinidad wrote,
"out of the 324 Coolies who came on board, I do not believe five, at
most, either know where they are going, or what is to be their occupation". She added, "My heart often yearned over them, in thinking of
the way they were entrapped, as many of them asked me to recommend
them to get a good situation on their arrival at the island."[30] Of the
324 passengers (274 of whom were adults) who left the Hooghly aboard

---

[28] Laurence, *A Question of Labour*, pp. 107–108.
[29] Bengal Government, "Coolie Export Enquiry 1838–1840", Appendix no. 4; reprinted
in UK (HC) 1841, XVI, nos 287 and 483.
[30] Captain and Mrs Swinton, *Journal of a Voyage with Coolie Emigrants, from Calcutta
to Trinidad* (London, 1859), p. 12.

the *Salsette* on 17 March 1858, 120 or more than one-third, died en route.

These two eyewitness reports fit with and illustrate that strand of the literature, contemporary and historical, that in language reminiscent of abolitionist accounts of the African slave-trade, has cast indentured migrants as victims of unscrupulous merchants and their procurers. It was accounts such as these that in 1840 disposed Colonial Secretary Russell against allowing resumption of Indian indentured migration to Mauritius and British Guiana, the lobbying of their sugar industries notwithstanding, on the grounds that it might "lead to a dreadful loss of life on the one hand, or, on the other, to a new system of slavery."[31] In 1839 three of six commissioners appointed by the Government of Bengal to investigate charges of abuse against that recently-suspended migration concluded that "the Coolies and other Natives exported to Mauritius and elsewhere, were (generally speaking) induced to come to Calcutta by gross misrepresentation and deceit practised upon them by native crimps styled Duffadars and Arkotties employed by European and Anglo-Indian Undertakers and Shippers who were mostly cognizant of these frauds, and who received a very considerable sum per head for each Coolie exported".They strongly advised against resumption of the migration, noting that "permission to renew this traffic would weaken the moral influence of the British Government throughout the world, and deaden or utterly destroy the effect of all future remonstrances and negociations [sic] respecting the slave trade".[32] Subsequently, other critics of the system, contemporaries and historians alike, have elaborated on this theme, arguing that indentured emigrants were victims of simple deception or, more broadly, of British revenue settlement and land tenure policies of the nineteenth century, and backing their argument with evidence from ethnographic surveys and other such enterprises of colonial rule in India.

Another strand in the literature, however, argues that whatever the reasons for their immiserated condition, indentured emigration represented a "Great Escape" for enterprising Indians, an opportunity to turn colonial subordination at home to their own advantage abroad – and that women, in particular, may have seized it as such.[33] Two others

---

[31] UK (HC) 1840, XXXIV, no. 121, Russell to Light, 15 February 1840.

[32] Bengal Government, "Coolie Export Committee", Majority Report (Chairman Theodore Dickens, Rev. James Charles, Russomoy Dutt), p. 2.

[33] P.C. Emmer, "The Great Escape: The Migration of Female Indentured Servants from British India to Surinam, 1873–1916", in David Richardson (ed.), *Abolition and its Aftermath: The Historical Context, 1790–1916* (London, 1985); Rhoda Reddock, "Freedom Denied: Indian Women and Indentureship in Trinidad and Tobago, 1845–1917", *Economic and Political Weekly*, 20–43 (26 October 1985), pp. 79–87; Pat Mohammed, "Writing Gender into History: The Negotiation of Gender Relations among Indian Men and Women in Post-Indenture Trinidad Society, 1917–1947", in V. Shepherd, B. Brereton and B.

appointed to the 1839 enquiry by the Government of Bengal disagreed with the findings of their three colleagues, and submitted dissenting reports of their own. J.P. Grant, who was later to be appointed Protector of Emigrants at Calcutta worried that "To confine the laborers of a Province to the soil of that Province, or the laborers of a collection of Provinces, such as our Indian Empire consists of, to the soil of the same, seems to me, but a lower degree of the barbarous system which attaches a serf to the lord on whose soil he was born, or imposes special restrictions on the movements of free coloured native subjects." Warning that "The prosperity or existence of whole Colonies, and the liberty of tens of millions of British subjects, are not light matters," Grant concluded that "If the recommendation of the [majority] Report is adopted, we have opinions before us that Mauritius must be ruined; and it is unquestionable that the mass of our Indian fellow subjects are no longer free men as before."[34] He proposed that the emigration be allowed, but under government supervision to minimize the risks of fraud, deception and kidnapping that he admitted had marred the migration under investigation (1834–1838). Elaborating on Grant's analytical framework, subsequent investigators, supporters and some historians have argued that Indian indentured emigrants had made the rational choice to take advantage of their imperial subject-hood and that, minor and removable obstacles aside, had been able to maximize opportunities to an extent that in India, paralysed by tyrannies of caste and tradition, would have been impossible.[35]

Represented both as victims and as rational, indeed wily, maximizers of opportunity throughout the history of indentured emigration, Indian indentured emigrants probably included fair shares of both. Complicating the picture is evidence that awareness of conditions in overseas colonies grew, not only because recruitment appears to have been concentrated in certain areas, but also because migrants were returning to India, either to settle or to visit – and sometimes to act as recruiters themselves.[36] Recent research indicates that multiple trips between India and the Caribbean by people who had made the initial voyage under indentures were not uncommon. In 1851, the first year Indians were eligible for repatriation, twelve of those who took the opportunity to return to India came back to British Guiana within the year. Based primarily in

Bailey (eds), *Engendering History: Caribbean Women in Historical Perspective* (New York, 1995), pp. 20–47.
[34] Bengal Government, "Coolie Export Committee", in James P. Grant, Minute Dissenting from Majority Report.
[35] J. Geoghegan, *Note on Emigration from India* (Calcutta, 1873); D.W.D. Comins, *Note on Emigration from the East Indies to Trinidad* (Calcutta, 1893); UK (HC) 1910, XXVII, 1, pp. 17, 58–59; Emmer, "Great Escape".
[36] Marina Carter, *Servants, Sirdars and Settlers: Indians in Mauritius, 1834–1874* (Delhi, 1995).

colonial immigration and Indian Emigration Department annual reports and other documents, K.O. Laurence's research suggests that between 1875 and 1894, 3,479 Indians re-migrated to British Guiana, with another 2,347 migrating there after having served out indentures in another colony. Over the same period, 866 Indians re-migrated to Trinidad, with another 1,753 migrating there after having served in another colony. In 1893, 306 Indians returned under indentures to British Guiana, along with 253 who had been indentured in other colonies.[37] Conditions in India, specifically in the areas of primary recruiting for British Guiana and Trinidad, were not unchanging or unchanged by this migration.

In 1883 George A. Grierson was assigned to inspect and report on the condition of recruitment depots throughout Bengal Presidency. His report and diary suggest that returned migrants were common in some districts from which others were recruited. In Shahabad, for example, in which district a relatively high proportion of recruits were registered (and one of the few districts in which the bulk of those registered also resided), Grierson claimed that there had been "a healthy inflow of returned emigrants, which has made emigration so popular as it is".[38] He felt that returned emigrants could make admirable recruiters, if they had been successful in the colonies, and puzzled over colonial employers' failure to capitalize on this resource, so effectively exploited by Assam tea estates.[39] He did, however, encounter one recruiter who had been in an importing colony, although not necessarily as an indentured migrant himself. Ghura Khan, who ran a sub-depot near Baksar, had been born in British Guiana, and returned to India with his mother in 1858 to live with his uncle, after his father's death. He re-emigrated to the colony with seven other family members in 1861. On his mother's death in 1872, he returned to India, and had been about to re-emigrate again when the agent for British Guiana persuaded him to stay on as a recruiter.

In the course of his inspection tour, Grierson met a number of returned emigrants, and recorded what he remembered of his conversations with them in his diary. For the most part, those he met and reported on (they had gone to Mauritius, Jamaica or British Guiana) had managed to save money overseas. Some had corresponded with their families and sent remittances home, and these had all been received. Indeed, he wrote, "In every village to which I went, three or four letters, which were shown to me, had been received, during the past year or two, from one colony or another. To all these, I was told, answers had been despatched."[40] Grierson added that ensuring ready means of communica-

[37] Laurence, *A Question of Labour*, pp. 127–128.
[38] George A. Grierson, *Report on Colonial Emigration from the Bengal Presidency* (Calcutta, 1883) [hereafter *Colonial Emigration*], p. 42.
[39] Grierson, *Colonial Emigration*, pp. 42, 34; Carter, *Servants, Sirdars and Settlers*.
[40] Grierson, *Colonial Emigration*, Diary, 8 January 1858.

tion between emigrants and those they left behind would facilitiate recruitment and improve the standing of indentured emigration in districts where, unlike Shahabad, it was not already good.

Some of the returned emigrants Grierson met had spent all their money, and were re-indenturing. Others, like Gobardhan Pathak, Nankhu, Tulsi Bhagat, Sukhiya and Ghura Khan had invested it in land or shops on their return, and in "getting back into caste", to which end they had apparently spent between Rs. 100 and Rs. 300. Thanks to such cases, Grierson concluded, in districts like Shahabad and Patna,

with regard to colonial emigration, the main facts are clearly and universally understood; namely, that a coolie goes out for five years; that if he stays for ten he gets a free passage home; that he is well treated, his caste respected, and comes home rich. The climate of the colonies is delightful, work plentiful and highly paid; and that stories, circulated some years ago, about *mimiai ka tel* (the oil extracted from a coolie's head by hanging him upside down), are all lies. When people are asked how they know all this, the reply always is that so-and-so went off to the Colonies so many years ago, came back, abused Hindustan and praised the colony and went out again, this time with his wife and children.[41]

Grierson reported that "In Shahabad, where emigration is popular, the recruiters have little trouble. Twelve-sixteenths of the recruits search for the recruiters, and voluntarily emigrate. I have known instances of men coming forty miles to look for a sub-depot." However, he continued, "In other districts it is just the reverse. There, there are few returned emigrants, and little is known about the colonies", and recruiters had to beware of *zamindars*, anxious not to lose their people, as well as a hostile constabulary.[42] While Grierson may not have heard, or chose not to record, unfavourable accounts of indentured emigration from returned emigrants or from emigrants' relatives, such information was probably circulating in districts like Shahabad and Patna, along with the rest, and had an equally immeasurable impact on recruitment and migrants' adjustment to life as plantation labourers overseas.

Laurence's research and Grierson's notes suggest that by the 1880s, repeat migrants were likely to number among those sent out on each ship leaving Calcutta for the British Caribbean colonies. A Colonial Office publication of the same period suggests what this meant to some contemporaries. In 1889 J.M. Laing, a veteran surgeon-superintendent aboard ships transporting Indian indentured migrants to the British Caribbean, wrote for the edification of unseasoned colleagues a handbook on maintaining discipline and health aboard ships transporting indentured emigrants from India. When problems arose, as they inevitably would, he advised, "look out for some *return coolie* as the instigator.

---

[41] Grierson, *Colonial Emigration*, p. 18.
[42] *Ibid.*, p. 15.

They will often give themselves airs among the other coolies, who will naturally believe that they know all about it from having been on previous voyages, and they are generally too knowing or too great cowards to complain themselves, but put some other coolie up to doing so." He continued:

Sometimes Brahmins and other high caste Hindoos will come up and say that they cannot eat food prepared in the galley, and this, although they have been told before embarking that their food would be thus prepared. Often this man's prejudice (his caste has been broken by the mere fact of his having lived in the depot even up country) can be satisfied by putting him into the galley as a bandharrie, *if the complaint has not been made for that purpose* and there is a vacancy.

He added, in a footnote: "N.B.: There are a good many pseudo-brahmans about."[43]

Like surgeon-superintendent Laing, employers in the colonies were not always pleased about re-indenturing immigrants from India.[44] During the mid-1880s, sugar prices throughout the world fell as a result of sugar from bounty-fed European sugar beet production, and market wages in Trinidad and British Guiana dropped by as much as a third, to below the minimum stipulated for indentured labourers. Some estates employing indentured labour tried, illegally, to depress indentured workers' wages, or to increase the size of the tasks assigned them, which effected the same ends. Indentured workers who refused or failed to meet the new conditions imposed on them were brought in large numbers before the courts for punishment: fines or imprisonment. In the 1880s planters' complaints against indentured workers for such transgressions escalated, some employers attributing the unrest to re-indentured veterans among the indentured labourers.[45]

Employers in the British Caribbean shared Laing's suspicions not only of re-indentured returned immigrants, but also of high-caste, specifically Brahmin, immigrants. In 1889 the Government Secretary for British Guiana complained to the Calcutta agent, Robert Mitchell, that:

the introduction of priests, high castes, coolies, members of the learned professions, decayed gentry, beggars, dancers, acrobats, vagrant musicians, men of inferior physique or health, persons not previously accustomed to outdoor

---

[43] James M. Laing, *Handbook for Surgeons Superintendents of the Coolie Emigration Service*, CO/PRO 885/9 Miscellaneous, no. 75 (Colonial Office, 1889), pp. 41–42.
[44] UK (HC) 1910, XXVII, no. 2, "Emigration from India to the Crown Colonies and Protectorates", Minutes of Evidence, Warner, pp. 29–30; Tyran Ramnarine, "Over a Hundred Years of East Indian Disturbances on the Sugar Estates of Guyana, 1869–1978: An Historical Overview" [hereafter "East Indian Disturbances"], in Dabydeen and Samaroo, *India in the Caribbean*, p. 25; Laurence, *A Question of Labour*, p. 128.
[45] Ramnarine, "East Indian Disturbances", pp. 122, 125; Laurence, *A Question of Labour*, pp. 116, 132, 149.

manual, much less field labour, has been more numerous during the past five years or so.

In 1890 the Planters' Association of British Guiana passed a resolution instructing their Emigration Agent in Calcutta to prevent such recruits from indenturing themselves for terms in their colony. Mitchell, for his part, tried to persuade his employers that caste was not a very good indicator of migrants' ability or willingness to perform the kind of labour they required, and in 1896 the Colonial Office rejected British Caribbean employers' attempts to attribute the low wages actually earned by Indian indentured workers on their plantations to the workers' unsuitability and poor selection by agents in Calcutta.[46] Nevertheless, managers in the British Caribbean continued to suspect that pre-migration associations and hierarchical values shared by all migrants from India could undermine their own authority as employers or supervisors on the plantations. There is evidence that they tried either to break these "traditional" ties of deference and loyalty, or turn them to their own advantage.[47]

Implicit in all of this is an essentialist assumption about the culture and societies that migrants (whether enslaved, indentured or "free") left behind, and a static conception of culture.[48] One indication that the communities from which indentured emigrants were recruited were not unchanging or unchanged by decades of recruitment for indentured emigration is the emergence of emigration-specific cultural strategies, such as that described by Grierson in 1883. He noted that, "About caste, the people have invented a curious theory regarding ship-board life, which shows the adaptability of native customs." Asked how people from castes (Sonars, for example) whose members would not eat food cooked by Brahmins managed on board ships where most of the cooking was done by Brahmins, Grierson was told that "a man can eat anything on board-ship. A ship is like the temple of Jagannath, where there are not caste restrictions". He added:

I admit that this rather staggered me, but I have since enquired from respectable men, and without doubt this belief is spreading. It is said to have originated with the steamer journey from Calcutta to Orissa, which is one of the incidents of a pilgrimage to Jagannath. On board these ships the theory was first introduced, as one of the incidents of the pilgrimage, and is now being extended to emigrant ships, to the great benefit of the Colonies.[49]

Together with the rest of Grierson's report, this story suggests a number of things. One: that contemporary and scholarly assessments notwith-

[46] *Ibid.*, pp. 115–118.
[47] Ramnarine, "East Indian Disturbances", p. 125; Haraksingh, "Control and Resistance", p. 67.
[48] Peter van der Veer, "The Idea of Diaspora: South Asians Overseas", in Peter van der Veer (ed.), *Nation and Migration: The Politics of Space in the South Asian Diaspora* (Philadelphia, 1995), p. 4.
[49] Grierson, *Colonial Emigration*, Diary, 8 January 1883.

standing, caste was not a good predictor of people's willingness to emigrate under indenture. Two: that at least in the Bhojpuri-speaking region of India, rural populations were by no means stationary, and cultural forms and practices by no means unchanging. People were on the move, performing pilgrimages, looking for employment on both seasonal and longer terms, migrating to and from agricultural regions, towns and cities. Three: that familiarity with conditions in overseas colonies was increasing in some recruitment areas. However, the areas in which concentrated recruitment for indentured migration took place changed over time, along with local factors ranging from competition over labour with recruiters for tea estates in Assam and coal mines in Chota Nagpur and elsewhere, as well as railway construction further afield.[50] By the twentieth century, recruiters were going as far afield as Delhi to fill colonial demand for indentured labour, and meeting with the kinds of hostility Grierson observed in parts of Bengal Presidency in 1883.[51] Even if people in some regions were increasingly aware of what indenturing involved, those in or from other regions were not necessarily so situated. In other words, there was not necessarily a steady improvement over time in migrants' preparedness for indentured migration. However glorified Grierson's image of the colonies and planta-tion labour, his report and diary suggest that by 1883 conditions of indentured emigraton were not entirely unknown in the districts from which most emigrants were recruited. All these myriad factors had implications for the ways employers of Indian indentured migrants treated them, and for their affiliations and institution-building both on and off the plantations.

Historians have sought to decode data on caste and regional origins as if they will explain present-day Caribbean-Indian communities and cultures. Regarding Indian women, migrants and settlers alike, the tend-ency is especially pronounced, and casts into stark relief the problems with the entire enterprise. Statistical data compiled from emigration and immigration records suggest that the majority of migrating women were not accompanying male relatives. Other documentary evidence suggests that colonial officials, plantation personnel and other observers in India, on the migration ships and in the importing colonies viewed alliances between indentured men and women with considerable scepticism, char-acterizing them as illegitimate unions springing from depot and ship conditions and Indians' lust and immorality, indicative of migrants'

---

[50] Dirk Kolff, "Indian Expansion and Indian Diaspora: The Original Context of Emigra-tion", unpublished paper, ISER-NCIC Conference on Challenge and Change: The Indian Diaspora in its Historical and Contemporary Contexts, University of the West Indies, St Augustine, Trinidad, 13 August 1995; Ian J. Kerr, *Building the Railways of the Raj 1850–1900* (Delhi, 1995).

[51] UK (HC) 1910, "Emigration from India to the Crown Colonies and Protectorates", Report, pp. 17–18.

degraded condition and corrupting influence.[52] Some recruiting agents in India complained bitterly that Indian magistrates interfered with the registration of women and the embarkation of emigrant ships because they were convinced that the women were either being coerced into indentured emigration, or fleeing the authority of fathers or husbands. Opponents of indentured emigration charged that recruits were being "scripted", told by "up-country" recruiters how to respond not only to magistrates', doctors', and Protectors' questions, but also to those that colonial emigration agents might ask. Grierson's field notes suggest that records on recruits were poorly maintained, sometimes clearly fraudulent and intended to meet requirements rather than to record recruits' vital statistics.[53] None the less, many historians, like most contemporary observers, have concluded that migrating women were either hapless victims – kidnapped, seduced, or possibly widows escaping unbearable conditions at home – or (already) prostitutes, fallen women, the "sweepings of the bazaars" and lock hospitals.

Others have evaded such characterization, instead focusing on exploring some of the implications of the unequal sex ratio that, for the duration of indentured periods, characterized this migration predicated on the assumption that men made better plantation labourers than women. Rhoda Reddock and Patricia Mohammed have suggested that under these conditions Indian women were vulnerable to exploitation by sex-starved men (Indian, white, or Afro-Caribbean) on colonial plantations, and to patriarchally-minded Indian men in Indian villages off them. They also suggest that in the context of Indians' isolation on and near plantations where they came to represent an increasingly large proportion of the labour force, Indian women's scarcity could give them more control over their own labour and sexuality than they could hope to have in less anomalous circumstances. They argue that in colonial Trinidad, Indian labour and culture appeared devalued and emasculated by indenturing and isolation on plantations, juridical marginalization and colonial policy. For example, like many contemporaries, they point out that colonial law recognized only those marriages between Indians that were performed by a Christian clergyman or registered by an authorized civil servant such as the Protector of Immigrants. According to Reddock, no marriages were registered until 1887, and even after that few unions between Indian men and women conformed to these legal standards, thus contributing to the perception that Indian immigrants were amoral and promiscuous. Marriages performed by Muslim and Hindu clergy were not recognized by law until 1936 and 1945 respectively, but Indians

---

[52] Swinton and Swinton, *Journal of a Voyage*; Comins, *Note on Emigration*; "Emigration from India to the Crown Colonies and Protectorates", Report, Minutes of Evidence, Appendices.
[53] Grierson, *Colonial Emigration*, p. 69; UK (HC) 1910, 2, "Emigration from India, etc.", Minutes of Evidence, Bolton, p. 191.

campaigned for recognition from the last quarter of the nineteenth century. Reddock and Mohammed argue that in campaigning to get those marriages performed according to Muslim and Hindu custom and laws recognized by the colonial state, Indian men were reclaiming the patriarchal authority they had lost in the course of emigration and indentured labour on sugar plantations.[54]

Reddock argues persuasively that culture and community formation must be seen as discursively constituted by struggles among not only immigrant and creole-Indian men and women, but also between them and other segments of Trinidad's population. However, in so far as these studies assume for Indian women indentured migrants the pre-migration condition of domestic-patriarchal and rural-agrarian bondage, they reproduce and reinforce assumptions about the static quality of Indian culture and Indian people introduced and elaborated since the mid-nineteenth century. By extension, they then also contribute to making Indian indentured migration overseas seem anomalous in, separate from, and only marginally significant to Indian labour history specifically, and to the contours of Indian colonial history more generally.

Implicit in the "new system of slavery" narratives is the assumption that traditionally, in other words before British intervention, people in the recruiting regions were largely stationary, and that indentured emigration was just another facet of the ongoing displacement and immiseration precipitated by colonialism. Uprooted, these migrants to overseas colonies like Trinidad and British Guiana struggled to reproduce remembered village communities to the best of their abilities, the unpromising ground of local plantation conditions permitting.[55] Implicit in the Whiggish "great escape" account of emigrants' motivations is the functionalist and modernization notion that, freed from the heavy hand of custom, these Indian indentured migrants transplanted in their new worlds those cultural forms and features they valued, rejecting oppressive features of Indian society.

Neither alternative seems satisfactory on its own. While a continuous history of massive deception seems implausible, there is also evidence that cases of abduction and entrapment continued throughout the seventy years.[56] Further, people in the recruiting districts were not unaffected by land and revenue settlements, industrial and agricultural developments,

---

[54] Reddock, "Freedom Denied"; Mohammed, "Writing Gender into History".

[55] Chandra Jayawardena, "Ideology and Conflict in Lower Class Communities", *Comparative Studies in Society and History*, 10 (July 1968), pp. 412–446; Ramnarine, "East Indian Disturbances"; Haraksingh, "Control and Resistance", Brinsley Samaroo, "The Indian Connection: The Influence of Indian Thought and Ideas on East Indians in the Caribbean", in Dabydeen and Samaroo, *India in the Caribbean*, pp. 43–60.

[56] Haraksingh, "Control and Resistance", and "Structure, Process and Indian Culture in Trinidad", in Howard Johnson (ed.), *After the Crossing: Immigrants and Minorities in Caribbean Creole Society* (London, 1988), pp. 117–119.

railway construction and other effects and technologies of colonial rule.[57] All of this may have had implications for community-formation among Indian indentured migrants and their descendents in the British Caribbean and elsewhere, although those predicated on push and pull models of motivation for emigration are unsatisfying, in part because such causation models seem clumsy. It is problematical to trace present-day cultural values and practices of Indo-Caribbeans back to origins in pre-migration India when the migration took place over an extended period, and when the bulk of migrants appear *not* to have travelled as families or village groups. More compelling is the suggestion that crucial institutional and political developments took place dialogically in the period between the 1880s and 1947. This period saw the founding of the Indian National Congress (1885) and related oppositional movements, and missionary activity by both Arya Samaj and Sanatan Dharm among overseas Indian communities. Indeed, the significance of communities of Indians overseas for the emergence of Indian nationalism and its strategies in the subcontinent, as well as the significance of these for crystallization of Indian identities in overseas British (and other European) colonies is relatively unexplored, although suggestive.[58]

Conclusion

I alone am today alive.
I remember logies, barrackrooms, ranges,
nigga-yards. My grandmother worked in the field.
Honourable mention.

Creole gang, child labour.
Second prize.
I recall Lallabhagie, Leonora's strong children,
and Enmore, bitter, determined.[59]

Mahadai Das, "They Came in Ships"

[57] Bernard S. Cohn, *An Anthropologist among the Historians and Other Essays* (Delhi, 1990); Gyan Prakash, "Writing Post-Orientalist Histories of the Third World: Perspectives from Indian Historiography", *Comparative Studies in Society and History*, 32 (April 1990), pp. 383–408; Nicholas B. Dirks, "Castes of Mind", *Comparative Studies in Society and History*, 37 (Winter 1992), pp. 56–78.

[58] Prabhu Mohapatra, "Longing and Belonging: Dilemma of Return among Indian Immigrants in the West Indies 1880–1940", paper presented at the ISER-NCIC Conference on Challenge and Change: The Indian Diaspora in its Historical and Contemporary Contexts, University of the West Indies, St Augustine, Trinidad and Tobago, 14 August 1995; John D. Kelly, *A Politics of Virtue: Hinduism, Sexuality, and Countercolonial Discourse in Fiji* (Chicago, 1992); Samaroo, "The Indian Connection"; Peter van der Veer and Steven Vertovec, "Brahmanism Abroad: On Caribbean Hinduism as an Ethnic Religion", *Ethnology*, 1 (1991), pp. 149–166; Steven Vertovec, *Hindu Trinidad: Religion, Ethnicity and Socio-Economic Change* (London, 1992).

[59] Leonora and Enmore were plantations in British Guiana that had employed large numbers of Indian workers, indentured and unindentured, and which were the sites of frequent, sometimes bloody "disturbances and strikes" between 1870 and 1905: Walter

Popular and scholarly concern with origins implicitly denies agency to migrants and their descendants and, more generally, to people in history. It overshadows the processes and struggles whereby people living in Trinidad from 1845–1917 constituted themselves at various times and in various places along the multiple and sometimes overlapping axes of sex, age, marital status, "race" or ethnicity, conditions of migration and time of arrival, relation to the means of production, sexual orientation, and so on. This article has suggested that, while the documentary evidence on migrants' backgrounds and origins are voluminous, they are also unevenly reliable, and problematically presume unchanging material and discursive conditions in Indian recruitment zones over a period of more than seventy years. The very processes, ongoing, of recruitment and immigration challenge notions of stasis in both sending and receiving regions' economies, social relations and cultures. Further, these regions were not autonomous, but, rather, linked with and through colonial and imperial alliances, rivalries and discourses that were themselves fluid, unstable, emergent.

Knowledge, however imperfect, of conditions on the other side of the world was accumulated and disseminated not only in the migrations and memories of repatriating and repeat-emigrants from India to the British Caribbean colonies, but also in the form of data like Grierson's report and other writings: scholarly, popular and administrative reports, censuses, surveys, maps and digests of all of these, as well as in the circulating personnel of imperial administration, from soldiers to governors. The implications of all this information for the ways Indians were legislated on, administered, punished and rewarded and, by extension, for the ways in which they responded to and negotiated these efforts are provocative, although as yet little explored. If migrants' communities and cultures took on what appear to be distinctively Indian forms, the extent to which such forms were privileged by employers and by government administrators – as well as by other people and interests – in both India and the Caribbean colonies needs to be considered. After all, Indians' perceived difference from Afro- and Euro-Caribbean people was one of the reasons for their being in the Caribbean in the first place. What this difference meant, and the ways it was staged and performed itself differed and changed along with the circumstances, resources and agendas of the women and men who invoked or rejected it.

Rodney, *A History of the Guyanese Working People, 1881–1905* (Baltimore, 1981), pp. 151–173.

Unsettling the Household: Act VI (of 1901) and the Regulation of Women Migrants in Colonial Bengal

SAMITA SEN

The advent of capitalism has traditionally been associated with a transformation of the economic and political functioning of the family. Capital is presumed to weaken, certainly to modify, gender and age hierarchies by undermining the productive role of the household. The labour market takes over the organization of work and age of consent legislations undermine parental authority in order to create the new legal subject capable of entering "free" labour contracts. The family, though it remains outside the norms of capitalism, primarily undertakes the physical and social reproduction of labour within the capitalist sphere. Such a transformation of the "family" is, however, not inevitable. In nineteenth-century India the colonial state, though avowedly committed to a free market in labour, in practice often upheld familial claims on women's labour and sexuality. As a result, gender and generational controls within the family were enhanced rather than weakened.

Capitalist development in India was premised upon a simultaneous exploitation of domestic and capitalist relations of production. Colonial capitalism found it unnecessary to strip the domestic unit of its perceived economic functions. Under colonialism, the domestic organization continued to undertake both a vital part of the production and the physical reproduction of labour outside the capitalist sphere. Thus the accommodations between the family and the labour market acquired a distinctive character. The gender division of labour did not follow clearly demarcated domains of production and reproduction. Women were neither to provide cheap labour for capital, nor were they "domesticated" to provide a reserve army of labour. The household itself remained the site for the adjustments between productive and reproductive uses of women's labour.

Indeed, the familial deployment of labour suited the colonial state more than a labour market augmented by young men and women "free" from familial control. The small family farm was crucial to colonial economic policy and the viability of small peasant agriculture depended on unremunerated family labour. Sugata Bose has argued that capitalist development itself "rested heavily on the forcing up of labour intensity within family units actually tilling the land". Consequently, from the 1860s, two significant processes transformed the functioning of the rural household: the increase in the unpaid component of women's and

International Review of Social History 41 (1996), pp. 135–156

children's labour and the decline in its paid component.[1] The division of labour in the household economy sharpened – control of capital and capital-intensive labour was concentrated in the hands of men while women undertook labour-intensive tasks of low status and poor reward.[2]

The family arrangements the colonizers inherited could not just be taken over, they had to be adapted to these new needs. To that end, new legal measures were introduced to buttress family authority. Colonial laws repeatedly interceded to elevate the powers of the male head of the family through regulation of inheritance and marriage laws. A range of legal and administrative initiatives were aimed at enhancing familial control over women's bodies – their labour and their sexuality.[3]

The convergence between the reinforcement of gender hierarchies within families and the sharpening gender division of labour in the household was reflected in the pattern of migration. In long-distance migration to cities and plantations adult men predominated. This was especially the case in "free" migration to the cities. The rural household, especially women and children left behind by migrants, remained responsible for reproducing, partially or wholly, the urban workforce. While industrial capital benefited from employing the labour thus reproduced, it made no direct contribution by way of wages or as revenue. When men went to the city to earn cash wages, the women and children who stayed in the village had to eke out a living from the family farm, wage labour and unpaid "subsistence" activities. In areas like Saran in north Bihar, which was a major catchment area for Calcutta's labour market, women's visibility in the workforce rose sharply.[4] The worker

---

[1] Sugata Bose, *Peasant Labour and Colonial Capital. Rural Bengal Since 1770*. New Cambridge History of India, III-2 (Cambridge, 1993), pp. 66–111.

[2] Nirmala Banerjee, "Working Women in Colonial Bengal: Modernization and Marginalization", in Kumkum Sangari and Sudesh Vaid (eds), *Recasting Women: Essays in Colonial History* (New Delhi, 1989), pp. 283–288 and "Women's Work and Discrimination", in Nirmala Banerjee and Devaki Jain (eds), *Tyranny of the Household: Investigative Essays on Women's Work* (New Delhi, 1985), pp. 110–121. Mukul Mukherjee, "Impact of Modernisation of Women's Occupations: A Case Study of Rice Husking Industry in Bengal", in J. Krishnamurty (ed.), *Women in Colonial India: Essays on Survival, Work and the State* (New Delhi, 1989) and idem, "Mechanisation in Food Processing and Women's Employment", in Mira Savara and Divya Pandey (eds), *Between the Farm and the Thali: Women and Food Processing* (Bombay, 1990). For an investigation into progressive gender inequities in distribution of household resources see Amartya Sen, "Family and Food: Sex Bias in Poverty", in idem, *Resources, Values and Development* (Oxford, 1984).

[3] M.R. Anderson, "Work Construed: Ideological Origins of Labour Law in British India to 1918", in Peter Robb (ed.), *Dalit Movement and the Meaning of Labour in India* (New Delhi, 1993), pp. 87–120; Bernard S. Cohn, "Law and Colonial State in India", in J. Starr and J.F. Collier (eds), *History and Power in the Study of Law* (Ithaca, 1989).

[4] L.S.S. O'Malley, *Bihar & Orissa District Gazetteer*, Saran (Patna, 1930), p. 86.

in the city could return to the village when he was ill or unemployed and when he eventually retired.[5]

Such arrangements suited the textile industries, jute and cotton, because they gave their male labour force the two characteristics most required – cheapness and flexibility.[6] But this is not to say that the emerging capitalist enterprises made no demands on women's labour. In eastern India, by the end of the nineteenth century, there were three clusters of large-scale capitalist enterprise. The jute industry grew in and around Calcutta: women workers were not supposed to have any gender-specific skill to offer this industry; they rarely exceeded 14–16 per cent of this workforce. Coal mining prospered in the Raniganj-Jharia belt and the tea plantations were making rapid headway in north Bengal and Assam. The mines adapted "family" labour, employing in the 1910s and 1920s about 27–28 per cent women and children in their workforce. The tea plantations, concerned with a settled and stable workforce and preferring cheap labour for plucking leaves, employed as many or more women as men.[7] In the late nineteenth and early twentieth centuries the tea plantations, especially those in Assam, and the colonial planta-tions overseas were devising ways and means of recruiting more women.

The possibilities of women's long-term and long-distance migration upset the desired gender equations within the family and the accom-modations between the productive and reproductive uses of women's labour. Attempts at large-scale recruitment of women for plantations raised a storm of debate, and all the parties involved in the controversy sought the Government of India's intercession. The planters were sup-ported by the Imperial Government in demanding better facilities for recruiting women. Local elites supported by local state officials demanded legal restrictions on recruiters and on women's freedom to enter labour contracts. This essay will focus on one legislative interven-tion of the government: the Assam Labour and Emigration Act (Act VI of 1901). The government clearly vacillated between the con-flicting demands made on it. The Act seemed to give by legislation power to the head of the household to restrain women's migration and recruitment. But by administrative fiat and through the racial alliances

<hr>

[5] Samita Sen, "Women Workers in the Bengal Jute Industry, 1890–1940: Migration, Motherhood and Militancy" (Ph.D., Cambridge University, 1992). For a discussion on the role of remittances and the links between the jute working class and the rural economy, see Gail Omvedt, "Migration in Colonial India: the Articulation of Feudalism and Colonial-ism by the Colonial State", *Journal of Peasant Studies*, VII, 2 (1980).
[6] For the Bombay cotton textile industry see R.S. Chandavarkar, *The Origins of Industrial Capitalism in India: Business Strategies and the Working Classes in Bombay, 1900–1940* (Cambridge, 1994). For the Calcutta jute industry, see Sen, "Women Workers in the Bengal Jute Industry" and O. Goswami, *Industry, Trade and Peasant Society: The Jute Economy of Eastern India, 1900–1947* (New Delhi, 1991).
[7] Banerjee, "Working Women in Colonial Bengal".

of administrators and agents, the effects of these laws were often nullified.

The recruitment of women for tea gardens and overseas plantations

The migration decisions of the peasant household were influenced by the increasingly critical role women played in the rural subsistence sector. A clearly gendered pattern of migration emerged in the nineteenth century. Individual and group migration of women predominated in seasonal inter-district movement of labour.[8] Such migrations were part of the household's labour deployment strategy and did not threaten familial control. Long-distance and long-term migration, however, posed a conflict with women's subsistence and reproductive activities. Women and children's labour was more profitably – for the urban employer and the peasant household – retained in the village. When rural resources were exhausted, whole families undertook permanent migration. However, women sometimes did migrate alone – without their families – when they were denied access to household resources. Widows, childless women, deserted wives, wives in unhappy marriages and women entering extra-marital sexual relationships often found migration their only option. Some went to the cities, some to the colonies and some to the Assam plantations. Most such migrants repudiated the "rural" connection that women migrating in families and single male migrants were able to retain.[9]

In the early years, and until the 1920s, urban and industrial employers hired widows and deserted wives, though their proportion was always low, declining over time.[10] As the industries switched to employing more workers from Bihar and Uttar Pradesh (UP), women's share in the workforce declined more sharply. The numbers of these single female migrants who came to the cities were, compared to the men, very small. As far as the urban employers were concerned, there was a large available supply of male labour, and they thus made no serious attempt to tie labour down by contract. Their proximity to Calcutta ensured a ready supply of workers at the mill gates. They did not have to contribute substantially to the costs of labour migration. It was more advantageous to have a proportion of "floating" labour that could be hired and fired according to the requirements of the international market. In contrast, planters, both in Assam and the overseas colonies, depended heavily

---

[8] O'Malley, *Bihar & Orissa District Gazetteer*, Saran, p. 30.
[9] Report of Dr Dagmar Curjel on the conditions of Employment of Women Before and After Childbirth, 1923, unpublished, West Bengal State Archives (hereafter WBSA), Calcutta. Commerce Department Commerce Branch, April 1923, B77 (hereafter Curjel Report).
[10] *Indian Factory Commission*, 1891. The proportion of women in the jute labour force began to decline from the 1920s. Sen, "Women Workers in the Bengal Jute Industry".

on tying down workers. Their problem was to ensure a steady supply of labour and to do this they had to invest heavily in recruitment which was covered by penal contracts.[11]

The export of Indian workmen under indenture to colonies in Australia and the Caribbean began in the 1830s when the abolition of slavery created a demand for cheap and controllable labour. Initially, women constituted a minuscule proportion of such workers.[12] The planters in the receiving colonies were not particularly interested in women. They wanted direct labour and men were thought more productive and capable of heavier workloads. Besides, they depended on migration itself to replace workers. To ensure a self-reproducing workforce they would have to incur some additional costs. They would have to encourage family migration which meant financing the migration and maintenance of some dependants – particularly wives and children. Even if wives were inducted as workers, there would be inevitable "financial disabilities due to the financial risks of child-bearing and rearing".[13] However, the representations of the receiving colonies proved serious especially since they gained the support of the Home Government. Colonial governments complained that large numbers of "single" Indian workmen caused high rates of crime and social dislocation. In the 1860s the Government of India attempted to alleviate the situation by fixing a minimum of 40 women to every 100 men (except in Mauritius which allowed 33 women for every 100 men) per shipment.[14] London continued to push for a stable and settled community of Indian workmen and women in the colonies. In 1875 Lord Salisbury preferred settlement and colonization rather than temporary labour engagements. He argued for "the emigration of a sufficient proportion of women of an honest and decent class".[15]

In the late nineteenth century even the Caribbean planters began to exhibit more interest in women immigrants. The pulls between short-term preference for adult male immigrants and the long-term advantages of

---

[11] The Workmen's Breach of Contract Act (Act XIII of 1859) was strengthened and reinforced by Act VII of 1873 and Act I of 1882.

[12] In the first batch there were some 6,000 men and 100 women. For more details see Hugh Tinker, *A New System of Slavery: The Export of Indian Labour Overseas 1830–1920* (Oxford, 1974).

[13] Rhoda Reddock, "Freedom Denied. Indian Women and Indentureship in Trinidad and Tobago, 1845–1917", *Economic and Political Weekly*, XX, 43 (1985); Jo Beall, "Women under Indenture in Colonial Natal, 1860–1911", in C. Peach and S. Yettovec (eds), *South Asians Overseas. Migration and Ethnicity* (Cambridge, 1990).

[14] These ratios changed over time and for different colonies several times in the nineteenth century: Bridget Brereton, "The Experience of Indentureship 1854–1917", in John La Guerre (ed.), *Calcutta to Caroni* (Longmans Caribbean, 1974). Also see Brian L. Moore, "Mating Patterns and Gender Relations Among Indians in Nineteenth-Century Guyana", *Guyana Historical Journal*, III (1991), pp. 1–12.

[15] Lord Salisbury to the Governor-General of India in Council, 24 March 1875; *Report of the Indian Jute Manufacturers' Association* (Calcutta, 1899).

a self-reproducing cheap and stable workforce became evident when planters feared an end to labour emigration from India. They began to pay a premium for women recruits.[16] It was when the sugar crisis in the late nineteenth century began to bite that the planters began to be seriously interested in "family". Lower wages and shorter indentures failed to solve their problems. They began to encourage cane farming in small family holdings. The women did most of the regular field work, producing cane and undertaking subsistence food production. Men worked in the estates and provided additional labour on the farms during harvests and in their spare time. This allowed a further depression of wages, a ready reserve of labour and an alternative source of cane.[17]

The tea planters of Assam had from the beginning encouraged family migration.[18] Their main catchment area had thus become the tribal belts of Bengal, Bihar and Orissa where periodic scarcities prised out whole families towards Assam and the Sunderbans.[19] The tea plantations were located in uninhabited, inhospitable and inaccessible areas. The planters could not, like the jute mills, draw on migrants attracted to Calcutta's expanding labour market. They had to invest men and money to organize recruitment and ensure a sufficient supply of labour. But their recruitment was not organized under agents as in the case of the overseas plantations.[20] The Commercial Association was particularly worried by the unpopularity of Assam among migrants, especially women, who seemed to prefer to go to the colonies or remain in Calcutta. In the 1860s the emigration to tea districts was in fact less than 10 per cent of the total overseas emigration. The tea lobby repeatedly sought to highlight "Indian" commercial interests against the larger "imperial" interests that Salisbury had so forcefully represented.[21]

The tea planters were in fact interested in captive labour. More importantly, in the longer term they were looking towards a stable and self-reproducing labour force. Women migrants as potential reproducers of labour were essential to their calculations. They were thus the first industry to offer rudimentary maternity leave and benefits.[22] Besides,

[16] Reddock, "Freedom Denied".

[17] *Ibid.* Also see Tinker, *A New System of Slavery.*

[18] Radhakamal Mukherjee, *The Indian Working Class* (Bombay, 1945), pp. 15–20.

[19] For a well-documented account of this migration see Haraprasad Chattopadhyay, *Internal Migration in India. A Case Study of Bengal* (Calcutta, 1987). The other major stream of migration to Assam was from East Bengal. Peasant families resettled in Assam to undertake the reclamation and cultivation of waste land. The low wages in the tea plantations could not attract these peasant migrants or the local peasantry. There was also a concentration of tea plantations in North Bengal. Ostensibly these were supplied by "free" migration as opposed to the indentured migration that obtained in Assam.

[20] The "free contracting" system came to be regulated from 1863 by the Inland Emigration Act (Bengal Act III of 1863).

[21] WBSA, General Emigration, January 1862, A6.

[22] Curjel Report.

and more importantly, women's labour was valued for subsistence farming and for the labour-intensive task of plucking leaves. This latter task could not be mechanized easily and without enormous outlay of investment. The cheap and "nimble" fingers of women and children were an added bonus for planters which they were loath to relinquish. When "family" migration failed to meet their requirements, "unattached" men and women were encouraged to "settle" in families in the plantations.[23] They could not wait for the "free" operation of the labour market to bring forth women. They extended their own coercive apparatus developed with the collusion of the colonial state specially to target women's recruitment.

In the late nineteenth and early twentieth centuries thus there were increased efforts to recruit women for overseas and Assam plantations. Agents for colonial recruitment, tea garden *sardars* and *arkathis* complained of the scarcity of women willing to migrate under contract.[24] In the case of the colonial recruiters, the Emigration Branch of the Government of Bengal opened a special file entitled "Short Shipment of Females" to accommodate the numerous applications from agents for permission to ship labour even when the proportion of women did not meet the statutory requirements.[25] Enquiries in the North-Western Provinces and Oudh and in Bihar into the system of emigration from British India to the colonies revealed that, "admitting that the proportion of 40 women to 100 men was by no means excessive [. . .] this proportion could not be readily obtained except at the expense of serious abuses".[26]

Colonial recruiters, like plantation recruiters, met the statutory requirements by coercive methods.[27] Unable to find women recruits in

---

[23] WBSA, General Emigration, October 1889, A139–40.

[24] The colonies usually appointed agents in Calcutta and Madras who contracted out recruitment to sub-agents working on commission. The tea planters employed licensed labour contractors who were called *arkathis* and *Garden Sardars*, reliable workers who were paid fees and costs to bring more workers directly to the gardens. The *arkathis* were professional recruiters, while the latter were supposed to recruit only from local and family networks. Planters sometimes preferred *sardari* recruitment because it made labour supervision more effective. The government argued in favour of *sardari* recruitment on the grounds that it eliminated fraud. From 1919 only the *Garden Sardari* system was allowed. There were two types of *sardars* – those who worked independently and those who worked under the control of Licensed Local Agents appointed by the Tea District Labour Supply Association, other recognized associations and individual employers. The Act VI of 1901 granted these latter some special concessions under Section 91: *Annual Report on Inland Emigration under the Assam Labour and Emigration Act VI of 1916* (Calcutta, 1916).

[25] *Report on the Emigration from the Port of Calcutta to British and Foreign Colonies* (Calcutta, 1909–1918).

[26] Bihar State Archives (hereafter BSA), General Emigration, May 1885, Nos 6–8.

[27] E. Van Cutsem, Emigration Agent for Surinam to the Protector of Emigrants, Calcutta, BSA, General Emigration, May 1885, Nos 6–8.

the normal course, they resorted to kidnapping. Various charges of unscrupulous and coercive recruitment were brought against emigration agents and tea planters. In the last three decades of the nineteenth century attention focused on the "kidnapping" of women. A statistical estimate of the extent of fraud and coercion practised by recruiters is difficult to cull from the available evidence. However, there is little doubt that, increasingly, from the end of the nineteenth century, the "kidnapping" of young women figured as an officially recognized problem. The drastic methods adopted by recruiters provoked a characteristic debate between those who emphasized women's "familial" role and others who upheld her "right" to sell her labour.

The emigration agents offered a simple solution. The agent for Surinam, Van Cutsem, argued "that practically the only abuse in connection with emigration occurs in the recruitment of women" and that the "class of women being frequently sent to the colonies [. . .] are worse than useless".[28] The government, the agents believed, should relax the quota system. The Government of India was, however, under considerable pressure from London and the colonies to provide more women emigrants and a "better class of women". It was felt that social disorder was exacerbated by a large influx of "prostitutes" and "lax women". Agents pleaded that such were the only women available for migration. Salisbury was persuading the Government of India to protect the "habits of morality and decency of the Indian population of some of the Colonies" which was endangered "by the scarcity of honest women and want of family life" by promoting emigration of women "free from social prejudices" and "of agricultural and labouring classes".[29]

The collective weight of these representations prompted the government to attempt an investigation into the ways of facilitating more women's migration. Major Pitcher and Mr Grierson were appointed by the government to assist in recruiting women. They gave some specific recommendations: that the surplus women in one shipment should count towards the supply of the next; that separate accommodation and medical examination should be provided under the supervision of female personnel; and that licensed women recruiters should be employed for recruitment of women. But their two main recommendations were the most controversial. Against the tenor of official opinion that allegations of "kidnapping" should be investigated thoroughly, they argued

that the system of enquiry through the police after missing female relatives should be stopped: the single women should be either detained at the depot for week or ten days, or the enquiry should be made through the Civil Executive Agency.[30]

---

[28] BSA, General Emigration, March 1885.
[29] Lord Salisbury to the Governor-General of India in Council, 24 March 1875; *Report of the Indian Jute Manufacturers' Association* (Calcutta, 1899).
[30] BSA, General Emigration, May 1885, Nos 6–8.

This was in line with their strong contention that the only way to facilitate the emigration of "respectable" women was to "generally concede women more liberty of independent action than is allowed them at present". They were thus in favour of repudiating the right of fathers and husbands to influence individual women's migration decisions.[31]

The patriarchal response – "kidnapping" or "voluntary" flight?

In the 1840s the Government of India had been relatively unperturbed by the criticism that male immigration to the colonies left families stranded.[32] It had taken the combined representations of the Home Government and officials in the receiving colonies for the government to look into the question – not because the families left behind were vulnerable but because of the social "instability" in the receiving colonies and the planters' increased interest in women's productive and reproductive labour. Their solution too did not take account of the families of male migrants left behind in India. The quota system they introduced was more directed towards redressing the sex imbalance in the colonies. It allowed, and indeed prompted, a higher incidence of fraudulent recruitment of "unattached" women to make up the quotas when families proved difficult to recruit. The solution itself raised other intractable problems. The government found it impossible to take the same insouciant approach to the question of families left behind by women who migrated alone as they had in the case of families "deserted" by adult male emigrants.

In recommending greater autonomy to women migrants and dismissing the claims of the family to control women's migration decisions, Grierson and Pitcher seemed to have represented a minority opinion in official circles. Many local officers in labour catchment districts agreed that women's migration outside the family context was deviant. They believed that such migration, voluntary or involuntary, threatened familial control over women's labour and sexuality. They had to deal with increasing numbers of cases of missing wives and daughters. Many district level functionaries began to call for stringent legislative restraints on recruiters to protect the interests of fathers and husbands. A magistrate wrote from Chhotanagpur: "To protect husbands from the wiles of the coolie recruiter, there should be some [. . .] order [. . .] regarding the registration of married women."[33] The arguments advanced by officials

---

[31] *Ibid.*

[32] In the 1840s, the Protector questioned 48 returning emigrants. Apparently, the men "reposed perfect confidence" that their wives and children were cared for in their absence. McFarlen argued that it was not uncommon for men to go away as sepoys, bearers or to Calcutta to do odd jobs: D. McFarlen, *Memoranda of 48 Examinations of Mauritius Labourers returned to Bengal in the "Graham"* (Calcutta, 1841).

[33] WBSA, Judicial Police, August 1873, A95–98.

to restrict the emigration of women clearly spelt out the two most problematic aspects of unregulated recruitment. The possibility of emigration, it was often asserted, widened women's sexual choices, thereby undermining their control and containment within marriage. In such arguments, the line between illegitimate and exploitative sexual relations were often blurred: exploitation was seen to be the invariable and inevitable consequence of illegitimate sexual liaisons. The other line of argument concentrated on the domestic role of women. The concerned elite Indian men and British officials drew moving and poignant portraits of the deserted husband, the uncared home and the abandoned child. In both narratives, the key was marriage and the deployment of women's labour and sexuality which were in danger of disruption by women's emigration. One magistrate complained that the kidnapping of young women was causing

great hardship and distress in many families [. . .] the frequent practice of cooly recruiters inveigling away married women from their husbands and children, which latter are in some cases of such tender age as to be exposed to great risk of dying from being deprived of their mother's milk and care.[34]

The coercive recruitment tactics of plantations and emigration agents had hardened patriarchal opposition to women's migration. Objections to women's recruitment for dispatch to Assam and the colonies poured forth from various quarters. The critical questions thrown up in the debates that followed were: whether women's migration was actually "voluntary" and, if so, whether women were to be allowed such "voluntary consent". There were those who believed that women would not and could not voluntarily abandon home and family to migrate to distant tea gardens or overseas colonies where they had to work long hours in appalling conditions. Moreover, in the plantations, the women became victims of sexual harassment and molestation. In these views, poverty, violence and sexual anarchy were inextricably bound to plantation life. The many objections to women's "voluntary" migration turned on four arguments: that recruiters often forcibly "kidnapped" women for Assam and the colonies; that even when the women appeared to have consented to migrate, their recruitment constituted "kidnapping" because they were deceived about the conditions of life and employment; that these conditions were so degrading that no women would, knowingly, opt for migration to Assam or the colonies; and that, moreover, even when no fraud was perpetrated, women, especially married women, were not entitled to enter into contract without the consent of their guardians. The last two arguments often came together when presented by British officials and elite Bengalis. Emigration to Assam or the colonies was seen to offer women an opportunity for economic independence and a

[34] *Ibid.*

means of exercising their sexual choices which undermined the institution
of marriage and the maintenance of familial control.

In the 1870s, a district judge heard a case against Sheikh Panchoo, a
recruiter, who was charged with the kidnapping of Nobin Mochi's wife.
The woman in question was 20–22 years old. She testified that she had
left Nobin "voluntarily". Moreover, it could not be proved that she was
married to Nobin "even by nika marriage". The judge was unable to
convict but he was sympathetic to Nobin. Such recruitments, he felt,
were "against law and morality". Jaggo Mahto had been charged with
the abduction of 11-year-old Geerdharee Bhooyan. Nothing could be
proved, but the magistrate felt that since the result of emigration was
often that

the women, thus leaving their husbands, go into the keeping of other men, and
that the act of enlistment though not illegal at the time becomes tantamount
to inducing a married woman to leave her husband for an immoral purpose
which the recruiter knows full well will be the result and he can recruit such a
woman with perfect impunity.[35]

The magistrate, therefore, recommended that "a clause should [. . .]
be inserted in the recruiter's licenses prohibiting their enlisting married
women without the consent of their husbands".[36]

The enticement of married women "for immoral purposes" was already
a cognizable offence under the Indian Penal Code. It was not clear,
however, whether such a clause could be used against recruiters. A
district magistrate of Chhotnagpur, which was one of the main recruiting
grounds for tea labour, argued that the spirit of the law would be
violated if a clause designed to deal with the sale of women into
prostitution was stretched to cover labour contracts. But to him, as to
many others, there was little difference between the practice of prostitution and the non-marital or extra-marital sexual relationships into which
women entered when they reached the tea gardens or the colonies. He
argued that since Section 366 of the IPC could not be applied to these
cases, other similar legislative or administrative measures had to be
taken to prevent "enticement" of married women.[37]

Charges of enticement were still easier to handle than "abduction"
and "kidnapping". A charge of enticement could on occasion be made
to stick even if the women's willingness to be thus "enticed" remained
questionable. Many cases of "kidnapping" and "abduction" were, however, brought to nought because women were willing to declare their
consent before the magistrate. By definition, "abduction" and "kidnapping", except when they involved minors, assumed forcible apprehension
against the will of the "victim". Thus when a *sardar* was charged with

[35] *Ibid.*
[36] *Ibid.*
[37] *Ibid.*

the kidnapping of three young women, the registering officer recorded
that though there had "[. . .] undoubtedly been great deceit practised
by the accused [. . .] the offence of kidnapping had not been established".[38] Many cases came to hinge on proof of the nature and extent
of deceit practised by recruiters. It was generally believed that

presents of ornaments and clothes and the glowing accounts the recruiters give
of the ease and luxury the women will enjoy in the tea districts which contrasted
by them with the hard fare and work to be done at home often succeeds in
inducing them to leave their families [. . .].[39]

Such official representations found echoes in the writings of elite
Bengalis. In the 1870s and 1880s Dwarkanath Ganguly and Ramkumar
Vidyaratna wrote in the *Sanjibani* harrowing accounts of sexual harassment in the Assam gardens.[40] The violation of "Indian" coolie women
by European men provided a potent symbol of colonial exploitation and
oppression.[41]

Ganguly believed, like some British officers, that "recruitment" was
"tantamount to inducing a married woman to leave her husband for an
immoral purpose".[42] Recruiters, goaded by plantation managers, practised great deception to recruit women who were susceptible to the
attraction of wages and a good life. In a fictionalized account of his
experiences, *Kulikahini*, Ramkumar Vidyaratna described in detail the
recruitment of a peasant woman, Adarmani. The recruiters seduced her
by holding out attractions of rich clothes, ornaments and comforts which
provided a stark contrast with her misery and drudgery in the village
home. The author made it clear that in succumbing to these wiles
Adarmani was not only revoking male authority but was inviting its
terrible consequences.[43]

The Act of 1901 – constraints on women's recruitment

In the closing decades of the nineteenth century, then, there were
various interests competing for labour in north India. Each staked their
claim to special patronage from the Government of India. The Home
Government condemned the Indian Government's indifference to overseas labour migration and accused them of not paying adequate attention

[38] *Ibid.*
[39] *Ibid.*
[40] Dwarkanath Ganguly, *Slavery in British Dominion*, ed. Srikumar Kunda, comp. K.L. Chattopadhayay (Calcutta, 1972).
[41] Samita Sen, "Honour and Resistance: Gender, Community and Class in Bengal, 1920–40", in Sekhar Bandopadhyay *et al.* (eds), *Bengal: Communities, Development and States* (New Delhi, 1994).
[42] *The Bengalee*, XXVIII, 4, 22 January 1887, reproduced in Ganguly, *Slavery in British Dominion*.
[43] Ramkumar Vidyaratna, *Kulikahini* [Sketches from Cooly Life] (Calcutta, 1888), pp. 6–7.

to larger imperial interests. The tea planters sought to represent "Indian" capitalist interests and based their appeal for privileges in the labour market on the grounds that India could corner a part of the tea market dominated by the Chinese. The big landlords had been objecting to the depredation of their labour since almost the middle of the nineteenth century.[44] Along with such arguments the focus on the "abuses" of labour recruitment sharpened. The British official and elite Bengali outrage against the challenge to patriarchal family authority added further fuel to these debates.

The colonial state found itself committed to the protection of these conflicting interests. Despite the government's earlier disinclination for further labour legislation, in 1901 the Assam Labour and Emigration Act (Act VI of 1901) was passed. Ostensibly the Act was meant to reduce the role of *arkathis* and encourage *sardari* recruitment on the grounds that *sardars* recruited from locales where they were known.[45] Meanwhile, the various pressures to take special measures to avoid abuses in women's recruitment had to be taken into consideration. Even the Chief Commissioner of Assam, the province attracting women tea workers, drew attention to this problem.

It is [. . . the case] of the female waif or stray, the woman who has been deserted by her husband, the woman who has left her home after a quarrel, the first wife who has been superseded by a second, the wife of a Coolin Brahmin, and such like. Such women are often ready to go anywhere with anybody and to do anything, and they seem not unfrequently to fall the victims to the professional *arkati* or recruiter. They have [. . .] to be deceived by some false representation, and they are probably told that a home will be provided for them either as domestic servant or in a less honourable capacity, or perhaps the person who enlists one of them tells her that he will himself marry her or keep her as his mistress [. . .] It is only when she is put on board the steamer, and her deceiver leaves her that she is brought to understand what is before her, and the deception comes to light.[46]

The Superintendent of Police, F.H. Tucker, inundated with complaints, also advocated extensive examination of recruiting. The "big abduction cases" of 1885–1886 were a further goad.[47] The government found itself more than ever caught between the interests of British capital and the displeasure of indigenous elites, missionaries and some of their own officials. On the one hand, the Home Government and the Indian Tea Association wanted less regulation of women's recruitment and the curtailment of criminal enquiries after missing women by fathers and husbands. Grierson and Pitcher had recommended reforms along these

[44] WBSA, General Emigration, January 1862, A6.
[45] *Ibid.*, July 1904, A6–15.
[46] *Ibid.*, January 1890, A139–40.
[47] *Ibid.*, A42–4.

lines. On the other hand, the state had to address the questions raised by the collective weight of cases of kidnapping.

In the end the government's response was to run directly counter to Grierson's recommendations. Section 9 of the Act of 1901 empowered registering officers to refuse registration to and detain women who were emigrating without the consent of their "lawful guardian", husband or father or brother as the case may be. Several categories of recruits were defined who were to be discharged from the depots and not despatched to the colonies: those refusing to emigrate; the Brahmins, Vaishyas, etc., who had not worked as coolies; those whose relations asked for their release; those recruited in one district but registered in another; minors; and women whose husbands were living. These last four provisions, devised as a concession to concerns about the familial control of women, were meant to check the "kidnapping", "abduction" and "enticement" of women.

These provisions were meant to quieten fears that widening women's migration options would threaten familial control over their labour and sexuality. The local elites and officials had thus successfully invoked state aid to stake out family control. Many district officials argued that only legislation would protect the interests of husbands whose wives were "kidnapped" by recruiters. Not only did husbands and children need protection from the recruiter but women who wished to escape them had to be prevented or punished. The provisions of the Act of 1901 were justified on the grounds that

the deportation of wives against the will of their husbands should be absolutely prohibited, and [. . .] Magistrates would be absolutely justified in refusing to pass any woman so situated [. . .] A married woman may be said to have entered into a contract with her husband which precludes her from engaging in services to another party for a term of years without his consent.[48]

The Lieutenant-Governor agreed that it should be a penal offence for a wife to be recruited without permission of husband or guardian.[49] From the mid-nineteenth century, the British sought by statutory intervention to restrain women's mobility, their ability to escape unhappy marriages or resist familial authority. An increasingly orthodox interpretation of marriage became the key to reinforcing male authority in the family, both as a guarantee of political stability and as a means of curbing women's resistance to coercive extraction of labour. This disability in particular affected low-caste women adversely since their marriages often resembled forced labour arrangements and the prevalence of divorce was the only avenue of escape open to some of them.

A provision for restitution of conjugal rights, which the Lieutenant-Governor had rejected in 1800, was introduced by judicial decision in

[48] WBSA, Judicial Police, August 1873, A95–8.
[49] *Ibid.*

1867 and later incorporated in the Code of Civil Procedure (1882) Section 260 and 1908 CCP (Order 21 under Rule 32). Men were thus permitted the use of courts to restrain wives who wished to migrate to Assam, the colonies, to cities and towns or even to live with other men. The control of women's work within the family was thus enhanced.

It was curious, however, that the Lieutenant-Governor subscribed to the notion that a woman by marriage "entered into a contract". The British Indian courts had held that Hindu marriage was, in fact, a "sacrament". "Hindu" marriages were thus set apart from Muslim and Christian marriages. The Madras High Court therefore ruled that even separation from a husband did not constitute grounds for divorce and/ or remarriage by a Hindu woman as long as her husband lived. Hindu men did not require divorce since polygyny was given full legal status. Polyandry was, however, completely rejected. In addition, "customary" divorces among low-caste women were criminalized and their second marriages were rendered invalid. The husbands by such marriages became vulnerable to charges of "abduction" and "seduction" and the women could be indicted for bigamy. All these were criminal offences. Despite the widespread practice of *nika* among lower castes in Bengal and Bihar, colonial officials held that it was a Muslim custom and would not apply to Hindu women.[50] For Muslim women too the right of initiating divorces was being eroded, though the dissolution of a marriage at the man's instance was widely accepted. Thus while the characterization of all marriages as contractual went against the tenor of the colonial legal discourse in the late nineteenth century, in this particular instance such an interpretation was in tune with the general movement towards a rigidification of gender hierarchy.

The Act of 1901 gave men – fathers and husbands – an additional means to restrain runaway women. It was often invoked to stop women who sought to escape, either alone or with lovers. It was recognized that in every district of the province there were cases of "kidnapping" related to girls being "carried away by their paramours", or taken with the object of marrying them without consent of the family. The extensive use of the term "kidnapping" not only emphasized the legal status of women as minors, but the term had to be given a new legal meaning

---

[50] The term *nika* was derived from an Arabic word meaning marriage. In nineteenth-century Bengal, many Muslims called the first marriage *shadi* (meaning delight) and ritually celebrated. According to colonial officials, the second marriage was called *nika* and, even among Muslims, influenced by Hindu notions of second marriage being disgraceful, performed with less ceremony. Among the lower castes, divorcees and widows were allowed to remarry. Many of them (including some Vaishnava sects) seemed to have termed their second marriages *nika*, though they were also termed *sanga* or *sangat* or even *sagai*. Some colonial officials argued that such a second marriage was concubinage in the case of a divorced woman, but because of its wide acceptance it should not be made a penal offence: WBSA, General Miscellaneous, April 1874, B1–15.

to account for women who consented to their "kidnapping". Since legal restraints on women's mobility construed voluntary flight as "kidnapping", the "offence" became impossible to establish.[51]

The attempt to establish kidnapping by arguing that the women's "consent" was invalid when obtained by deceit was obviously fraught. Doubtless deceit and fraud were the stock-in-trade of recruiting agents. They held out (usually false) prospects of high wages, good working conditions and even marriage. It is also certain that some women did choose to migrate to the gardens of Assam or to distant colonies. A recruit, Jainaff Bibi, rescued from a depot in Calcutta testified that, though she had been deceived, she had accompanied the recruiter willingly.

I fell in love with a man named Jame. He was perhaps one of the cooly recruiters. He said that he would get me admitted into a cooly depot and then after securing my discharge by paying the usual fee of Rs. 30 on my arrival in Calcutta, would marry me under the nika form, so that my own people might not claim me.[52]

The pressure to recruit only adult women of "respectable antecedents" exacerbated the issue. The legal formalizing of familial rights over women's mobility made it relatively easier for women who were marginalized in the family or deprived of familial resources to migrate than married women, whose recruitment was more likely to be challenged. Recruiters were forced to seek out "women who were either of bad repute, or were involved in domestic troubles" to make up the required proportion.[53] Young girls and widows often fled from home because of ill-treatment or domestic strife and fell victim to unscrupulous procurers and labour recruiters. Sometimes married women sought escape from the harassment of a husband or in-laws, or a quarrel might trigger off flight. Such women had little access to resources outside the family and emigration might have seemed a viable option providing some economic independence. Munni was a Rajput from UP. She was 18 years old and married to a 9 year old: "I was therefore never on good terms with the members of my father-in-law's family [. . . M]y mother-in-law gave me much trouble and never sent me to my father's house."[54] She had run away from home and had been decoyed by a recruiter. Rampyari Halwayin had fallen on hard times because "[. . .] about a year ago my husband has gone away, I do not know where" and in her search

[51] WBSA, Judicial Police, August 1873, A95–98.
[52] Translated from *Bharatmitra*, 28, 29 and 31 October and 1, 2, 4 and 5 November 1913. WBSA, Finance Emigration, November 1915, B5–7.
[53] *Report of the Inter-Departmental Conference held in London in 1917 to Consider Proposals for a New Assisted System of Emigration from India to British Guiana, Trinidad and Fiji*, WBSA, Commerce Emigration, July 1918, A1–16.
[54] *Ibid.*

for work she had found her way to the depot.[55] The Act of 1901 did little to reduce such recruitments. In 1913 five cases were cited against recruiters. One widowed and orphaned girl who quarrelled with her aunt, another 25-year-old woman who fell out with her mother-in-law, another who left with her son because her husband took another wife with whom she did not get along. In all these cases, the women were promised employment in Calcutta and then decoyed to a tea garden.[56] While some of these women were actually taken to plantations or to the colonies, others who managed to escape or were released could not return to their village home. They found their way to the tenements of Calcutta and the jute mill towns.[57]

The Act had sought to resolve the controversy over the legal definition of "voluntary consent" by altogether denying women the capacity to consent and by deferring that right to the husband/guardian. This raised other complicated questions: the issue of guardianship in case of widows and deserted wives and, more important, widely practised customs of divorce and remarriage.

In the end, legal confusions about "consent" helped towards confounding the provisions of the Act. The magistrates were often unable to prevent even enticements and kidnappings. In 1901 so many women recruits presented to the registering officer were suspect that the Commissioner of the Chhotanagpur division felt that the practice of detaining the women in the *thana* was undesirable and inadequate, especially since some women were delivered of children while in custody.[58] In the Central Provinces, in 1904–1905, all prosecutions regarding illegal recruitment related to the enticement or kidnapping of young women.[59] In 1913, out of 49 persons who were rejected for registration at Naihati, 13 were young women who could not prove that they had the consent of their lawful guardian.[60] "During the present season, 120 coolies were kidnapped many of them young, married women", said an article in *Capital* in February 1911.[61] The figures in government reports are too fragmentary to allow us to estimate whether such cases actually decreased after the Act of 1901. Without doubt, however, the frequency of incidents of "kidnapping" and "abduction" continued to trouble district authorities in recruitment districts. Their reports for 1911 and 1912 give some

---

[55] Statement, Alipore Court, 11 May 1911. WBSA, Finance Emigration, November 1915, B5–7.
[56] *Ibid.*, February 1913.
[57] Sen, "Women Workers in the Bengal Jute Industry".
[58] Special arrangements had to be made with the local Lady Dufferin Fund Committee. WBSA, General Emigration, December 1901, A23–30.
[59] *Report on the Working of the Inland Emigration Act in the Central Provinces for the Year Ending 30 June, 1905.*
[60] WBSA, Finance Emigration, December 1913, A1–3.
[61] Extract from *Capital*, 9 February 1911. WBSA, General Emigration, January 1912, A1–32.

Table 1. *Number of cases of abduction by recruiters registered during 1911–1912*

Date	Region	Total cases against recruiters	"Abduction" cases	Percentage of "abduction" cases to total cases
July–Sept. 1911	Orissa	4	2	50.00
	Chota Nagpur	34	20	58.82
Oct.–Dec. 1911	Orissa	1	0	0
	Chota Nagpur	11	7	63.63
	Bhagalpur	3	1	33.33
	Burdwan	6	3	50.00
Jan.–March 1912	Burdwan	2	1	50.00
April–June 1912	Burdwan	5	3	60.00

Sources:
1 WBSA, General Emigration, June 1911, B7–24, File 5R-1.
2 *Ibid.*, December 1911, B4–19, File 5R-1.
3 *Ibid.*, February 1912, B43–58, File 5R-1.
4 *Ibid.*, May 1912, B48–57, File 5R-1.
5 *Ibid.*, August 1912, B27–39, File 5R-1.

indication of the extent of kidnapping of young women by recruiters. These figures can only be the tip of the iceberg, for it is likely that the majority of cases never found their way into courts and thence into government returns.

The recruiters fight back

However ineffective in achieving its avowed purpose, the Act made women's recruitment more difficult and expensive, especially for emigration agencies. They argued that between the need to maintain a steady number of women recruits and the provisions of Section 9, they were being squeezed from both ends. To entitle recruits to demand release from the depots after the recruiter had paid advances and transportation costs was to violate the spirit of the contract that underlay recruitment practices. Besides, the compensation they were paid was insufficient, especially in the case of women who were more expensive to recruit and were given more opportunity to revoke their contracts.[62]

A serious problem in applying the law on the ground came from another quarter. Section 9 was rendered relatively ineffective by the powerful lobbies interested in cheap female labour. A technical issue, the clause requiring a "lawful guardian" to register a complaint to the registering officer, became the ostensible ground of conflict between some local officials and the plantation and recruiting agencies. In 1903 J.N. Gupta, Magistrate of Bankura, suspected that a woman brought

[62] L. Grommer, Emigration Agent for Surinam to the Protector of Emigrants, 24 April 1914. WBSA, Finance Emigration, November 1915, A22.

before him for registration did not have the consent of her guardian. A long-drawn and expensive process lay before him. To cut the procedure short, he ordered that women needing to be registered would have to obtain a certificate from their local *panchayat* stating clearly that they wished "to enter labour contracts with the consent of their husbands or lawful guardians".[63] Gupta's object was to "put a check to fraudulent recruitment by misrepresentation, coercion, undue influence". He argued that it was incumbent upon him "to prevent women from being cajoled away" especially since sections 34 and 69(2) of the Act had "laid much stress on the subject of making enquiry into all suspected cases of labour contract by women against the wishes or without the consent of her husband".[64] The Tea Districts Labour Supply Association, however, thought otherwise. They held that such a directive would not only not fulfil its objective, it would "hamper recruiting operations" by giving "in the hands of village panchayats" a power that would be "utilised in placing additional difficulties in the way of sardari recruitment under the Act to what already exist".[65] The government lent a sympathetic ear and O'Malley, the Secretary to the Government of Bengal, argued that "special enquiries should *only be made when there is positive reason for suspecting that a woman*, who is brought up for registration unaccompanied by her guardian, *is being 'cajoled away'*".[66] The government directed the withdrawal of the order. Silence on the part of the guardian was to be construed as consent: "the presumption is that the guardian (if there is one) consents unless he comes forward to object".[67]

H. Savage, a registering magistrate for many years, to whom the Governor referred the case, pointed out that if preventing enticement was the purpose of the law, this ruling defeated it. Rather, he argued, "the panchayat's certificate is the *lowest* evidence that a Magistrate would be justified in accepting as evidence of the consent of husband or guardian in their absence". The presumption that "the guardian consents unless be comes forward to object is made on the further assumption that the guardian knows what has become of the woman, which, if there has been cajolery, is just what he would not know".[68] This indeed was the hub of the matter. If silence was to be construed as consent, it was precisely cases of cajolery, enticement and fraudulent recruitments that would not be detected.[69] A magistrate would not be able to act on his own initiative. Women who were deliberately escaping oppressive marriages, alone or with their lovers, found it relatively easy

[63] WBSA, General Emigration, June 1903, A48–53.
[64] *Ibid.*
[65] *Ibid.*
[66] Italics in original. *Ibid.*, June 1904, A48–53.
[67] *Ibid.*
[68] Italics in original. *Ibid.*
[69] *Ibid.*, August 1904, A87–9.

to conceal the facts from the registering magistrates. Married women thus recruited, if apprehended in time, could still be released from the depot on payment of Rs. 30. The amount itself would have been hard enough to find. Moreover, the fact of marriage had to be proved with three witnesses. If the woman was already at a depot in Ranchi, Naihati or Calcutta, proving the "factum of marriage" was extraordinarily difficult and many deserted husbands found themselves unable to pursue their charges.

In the case of widows, orphans and adopted girls, there was still a more fundamental question to settle. Who were their "lawful guardians"? What gave the tea lobby an edge against Gupta was that the particular case in which he gave the order for compulsory *panchayati* certification involved the recruitment of a young widow. Hence, in his memo O'Malley added the parenthesis: "the presumption is that the guardian (if there is one) consents unless he comes forward to object".[70] It was often assumed that some widows, deserted and deserting wives were "single" women and if they were above the age of consent they were in fact competent to enter into labour contracts on their own behalf. The Emigration Report of 1912 thus categorized 69.45 per cent of migrants as "single women".[71] For some, especially elite Indian men, women's ability to take their own migration decisions constituted an illegitimate attack on the integrity of the family. They denounced the assumption that some women could be treated as "single" and therefore "free" to enter into labour contracts without permission from the male head of household. The Secretary of the Marwari Association, which had mounted a campaign against indentured labour, wrote to the Government of Bengal:

Women are decoyed as freely and with as much unconcern as men and registered as single, although women are never single in this country unless they happen to be widows. The object of registering them as such is evidently to show that they are free to act for themselves. But it is a well-known fact that women in this country are seldom free and are always under the guardianship of either their husbands or other relations.[72]

Even some registering officers who were faced with the everyday reality of rising abuses in recruitment of women were unimpressed by the specious arguments forwarded by the tea lobby and the recruiting agencies. The Deputy Commissioner of Ranchi felt that the real purpose of the 1901 Act was to ensure that "no woman was capable of binding herself by a labour contract if her husband or lawful guardian objects

---

[70] *Ibid.*
[71] *Report on the Working of the Inland Emigration Act*, (Calcutta, 1912).
[72] Babu Ramdeo Chotham, Honorary Secretary, Marwari Association, to the Secretary to the Government of Bengal, 5 August 1915. WBSA, Finance Emigration, November 1915, B5–7.

[. . .]" and that this obliged the registering officer to look carefully into the competency of a woman to execute a labour contract. He cited a case where a woman abducted by an unlicensed recruiter was paired off with another man and "to prevent any looking back on her part, got this newly formed couple to consummate their union in the jungle, where he first introduced them to each other".[73]

The recruiting agents, however, held fast to the technicality that under the Act the registering officer was not required to question *sardari* recruits, and had no power to enquire whether such women had the permission of their guardians. In a few cases where local officials took an initiative in cracking down on illegal recruitment, agents put up stiff resistance.[74]

In fact, most district officials were indifferent, if not actively in sympathy with recruiting agencies, many of which were owned and run by Europeans. Nanika's case received considerable publicity because it was taken up by a clergyman who had converted her to Christianity before her recruitment.[75] The Reverend A. Logsdail complained that contrary to the Tea Association's vituperations, local officials took little action in cases of illegal recruitment. Nanika had been recruited by Mata Sardar and taken to a tea garden as his "wife". She had been registered under a false name and as a resident of Maurbhanj where she had never lived. When her mother complained to the police and applied to the District Officer for maintenance for herself and Nanika's young daughter the case was dismissed summarily

without any inquiry whatever from the complainant [. . . T]he Police took the depot folk's account without testing its soundness [. . . No] women, or men either, [should] be taken off [. . .] without registration as so-called "free" coolies [. . .]. The petitioner asked for bread for herself and grandchild, she has been given a stone.[76]

Since the legislation had been undertaken primarily to reduce *arkathi* recruiting and promote "free" recruitment by *sardars*, some officials argued that enquiry into doubtful cases of recruitment by *sardars* would defeat the main purpose of the Act. Enquiries were not only inexpedient but unnecessary, since *sardari* recruitment was, by definition, "free" recruitment, and since the *sardar* recruited, with his limited resources, from his own locality within his known circle, such abuses were unlikely to occur.[77] Whatever the arguments advanced, that the Act was in

---

[73] H.C. Streatfield, Deputy Commissioner of Ranchi, to the Commissioner of the Chota Nagpur Division, 23 September 1901. WBSA, General Emigration, December 1901, A50–62.
[74] Emphasis in original. *Ibid.*, July 1913, B57–65.
[75] *Ibid.*, June 1905, A18–32.
[76] *The Statesman*, 15 October 1904.
[77] WBSA, General Emigration, December 1901, A50–62.

practice ineffective was evident from the continued reports of illegal recruitment. Even as late as 1912, the Magistrate of Gaya felt that the word "kidnapping" was being used frequently in connection with recruiters, both licensed and unlicensed, and that unless the most stringent checks were maintained there would be "instead of recruiters merely licensed kidnappers".[78]

Conclusion

The Sections 9, 34 and 69 had been included in the Act VI of 1901 to prevent women's fraudulent recruitment and to restrain women who sought to flee their families, voluntarily or because they had been deceived. These provisions were intended to propitiate patriarchal outrage. But the pressure from emigration agencies and various tea lobbies including the Indian Tea Planters' Association and the Tea Districts Labour Supply Association forced the government into various compromises. Registering magistrates were encouraged to wink at illegal recruitments which most of them did anyway. The Government of Bengal was more susceptible to the interests of recruiters than Delhi. By executive fiat, Calcutta neutralized the possibilities of rigorous enquiry into women's recruitment. It was precisely the kind of recruitment that the Act was meant to suppress that remained unchecked by the Government of Bengal's decision to hold by the rule that the husband/guardian would have to come forward before special enquiries could be made into a woman's recruitment. The controversy continued. From time to time, some district magistrates would attempt a more zealous application of the spirit of Section 9. The need to reconcile the interests of recruiters with familial claims over women's labour and sexuality remained an irritant until the practice of recruiting indentured labour was abolished.

[78] T.S. MacPherson, Magistrate of Gaya to the Commissioner of the Patna Division. WBSA, General Emigration, March 1912, A9–12.

Sordid Class, Dangerous Class?
Observations on Parisian Ragpickers and Their *Cités* During the Nineteenth Century

ALAIN FAURE

Everybody knows that refuse is a ragpicker's *raison d'être*. Continuous collection of the waste from big city consumption, along with the rubbish and the refuse, led to collection efforts that gradually brought about a wholesale trade and an industry for recycling these wastes back into production. Until the famous prefectorial decree of 24 November 1883, garbage was left on the public thoroughfares and collected by the dust carts of the licensed garbage collectors at daybreak. During the night, the bins were searched by the ragpickers, who constituted a unique category of workers known as *ramasseurs* (gatherers). They seemed to work with standard equipment from the beginning of the nineteenth century onwards. Each carried a hook, a basket suspended from the back (a "dummy"), and a lantern. They sought and garnered a wide variety of products, from fabric to cork, ranging through metals, bones and skins, each item serving a specific purpose, from the most commonplace (old papers and rags for paper production) to the most extraordinary (crusts of bread for the crumbs used by butchers for frying). Around 1900, the ragpicker's take consisted of all kinds of old papers, twine, rags for manufacturing paper (50 to 60 per cent), all types of bones (20 to 25 per cent), and an infinite variety of objects (15 to 30 per cent).[1] At this time, however, the rag industry changed dramatically as a result of technological advances (especially the new manufacture of paper from wood pulp). The subsequent collapse of most of the markets exacerbated the recent differentiation between ragpickers. Nevertheless, ragmen still siphoned off 13 per cent of the tonnage of garbage in Paris. Annual exports of this capital resource by the rag trade totalled 27 million francs.

Given this turnover and the categories of entrepreneurs (the master ragpicker, who purchased directly from the ragpicker, and the merchant, who sometimes headed large operations), the size of the rag industry in Paris was considerable. Moreover, the forces supplying this market were far from trivial. The history of ragpickers is in part characterized by their encounters with the police. In the eighteenth century, a series of ordinances by the general lieutenancy represented a futile effort to

---

[1] Office du Travail, *L'industrie du chiffon à Paris* (Paris, 1903), p. 40. For an extensive list of classifications, with price lists for merchandise gathered, see e.g. J. Barberet, *Monographies professionnelles*, Vol. 4, *Les chiffonniers* (Paris, 1887), pp. 103–104.

International Review of Social History 41 (1996), pp. 157–176

restrict their activities to a section of the night. As night-time wanderers on the streets, ragpickers had ambiguous interactions with prowlers. The 1828 ordinance transformed their industry into a regulated trade requiring badges.[2] Never rigidly enforced (the number of badges and the actual numbers practising the trade always differed considerably; moreover, people sold and transferred their badges), the ordinance fell into abeyance after 1872, the year the last badges were made. Numerous projects for reforming garbage collection effectively augured the disappearance of the ragpickers: based on a principle that reflected Haussmann's ideology, a decree from the government's "Défense nationale" in September 1870 ordered *concierges* to place boxes on public thoroughfares immediately before the dust carts rode by in the morning. As the old habits persisted, a new decree from Prefect Poubelle was necessary to impose the boxes in 1883. The corporation's vehement protests drew only a single concession from the administration: placement of the receptacle on the public thoroughfare one hour before the dust carts rode by, with authorized accessibility to the ragpicker during the interval. The occupational adjustment to this tremendous upheaval gave rise to two main categories of ragpickers during the 1880s. One category comprised the people who obtained permission from the *concierges* to enter the buildings and search the boxes (known as *placiers*). The other type consisted of the *coureurs*, who made do with the hour of grace and the boxes already explored by the first group.

Under the new regulations for rubbish collection, the *coureurs* perpetuated the old-style ragpickers, wandering collectors in the field of unlimited foraging. The *placiers*, on the other hand, introduced a stationary element to the trade. A remote disciple of Le Play viewed this process as the transition from collective property to individual property in the workplace.[3] The same formulation might be applied to the territorial system: the ragpicker with a claim to the rubbish from a given house came every morning at daybreak to collect the boxes and to transport them to the courtyard and subsequently (after rummaging through them) to the road. This individual also performed small services for the occupants, who paid him in "little packages". These sites were passed on as inheritances or sold at a price commensurate to the revenue from the dwellings included. *Coureurs* equipped with spiked sticks or bags (they had stopped using the baskets by then) often made extremely long

---

[2] Considering that "the offenders fool the police surveillance by arming themselves like the ragpickers with a hook that they use to steal and to kill, a basket in which they can easily conceal stolen objects, and a lantern that enables them to recognize their surroundings [. . .]." (excerpts from the text of the ordinance by de Belleyme of 1 September 1828). Regarding the regulations until the modern era, see File DB 194 at the Archives de la préfecture de Police.

[3] Joseph Durieu, *Les Parisiens d'aujourd'hui*, Vol. I, *Les types sociaux de simple récolte et d'extraction* (Paris, 1910), p. 168.

rounds to search the bins already placed outside. They represented the lower ranks of the trade and had to settle for an inferior and chancier take: most *placiers* owned a cart or a horse-drawn wagon, equipment that was beyond the means of the *coureurs*. Moreover, the old-style collector had enough time to return home to drop off his take at various points throughout the day.[4] The new regulation eliminated this convenient option and placed the individuals without designated sites at a greater disadvantage. It also gave rise to other categories of ragpickers, especially the *gadouilleurs*, ragpickers authorized to work on the wharfs for loading the town refuse into the pulverizing plants.[5] Thus, the trade featured a hierarchy: given this typically urban activity that resulted from the city waste, the rags were necessarily very sensitive to developments in public hygiene, of which the 1883 decree was a milestone.

The exact number of ragpickers was a subject of serious debate around the time the new regulations became effective. Throughout the nineteenth century, all estimates were very high: a police notice reporting 5,937 badges registered with the prefecture estimated the actual numbers of regular ragpickers at around thirty or even forty thousand men and women.[6] This last figure was also submitted by the representative of the trade committee to the Parliamentary Commission, known as the *Quarante-Quatre* (Forty-Four), which convened at that time to investigate the industrial crisis. Including the families, the representative counted up to 200,000 persons. Adding the workers employed by the master ragpickers and the merchants, as well as their families, the total was 500,000.[7] In 1886 the Paris Board of Health released its own assessment of 41,000 individuals (*placiers* + *coureurs*).[8] Once again in 1903, at the time of the survey by the Labour Department on the ragpicking industry, the figures quoted by the employers' organizations fluctuated between 20,000 and 22,000 ragpickers, while the numbers reported by the workers' organizations varied between 19,200 and 27,000.[9] According to these figures, which merit closer evaluation, the ragpickers trade was among the most numerous of all occupations in Paris. Overestimating the figures for these individuals was customary: even though ragpickers were not very well known, their operations were certainly very widespread. They

---

[4] The ragpicker studied by Le Play in 1849–1851 left home at six o'clock in the morning (seven in the winter) and returned at nine o'clock to eat; he then went on a new round from half past ten until five o'clock in the afternoon and from seven o'clock in the evening until midnight: *Les Ouvriers européens* (Paris, 1860), p. 272.

[5] Another category consisted of the dust cart ragpickers (454 in 1903), who helped manage the bins for low wages (known as the "21 sous") and the right to rummage through them along their route.

[6] Report from the chief of police for security of 8 May 1883. DB 194.

[7] *Commission d'enquête parlementaire*, p. 246.

[8] Conseil d'hygiène publique, De Luynes, *Rapport sur les dépôts de chiffons* (Paris, 1886), p. 4.

[9] Office du Travail, *L'industrie du chiffon*, p. 17.

were true journalistic resources as well as romantic or dramatic figures. In addition, their marginal reputation – bordering on the disconcerting – as innumerable soldiers of a nightly street brigade provides an inkling of the motivations underlying these over-evaluations. Moreover, the individuals in question tended to inflate their numbers to convince the authorities that restrictive regulations would harm a larger group than was actually the case.

An administrative reaction followed the backlash of the words of the ragpicker delegates before the *Quarante-Quatre*. An investigation ordered by Alphand, the Paris director of public works, based on the tonnage obtained and a count of the ragpickers entering the gates of the capital every day, yielded the figure of 7,050 ragpickers from all categories.[10] The most serious study was by Barrat, the Department's investigator, who divided the 4,950 people active in the trade into 2,000 *placiers*, 1,600 *coureurs* and 1,350 *gadouilleurs*. These distinct evaluations, which were conducted fifteen years apart, conveyed only the numbers involved, but were nevertheless nowhere near the conventional figures. As for the relative difference between the two estimates (2,100), it is difficult to determine whether this discrepancy arises from counting error or from the long-term effect of the regulation of 1883.

While these last two evaluations might seem very convincing because of the low figures mentioned, they actually reflect minimum numbers. They overlooked certain specific features of the trade: who were the ragpickers? How did they enter the business?

After all, rags were merely one of the wide range of possible street trades in an astonishing variety in Paris as in all large cities: one of several trades, but undoubtedly the most important. These non-wage activities served a well-known purpose: the unemployed, meaning any individual without savings and lacking a regular source of income for any reason, could occasionally rely on such work. Barrat wrote that the distribution of the different categories of ragpickers varied over the course of a year (Table 1).[11] The inflated proportion of *coureurs* in the winter is attributable to the lull in various occupations, especially in construction. The only equipment required for becoming a *coureur* was a bag and a strong pair of legs. Of course, the number of *placiers* was fairly stable. Around 1909, Durieu, who wrote a book about ragpickers, encountered a number of these moonlighting ragmen, such as the former captain of a passenger steamer who lost his job because of a strike and divided his year between a position as a stock clerk at the bonded warehouses and ragpicking in the suburbs, or even the young plumber without work, the son of a trade union activist and a trade unionist

---

[10] Including 4,000 *placiers*, 2,000 wandering *coureurs* or *rouleurs*, 1,050 ragpickers and second-hand dealers. Quoted by Barberet, *Monographies professionnelles*, 4, p. 83.
[11] Office du Travail, *L'industrie du chiffon*, p. 14.

Table 1. *Distribution of the different categories of ragpickers*

	Winter	Summer
Placiers	30%	40%
Coureurs	60%	30%
Gadouilleurs	10%	30%

himself.[12] This observer was also struck by the sense of shame among the *coureurs* he approached: "They feel as if they are pariahs. They voluntarily remain in seclusion and dislike being treated as ragpickers." A carpenter, a one-time home-worker who had failed, described his first experience with the trade: "Many people, who, like myself, were unemployed during the winter of 1860 to 1861, started working as ragpickers. I began at night because I feared encountering acquaintances. To avoid being recognized, I covered my head with a wide-brimmed hat that I carefully pulled down over my eyes."[13] If this individual acquired a taste for his new occupation, imagine how many others must have found the rag trade providential! The considerable numbers of people in this line of business that are conventionally presented and quoted above may provide a rough indication.[14]

As a sign of survival difficulties among workers in the big city, ragpicking served an additional function that was often unmentioned but nevertheless essential: the trade was the last resort for old workers, not as a temporary refuge, but for retirement purposes. The ragpickers described in various sources were often quite old and even ancient. Had things changed so much since the enactment of the regulations? Of the 1,841 individuals who obtained a badge from the prefecture between 1 September 1828 and 31 December 1829, 50.2 per cent were over 40 (63 per cent among the women).[15] The situation probably had changed a

[12] Durieu, *Les Parisiens d'aujourd'hui*, pp. 126–132.
[13] Quoted by Barberet, *Monographies professionnelles*, 4, p. 102. These "Notes d'un chiffonnier" were imparted to Barberet by Desmarquet, one of the witnesses in 1884.
[14] In the nineteenth century, the rag trade was a choice refuge both for aristocrats and for foremen from failed industries. The origins undoubtedly date back to the melodrama of Felix Pyat, *Le chiffonnier de Paris* (1847) and his character the Comte Crion-Carousse, who took up a basket on his back by sheer coincidence. The work has a moralizing theme and is rife with expected turns of events: punishment for wealth acquired improperly, vanity of earthly goods, etc. Nevertheless, an element of truth prevails: Georges Mény (in the *Chiffonnier de Paris* (Paris, 1905)) refers to the case of a descendent of du Mâconnais (an old family of aristocrats) who used his protection to claim the rubbish bins of Palais-Royal and the minister of the colonies. Before him, Privat d'Anglemont had described this special class of ragpickers as "philosophical bohemians, who had once been important and who had, through various misfortunes – almost always involving misconduct – become trapped in a downward spiral culminating in the dregs of society": Privat d'Anglemont, *Paris inconnu* (Paris, 1861), p. 53.
[15] DB 194. This file comprises ten registration forms dated between 1849 and 1863: the average age was 45.5. Two applicants listed a previous occupation.

lot, as the badges were originally intended especially for old people with no means, although this particular aspect of recruitment undoubtedly persisted.

By this point, the ragpicking trade included true professionals: only these people figure in the calculations by Alphand and de Barrat. In summary, about 5,000 persons subsisted permanently from ragpicking (throughout the city area) around 1900. The effect of the conjuncture and of structural variations in employment in wage-earning occupations attracted waves of irregular workers who disproportionately inflated these figures.

In addition to being a trade with traditions, rules, and a history, the rag occupation was characterized by an original social environment. The authentic ragpicker was the son of a ragpicker: "Ragpickers raked through dustbins from father to son and from generation to generation. Children took up the basket at eight or ten years of age; they never learned a trade. How could people escape from this circle? They were born, lived, and died as ragpickers."[16] In 1861 Privat d'Anglemont wrote about the true ragpicker: "By the time he stood one metre high, dressed in rags, with a foraging cap over his ears, a pipe in his mouth, and a basket on his back, he would take a hook in his hand and delve into all the refuse to which people of authority allowed him access."[17] The most frequently mentioned traits of such individuals included their tendency to enter precocious relationships: "We see conjugal cohabitation between young girls of fourteen or fifteen and boys of sixteen."[18] Such love matches arose between adolescents from neighbouring families as soon as they were old enough to manage without their elders. Nevertheless, family values remained essential to one and all: "If a son leaves for the army, all the relatives, including distant cousins and their friends, gather to see the young soldier off; they take up a collection [. . .], every month, they regularly send him a bit of money."[19] The following description summarizes the sight of the departure of *placiers* at daybreak: "A procession of carts drawn by a poor lame donkey or an emaciated old horse [. . .] The ragpicker, his wife, his children – the youngest only four or five years old – and his '*nègres*' [20] perched on top with great difficulty."[21] The occasional *coureurs* mostly worked alone, although the regulars raked through dustbins in small family teams and gradually filled a large bag they left at a crossing.[22]

---

[16] Barberet, *Monographies professionnelles*, 4, p. 92. Further on, Desmarquet describes recruitment to the trade: "First, there are ragpickers by birth, who are the children of ragpickers and who have never practised any other trade" (p. 102).
[17] Privat d'Anglemont, *Paris inconnu*, p. 52.
[18] Barberet, *Monographies professionnelles*, 4, p. 94.
[19] Privat d'Anglemont, *Paris anecdote* (Paris, 1860), p. 320.
[20] The *nègres* were children hired by the ragpickers.
[21] G. Mény, *Le chiffonnier de Paris* (Paris, n.d.), pp. 8–9.
[22] *Ibid.*, p. 11. Four persons could thus gather an average of 200 kg. a day.

In addition to its role in perpetuating the trade, the tribal link indisputably had a cohesive effect on the ragpicking population; another aspect was the value attached to the trade: "Frequently," wrote Privat d'Anglemont, "these bizarre individuals say proudly: 'In our family, the basket goes from father to son, we have never been [wage] labourers.' They always felt very strongly that they had chosen a free occupation devoid of the constraints of wage labour: 'Some who might engage in different occupations rake through dustbins because they love their freedom. They prefer to live in poverty and to be their own masters.' "[23] Ragpickers took offence at any comparison to beggars – and abhorred submission to the discipline of regular work in equal measure. In 1884, for example, 294 ragpickers from the 13th *arrondissement* requested employment from the municipal cleaning service; they were offered jobs as sweepers. Only eight accepted the conditions of employment. The others responded as follows: "We work freely and do not wish to be enslaved, plenty of old people can do this work [. . .]. We demand to live from our independent occupation."[24] The *coureurs* that Durieu met expressed disdain for the *placiers*: working at fixed stations, they were obliged to show up daily or risk replacement and to be polite to the *concierge* and the tenants of the building. In short, they were no longer true ragpickers.

According to the traditional public image: "The ragpicker is a free agent *par excellence*, the philosopher of the macadam. He feels immense pity for the slaves of Paris, locked from morning to night in a workshop or behind a workbench!"[25] Free to plan his route, the sole master of his time, eating straight from containers and wearing the garb he happens to find, with neither extravagant needs nor ambition, the ragpicker has all the traits of a modern savage, reincarnating the instincts and lifestyle of our predator ancestors in the midst of urban civilization: "They represent primitive mankind in the big city, blissfully ignorant of laws, happy with nonentities, imbued with their vegetative way of life, retiring from society like a troglodyte of the caves." From another world, from another city [. . .] While most topical literature was sympathetic towards these people, as is easy with friendly savages who have simple and childlike dispositions, disconcerting references appeared as well: their ignorance of hygiene made contact with these individuals repugnant and dangerous. Moreover, they were never entirely disassociated from night prowlers. This ambiguous image was both alluring and repulsive and accounted for the marginal status of ragmen.

This representation, however, was far from realistic. Indeed, ragpickers had a taste for and a tradition of independence, but the impression that

---

[23] Barberet, *Monographies professionnelles*, 4, pp. 102–103.
[24] *Ibid.*, pp. 85–88; Mény, *Le chiffonnier de Paris*, p. 24.
[25] *L'Histoire*, 3 April 1870.

they were happy saprophytes of the big city is based on a myth. Their low profits forced them to work regularly. Perhaps savings did not figure within their system of values because they disdained this virtue among more settled circles. Nevertheless, practical circumstances undoubtedly precluded this activity as well. Family cohesion and general mutual aid in surroundings rife with trials and tribulations could entail myriad compromises in the struggle for daily bread, although certain limits existed. Especially during the 1880s, occupational upheaval curtailed the freedom of those involved: the *placiers*, as aptly stated by the *coureurs*, tended to serve as deputy *concierges* in apartment buildings. Such was the price of their privilege, with respect to both the *coureurs* and the former type of gatherers. On the other hand, this article will show that many ragpickers – *coureurs* and *placiers* alike – became directly dependent upon the master ragpickers and effectively turned into wage labourers.

The new regulations also instigated practices that conflicted with the idealistic vision of an unfettered life. The territorial system, which was strictly observed, depended on forceful encounters between licensed and unlicensed workers. Trespassing by a *coureur* in buildings on the turf of a *placier* would inevitably lead to a brawl. If necessary, nearby *placiers* would rush to assist their injured colleague, as they were equally interested in maintaining the hierarchies. In 1905 such an altercation brought three ragpickers before the court: the council for the defence argued that "according to the rules of the ragpickers corporation [. . .] the rights of 'ragpickers' were exclusive, reserved for certain persons and individuals entitled to sell and dispose of these rights." Durieu asked a *secondeur* (a ragpicker who replaced a *placier* when he was inconvenienced from performing his rounds) whether he had ever tried to appropriate the place for himself. Indignantly, the deputy *secondeur* responded: "Do you really think I would take the place of this man who has paid me 80 F!"[26] This system generalized pre-existing tendencies: well before 1883, some ragpickers had thought of reserving the rubbish of a house through an understanding with the *concierge* and, in return for small services, got the tenants to set aside discarded linen or leftovers from meals that thus escaped the baskets of competitors.[27] On the other hand, the *cités* (blocks of dwellings surrounding a courtyard and generally secluded from the street) of ragpickers had always negotiated a distribution of the neighbourhoods: "Once the territories had been assigned, the confines had to be observed. In the event of trespassing, repressive measures awaited the delinquents upon returning to their *cité*. Punish-

[26] Durieu, *Les Parisiens d'aujourd'hui*, p. 147.
[27] See Barberet, *Monographies professionnelles*, 4, p. 100; Privat d'Anglemont, *Paris inconnu*, p. 54. In 1872 the police commissioner for the Combat district noted that many of the 500 badges from his jurisdiction were linked to a site in Paris (Enquête parlementaire sur les ouvriers, Archives de la préfecture de Police, BA 400).

ment ordinarily consisted of a fine and, if necessary, a conscientious chastising, to use the standard formulation."[28] Little is known about this subject [. . .]

The picturesque descriptions of the savage creature in the literature thus concealed a complex being, deeply rooted in his surroundings. To what extent was he truly marginal? All the evidence gathered describes the ragpicking population as a special group that remained aloof from the other citizens: "They keep to themselves and discuss only their trade."[29] Fed and clothed largely through their proceeds, they kept their interactions with vendors – an essential activity among the proletariat – to an absolute minimum (with the sole exception of wine merchants, as alcoholism was their most prevalent behavioural characteristic). The offspring of ragpickers had a reputation for truancy, and the literature states that "uniting the progeny of ragpickers with the children of workers was virtually impossible". Durieu had some difficulty establishing contact with the subjects of his study, as borne out by this reflection shared by a couple of ragpickers whom he approached a bit too closely: "Surely, if he had had photographic equipment, he would have taken a picture for his mantlepiece."[30] The independence that the ragpickers associated with their work inevitably made them feel they were entirely different from the workers. Moreover, they obviously found poor neighbourhoods less lucrative. The very nature of their work discouraged any sense of solidarity among the ragpickers with respect to the people whose dustbins attested to poverty. "This is worker [territory]", declared a *coureur* to Durieu, with a note of arrogance, as they crossed a destitute quarter. Finally, beneath this marginal individual lurked an *aficionado* of order: the anarchists during the occupational upheaval instigated by regulations unsuccessfully tried to reach their audience. With tremendous respect and confidence in the justice of the delegates, they made lengthy statements before the *Quarante-Quatre*.

In this respect, the honesty of ragpickers was a subject of tremendous controversy. According to many authors of the picturesque literature, no citizen was more righteous: they scrupulously returned any item of value that wound up in a dustbin. The low figures for police arrests of these people are quoted extensively. In short, "the ragpickers of Paris were not victims of degradation as felt by haughty individuals".[31] More astute observers, however, believed otherwise. According to Durieu, the ragpickers deliberately kept unexpected discoveries, except if the gratuity was likely to exceed the value of the item in question. Surely the territorial system, where tenants of buildings knew the licensed operators

---

[28] Barberet, *Monographies professionnelles*, 4, p. 91.
[29] *Ibid.*, p. 93.
[30] Durieu, *Les Parisiens d'aujourd'hui*, p. 127.
[31] *La Paix*, 8 January 1892. As stated by Louis de Paulian, the author of an important work on ragpickers, *La hotte du chiffonnier* (Paris, 1885).

well, encouraged a more scrupulous approach. Among the *placiers*, however, especially with the children and the "*nègres*", petty theft was thought to be common.[32]

What do these contradictory statements suggest? Excerpts for 1907 and 1908 from the registers for the commissionership of the Gare (13th *arrondissement*), a quarter where ragpickers abounded, offer a clue: ragpickers are mentioned very rarely in connection with the types of crimes or offences considered. They appear twice among the thefts perpetrated by adults and only once in cases of rebellion and insults against officers. The significance of these cases pales amid the considerable total numbers of such incidents.[33]

This information totally disproves any comparison of the ragpickers to the contemporary "dangerous classes" and elucidates descriptions elsewhere: the population of ragpickers led an introverted existence, satisfied its very limited needs from its meagre profits, and maintained little contact with other social groups. The group's cohesive nature ensured both strong individual integration and resolution of conflicts of interest between persons and families, whereas among outsiders they were often hauled on to the public square and were rarely successful with the commissioner. Regarding the distribution of neighbourhoods among the *cités* and their authority, the source added: "The police has no involvement or interest in these harsh disciplinary tactics." In 1883, a ragpicker submitting a written complaint to the prefecture about the infiltration of "criminals" in the trade demanded that henceforth the practice be restricted to licensed operators: in other words, the badge, which denoted legitimacy in the ragpicking business, ensured the absence of police intervention in the trade. Another ragpicker expressed the same sentiment even more specifically to a clergyman venturing into a *cité*: "We do not meddle with the bourgeois; they should resolve their issues themselves and leave us alone."[34] Territorial segregation, however, was among the most striking features of the occupation.

The nature of the work was of universal importance: after completing his gathering rounds, the ragpicker returned home and began the *tricage* process, which involved sorting and decomposing the proceeds (e.g. separating leather from the clasp of a wallet). The regulations of the decree of 1883 authorized this operation between 11 o'clock in the morning (the time of their return) and 4 o'clock in the afternoon and

[32] See Barberet, *Monographies professionelles*, 4, pp. 94–95.
[33] The first case of theft (15 November 1906) involves a ragpicker of the rue Nationale who had kept a package he found in a dustbin on the rue d'Aboukir containing certificates and securities; the second, rather interesting case concerns a ragman who traded second-hand goods accused of stealing a pair of trousers and a vest (valued at 5.5 F) from an individual. The insult to officers (23 March 1907) occurred in the Jeanne-d'Arc *cité*, a very specific area of the arrondissement.
[34] Mény, *Le chiffonnier de Paris*, p. 23.

assigned the rest of the afternoon to sales to the master ragpicker. Ragmen thus did a lot of their work at home. Every abode occupied by a tradesmen was therefore a small warehouse for rag scrap: the choice of residence among ragpickers thus depended upon advances in hygiene.

In the first half of the nineteenth century the ragmen lived in the city's central districts and the working-class areas, especially in the old 12th *arrondissement* and the neighbourhoods of Montagne-Sainte-Geneviève and Saint-Marceau: "Nearly all menial trades could be found there; the low rents and the numerous local wholesale rag merchants attracted most of the ragpickers in Paris", noted the Commission for unsanitary dwellings in 1851.[35] Their lives were generally closely connected with the rest of the population, despite a pronounced tendency to concentrate on certain abodes. The large construction projects marked the start of a progressive ragpickers' exodus from the centre (the first ten *arrondissements*, which constituted the bourgeois neighbourhoods of Paris) in the late 1840s. The complex movement proceeded in different directions and entailed various forms of district planning. From the Second Empire onward, the *cités* spread outside the city limits into the suburbs. A simultaneous trend, which prevailed during this era, involved the relocation of ragpickers from the centre to the neighbourhoods on the periphery (the ten higher *arrondissements*, which constituted the working-class neighbourhoods of Paris). Even in Paris, residential developments emerged in *cités* comparable to the suburbs or as subordinate, smaller concentrations fairly close to the *cité*, but on sites or territories owned by master ragpickers. Nevertheless, a general tendency began in the second half of the century: settlement by families formerly dispersed throughout the city in compact and highly individualized arrangements, thus leading to largely voluntary enclosure inside these local ghettos.

In addition to the contrast between the centre and the periphery, the spatial implantation of this population affected the urban-suburban context. In 1902 the figures gathered by the Labour Department on occupational organizations reflected the distribution of ragpickers' households shown in Table 2.

By the turn of the century, the share of ragpickers in the centre was of marginal significance. Along the periphery, they operated predominantly on the Left Bank. They apparently benefited from shifting their centre of occupational gravity (from the old 12th *arrondissement* to newer quarters), especially towards the 13th *arrondissement*: the considerable contrast between the assessments of the workers and the employers clearly shows that this *arrondissement* heralded the occupational resettlement in Paris.[36]

---

[35] *Rapport général sur les travaux de la Commission pendant l'année 1851*, p. 11.
[36] Office du Travail, *L'industrie du chiffon à Paris*, pp. 22–23. The absolute figures are of little interest: only the proportional distribution is significant.

Table 2. *Distribution of ragpickers' households, 1902*

	1 %	2 %
5th *arrondissement* (Saint-Victor)	3	4
13th (Gare, Salpêtrière, Maison Blanche)	25	33
14th–15th (Santé, Javel)	30	22
18th (Montmartre)	15	14
19th (La Villette)	9	8
20th (Belleville, Saint-Fargeau, Charonne)	18	19
Paris	100	100
Paris	47.8	50
Suburbs	52.2	50
Total settlement	100	100

1 = according to the employers unions
2 = according to the workers unions

At this early date, the suburbs provided a counterweight to the original urban hub. This evaluation falls squarely within the proportions previously introduced: in 1886 the Board of Health accounted for two-thirds of the ragpickers in suburban communities. In 1894 it was written that "Ragpickers have moved to the countryside, if Saint-Ouen, Pantin, or Clichy could possibly suggest an open prairie."[37] Recall that this situation had its distant origins in the beginning of the expulsion from the centre. Clichy in particular quickly became the residence of major settlements of ragpickers, such as the Germain *cité* (which was nicknamed Little Mazas[38]) and especially the Foucault *cité* (known as "woman in culottes"). Around 1850, Doré's rival purchased a vast area in the community and sublet portions to about fifty households.[39] In 1888, an actual ragpicker said that "Clichy is the place for studying the ragmen's customs".[40] The suburbs to the north of the capital accommodated the main concentration of this development outside the city limits, probably because of the significant urbanization of the zones adjacent to the Right Bank; on the other bank, the free spaces that were less important long restricted the ragpickers within the confines of the city.

Even though the encampments of the suburbs and the periphery both originated from the movement emanating from the centre, many signs indicated that the suburbs eventually became an outlet for the settlements along the periphery threatened by constraints. Statistics on warehouses containing rag scrap that belonged to the master ragpickers exemplify this rate by virtue of the function of the masters in ragpicker accommodations

[37] *Le Monde illustré*, 4 August 1894.
[38] "Given this name because its forty or fifty rooms are the size of a cell [at the Mazas prison]": Barberet, *Monographies professionnelles*, 4, p. 96.
[39] De Paulian, *La hotte du chiffonnier*, p. 55. This individual bequeathed the site to the community.
[40] Barberet, *Monographies professionnelles*, 4, p. 95.

(dwellings that they sometimes supplied, *cités* that were always close to the warehouses). In 1884 138 such warehouses existed within the city limits of Paris; by 1901, 135 remained. Simultaneously, the suburban establishments increased from 35 to 97: all growth in the profession thus took place outside the city between these dates.[41] On the Left Bank, the number of warehouses decreased from seven to four in the 14th *arrondissement* and from sixteen to eleven in the 15th *arrondissement*. Along with the 10th *arrondissement* in Paris (where merchant warehouses were located), only the 13th *arrondissement* experienced any increase (of the 12th through to the 20th *arrondissements*). By 1912, while the 14th *arrondissement* gained three additional units (rising from four to seven), the 15th and the 13th *arrondissements* experienced a considerable drop (from twenty to fourteen in the 15th and from eleven to six in the 13th). After 1900, this disappearance of industrial establishments probably coincided with the departure of ragpickers for the suburbs. Certain important districts had already vanished or had been dismantled. The regulations reflected the same trend: when Durieu conducted his survey, he noted that the *placiers* had practically monopolized the capital, thereby relegating the *coureurs* to the routes in the suburbs. The benefits that the *placiers* reaped from the territorial system thus gradually brought about the distribution of the general areas of settlement for the two major categories. Admittedly, many *coureurs* resided inside Paris (and many *placiers* lived outside). *Coureurs* wishing to avoid excessively long routes, however, eventually had to move to the suburbs, especially people engaged in the trade sporadically.

The ragpickers were a group of the populace that retreated to the suburbs even before 1914. While the numbers were relatively modest, the trend signified their rejection of both the bourgeois and the proletariat elements of city life. This case, which was probably unique, undoubtedly reflected the original characteristics of the occupation and resembled a veritable flight from the advancing urban sanitation drive: "Sanitation issues are totally alien to this segment of the population; the very word scares them. They regard the operation as a malevolent goddess dedicated to persecuting the poor ragpickers; in the interest of sanitation, the police betrays them with a view to improving the cleanliness of their dwellings and to restricting the number of pigs they are entitled to raise. I have often [. . .] heard the exclamation: 'You see, sanitation is our worst enemy'."[42] According to the investigator from the Board of Health, "when measures affect occupational practice in certain settlements, ragpickers prefer to move elsewhere (occasionally very far away from their place of residence), rather than to submit". Ragpickers consider sanitation experts their enemies: "Sadly, the arro-

[41] Office du Travail, *L'industrie du chiffon à Paris*, pp. 21–22.
[42] Durieu, *Les Parisiens d'aujourd'hui*, pp. 92–93.

gance of these poor souls leads to their abasement; they seem happy with the life they have built for themselves and immune to all laws of society; if we were to install them in a palace, they would soon turn the residence into an equally atrocious and pestilential abode as the one where they were born and where they hope to die."[43] A sordid class, a dangerous class [. . .]

Precautionary isolation then became the only solution, as advocated by the Board of Health: "Great interest existed in moving them away from the population centres and resettling them just inside or outside the Paris city limits [. . .] This emigration may be furthered by erecting well-built *cités* for workers outside Paris providing sanitary and low-cost accommodations to large numbers of these ragpickers."[44] The sanitation authorities had chosen to focus on their marginal nature and their tendency to live in groups. Recall that the desire to wipe out the occupation underlay the regulation of 1883: perpetuation and survival of these town savages was tolerable only in the event of a sanitary cordon.

What type of abodes existed in these *cités*? From the middle of the nineteenth century the centrifugal exodus essentially led to *cités*: the search for a vast open area, settlement through makeshift construction of hovels, and a progressively increasing population density that gave rise to an integrated arrangement. Privat d'Anglemont wrote: "As soon as one discovered a home or a site available for rent, all the others came to visit and quickly formed a settlement, a clan, a family, a type of mutual assistance society where they afforded one another generous support during hard times."[45] The ragpickers' *cités* were merely a specific type of improvised abode that arose along the periphery at the end of the nineteenth century: especially in this respect, the original population of these settlements consisted almost exclusively of ragmen's households. While the origins of these cities are quite obscure, the system of improvised dwellings already seemed very common: owners of vacant sites would divide the area into lots on which the tenants constructed their own homes. The case of the Foucault *cité* has been described above; the Doré *cité* in the 13th *arrondissement* was the most widely known. In 1886, the reporter from the Board of Health listed in addition to the Doré *cité* neighbourhood the Maufry, Fournier, Malbert (at Montmartre), and Hivert (Combat, 19th *arrondissement*) *cités* inside Paris: using proper names to designate the settlements indicates their origins beyond any doubt. This category comprised the Ile-aux-Singes, the cité des Mousquetaires, and the Cour des Miracles in the 15th

---

[43] Commission des logements insalubres, *Rapport pour l'année 1851*, p. 12.
[44] De Luynes, *Rapports sur les dépôts de chiffons*, p. 12.
[45] Privat d'Anglemont, *Paris anecdote*, pp. 307–308.

arrondissement.[46] In the 13th *arrondissement,* most of the inhabitants in the dwellings in the Butte-aux-Cailles development were probably ragpickers.

These concentrations of ragmen were the largest ever in Paris. The few available descriptions are striking. Regarding the Foucault *cité* at Clichy:

Picture a long rectangle or rather a wide alley lined with two-storey buildings on the right and on the left containing thirty rooms on each floor. Some rooms lack any windows and have a single door serving both as the entrance and as the window. The area is slightly larger than a prison cell. It contains neither a wooden floor, nor tiles, nor a stone surface. The furnishings vary according to the financial situation of the tenants. Nearly all own a stove made of pieces of scrap metal and bricks easily found in public dumps; the wealthiest have a bed, a table, and a chair, or rather objects that resemble a bed, a table, and a chair. Inhabitants with more modest means have only a bed. Many own nothing at all. In a corner of such rooms lies a heap of straw the inhabitants have gathered on the street on the day of their move. On this bed of straw, the ragpicker sleeps with his wife, his children, his dog [. . .] and his refuse.[47]

The improvised dwellings, which resulted from makeshift fabrication, where the initiative of materials, arrangement of the shanties, and interior decoration were left entirely to the users, gave rise to unusual urban landscapes that featured stark geometric constructions assembled from disparate elements forming curious combinations – especially in the *cités* of the ragpickers, who relied on the recovery of items for their livelihood. Photographs from the late nineteenth century reveal shanties with overlapping roofs and paths overflowing with the proceeds of the *triage* and even extending into the living quarters. At 85 rue Château-des-Rentiers, where a night shelter eventually arose, a confused shanty town existed around 1890; the small gardens adjacent to the dwellings, "helter skelter with the inhabitants, contained heaps of rags, all kinds of rubbish".[48] The description of the Maufry *cité* on the rue Marcadet was as follows: "While the general countenance of this development is indeed impoverished, it is not dull; myriad small details are apparent [. . .] Here, a stuffed crow is perched above the door of an abode; there, rocks are arranged in a curious window decoration; further on, a wall is covered with small glittering shards of mirrors."[49]

These *cités* offered the ragpickers far more spacious accommodations than their previous quarters in the centre. The facilities for *triage* and storage of the proceeds in the courtyards of the cottages may have

---

[46] An article in *Le Matin* (22 August 1908) estimated the number of ragpickers in this arrondissement at 2,000.

[47] De Paulian, *La hotte du chiffonnier*, p. 55.

[48] Octave du Mesnil, *L'habitation du pauvre à Paris* (Paris, 1890), p. 39.

[49] A. Coffignon, *Le pavé parisien* (Paris, n.d.), pp. 41–42.

motivated the exodus. Father Cordet's clan was an isolated but exemplary case.[50] Like his family, he was an old "patriarch" hailing from the Mouffetard neighbourhood near the Patriarches market. As "the indentations in these neighbourhoods inconvenienced the clientele", he proposed a dispersed *smala*-style household: "What if we join forces? We could live and work together; the able men and women would search out the goods, while the young and the old did the sorting." For 500 F (the amount of compensation for eviction), Father Cordet purchased a vacant site on Vaugirard. The united households (married youths and girls) constructed six ramshackle huts (of which two served for storing merchandise). Twenty-two people set up co-operative living arrangements in these huts, where each household had two or three rooms at its disposal. Father Cordet did not long for the days "before we were patriarchs", when, for lack of space, the proceeds had to be sold to the master ragpicker daily. As a group effort, the *tricage* operations improved, and the people could live from their reserves while waiting for the monthly sale, which was now directly to a merchant. While this small *cité* had a strong, virtually tribal link, the lifestyle emphasized characteristics common to other large *cités*: concentration of households, greater harmony between the activity and its fixed base of operation, collective life, and so on.

The collective lifestyle characterized the ragpicker communities. In the *cités* the homogeneous occupation and the links between families, along with the relatively similar incomes among the ragmen before the upheaval in the trade caused by the regulation of 1883,[51] arose from the very existence of these isolated environments. Mutual aid was an accepted practice: "When he grows aged and infirm, a ragpicker does not go to the hospital. His neighbours will not allow him to suffer. Rather, they help him and take up collections to satisfy his needs, enduring deprivation to offer him small comforts."[52] The willingness of the ragmen to take in stray children or the progeny of their neighbours (their "*nègres*") reflected both an interest in additional hands for gathering and a common practice of living and working together, as well as a form of public assistance for children. According to Durieu, the

---

[50] P. Bory, *Les métamorphoses d'un chiffon* (Abbeville, 1897).

[51] This equality was relative. Even before the distinction between *placiers* and *coureurs*, a hierarchy existed among the population of ragpickers. The arrangement was sometimes institutionalized, as in the Pot d'Etain entertainment facility on the border of Fontainebleau, which was divided into three halls: "la Chambre des Pairs" (reserved for people who owned baskets and hooks in good condition), "la Chambre des Députés" (for the common people), and the "cercle des vrais prolétaires" (for everyone whose equipment consisted merely of a bag). "Disciplinary penalties" were issued to anyone entering a hall restricted to people with greater means (*Le Monde*, 7 June 1872). In 1857, upon the establishment of a mutual benefit society, this hierarchy was replaced with a common banqueting hall, although it quickly reappeared (*Moniteur universel*, 5 November 1857).

[52] Privat d'Anglemont, *Paris anecdote*, p. 321.

ragpickers' offspring, despite their irregular school attendance, were gifted with a keen sense of observation and certainly did not scorn study: "They often seem to form a class of their own. The *concierge* at a *cité* of ragpickers showed me doors and walls covered with letters, figures, additions, and subtractions attesting to this system of mutual instruction and told me that upon learning something new at school, a young ragpicker would immediately share this knowledge with his chums."[53] Some observers marvelled at the fairly frequent religious practices in the *cités*, although these cases were restricted to ceremonial occasions (baptisms, first communions, burials) concerning the family and attended by the people in the neighbourhood.

The daily schedule reflected a common pattern in each *cité*; after *tricage*, the men left the courtyards and the cottages to gather at the shops of local or neighbouring wine merchants. A journalist who visited the Ile-aux-Singes one evening in 1869, when the area had reached its maximum, provided the following description: "Children clad in rags sought the warmth of the sunlight; women sat on the ground mending their husbands' tattered garments, while an inebriated refrain resounded from the gloomy taverns that inevitably abounded in such areas."[54] Alcoholism was more characteristic of the ragpickers than of any other group in the nineteenth century.

Inside Paris, the decline of these developments is difficult to date and probably began before the 1880s. Although details are lacking, sanitary grounds seem to have been the main reason, as mentioned previously. Large construction projects or demolition measures affected or eliminated several *cités*. New roads that were opened, which entailed the urbanization of zones where *cités* had arisen unhindered, were also decisive and certainly occurred in conjunction with the construction projects (as on the Ile-aux-Singes). Such settlements continued to be built in the suburbs (*cités* at Gennevilliers and Asnières, for instance). Within the city limits, however, new types of ragpickers' dwellings emerged, preceding total exclusion of the ragmen from the city.

Dismantling the *cités* led several ragpickers to stake out new sites for building. Initially, the construction gave rise to individual buildings without forming new settlements. Around 1905, the rent per square metre near the city limits varied from 1.50 F to 2 F per year.[55] The construction cost 100 F,[56] more if a coach house, a stable, and perhaps even a basement for the merchandise were added to the simple hovel. Only the *placiers* had the means to set up house in such fashion. In fact, many new settlements arose, although most were smaller than the

---

[53] Durieu, *Les Parisiens d'aujourd'hui*, p. 97.
[54] *Ville de Paris*, 5 October 1883.
[55] In Gentilly: 0.25 to 0.50 F; in Saint-Ouen: from 0.60 to 0.90 F: Office du travail, *L'industrie du chiffon à Paris*, p. 12.
[56] Mény, *Le chiffonnier de Paris*, p. 12.

cités, and the master ragpickers usually built and let the accommodations. The pointe d'Ivry neighbourhood in the 13th *arrondissement* typified such habitats. On the rue des Hospices, at a site belonging to the Ouest railway, the subtenant (who was a master ragpicker) appointed another ragpicker as a caretaker to collect the rents for the lots on which three ragmen's households had built shanties:[57] this case also involved make-shift constructions. At 48 avenue de Choisy, a large building in a courtyard contained the warehouses of the master ragpicker – who was also the owner – and single-room accommodations rented to ragmen by the week (from 2.50 F to 2 F). This *cité* provided shelter for 51 people. On the rue Baudricourt three sides of a huge quadrilateral structure contained 77 dwellings. The master's residence occupied the fourth side; a large shed in the centre served as a warehouse for rags: 64 people lived there. While this arrangement was not the first effort by the master ragpickers to concentrate their suppliers in their midst, they succeeded only as a result of the dislocation of the large *cités*.

In the preceding cases, as with all situations of the same type, the ragpickers or tenants processed their proceeds daily at the site on their master's scales. Dependence on such an intermediary had always characterized this occupation where the vast majority lived from day to day; the master ensured continuity, being indebted to him is frequently mentioned among the evils of the ragpicking trade.[58] By providing accom-modation, the masters tightened their control considerably: the ragmen were on the verge of losing their independence; in some small *cités*, they were merely wage-earners for the masters, who became their bosses. An individual testifying before the *Commission des Quarante-Quatre* described the situation as follows: "The masters rent the sites to us at very high rates, higher than on the rue de Rivoli: we are allocated filthy premises; we are sweltering in the summer and freezing in the winter [. . .]Most mobile ragpickers are forced to board with their masters, who are usually wine merchants. They have to purchase necessities from him. Otherwise, the master ragpicker may refuse to take their wares or may give them notice."[59] In this respect, an existing practice became widespread at the expense of ragmen who did not own their accommoda-tion and did not pay promptly: first their door would be removed, next the roofing in the case of shanties, "this was the equivalent of dismissal;

---

[57] Rents: 7 F weekly, 6 F monthly, 5 F monthly. Du Mesnil, *L'habitation du pauvre à Paris*, p. 264.

[58] Ragpickers often sold their take on the basis of "gross weight": the product that dominated the lot determined the price. The ragmen had always objected to this unfair system. The masters attributed its need to the heavy losses after processing. On the other hand, ignorance of the wholesale prices (if only because of the considerable range of products) always made the ragmen believe that these natives of Auvergne (who had a reputation for swindling their subordinates in business) were taking advantage of them.

[59] *Commission d'enquête parlementaire* (1884), p. 246.

it was the only way to get ragpickers to leave, as the police never ventured into the *cités*".[60] This particular procedure soon came into general use in the small *cités* run by the masters.

Whether they were *placiers* or *coureurs* (the inexorable decline in the number of *coureurs* practising their trade in the capital is noted above), ragmen in Paris had increasing difficulty earning a living. The disappearance of the large *cités* eliminated a major share of the freedom of these people who roamed the city. Preserving their independence required crossing the city limits, building their shanties on some obscure site,[61] or joining the major *cités* of the northern suburbs. By the end of the nineteenth century, the circumstances of the trade had begun to change. Entirely new institutions arose: selling co-operatives (intended to circumvent the intermediary role of the masters) and trade organizations.[62] The dismembered tribe sought to regain the lost element of cohesion. Manumission from the masters for the ragpickers residing in Paris added a new dimension to the process initiated by the division according to *coureurs* and *placiers*: the solidarity within the community of *cités* and the economic homogeneity were no more. Nearly all these consolidation efforts failed.[63] A journalist shared the following observation concerning an effort to establish a co-operative in Grenelle in 1908: "In our trade, the strongest will always have the upper hand."[64]

The ragpickers undoubtedly resented these forms of organization that were characteristic of wage-earners; their accepted marginality coincided with a sense of satisfaction with their fate that was too deeply rooted for the concerned individuals to approve of these tokens of goodwill. Moreover, the dispersion of ragmen in small units in the *cités* of the masters was a considerable obstacle. Even the large *cités* in the suburbs lacked the cohesion of the former Parisian *cités*, as illustrated by Durieu's visit to Gennevilliers. Neighbourly relations were more restrained: "every man for himself", stated a *placier*, emphasizing that nobody had helped him and his family when he suffered an extended illness.[65] Was the "well-being" of these households of *placiers*, with their settled way of life, as this author writes, indicative of true entrepreneurs who owned

---

[60] Mény, *Le chiffonnier de Paris*, p. 13.

[61] Such was the case among certain *coureurs* studied by Durieu, *Les Parisiens d'aujourd'-hui*, pp. 126–137.

[62] See Office du Travail, *L'industrie du chiffon à Paris*, pp. 79–83.

[63] Exceptions occurred in certain very specific sectors of the occupation: nearly all dustbin ragpickers were unionized (they were semi-wage-earners), as were their counterparts in pulverization plants. According to Durieu, the union succeeded in regulating the work at the Issy plant (only for the choice positions). This solidarity is attributable to the exceptional conditions: "At the Saint-Ouen plant, the ragpickers were there to stay and set up extremely inconvenient warehouses for rags": *Rapport sur les opérations du service d'inspection des établissements classés* (1907), p. 31.

[64] *Le Matin*, 22 August 1908.

[65] Durieu, *Les Parisiens d'aujourd'hui*, pp. 156–169.

subterranean warehouses, horses and carts, and were liable for real estate taxes? At any rate, as certain ragpickers loved to repeat on the eve of the war: "Jealousy entered the occupation."

It should be remembered that the emergence of these small units preceded the exclusion of ragpickers from the city. By 1914, the ragpicking diaspora, from the centre to the periphery, and then to the large *cités* in the suburbs, was almost complete. Progressive detachment and gradual repression characterized the ragmen in Paris during the second half of the nineteenth century. This historical process involved an exceptional degree of marginality for the actors. Among the paradoxes, this occupation, which had been decidedly urban, was gradually driven out of the city. To the extent that the freedom to practise entailed a certain state of public hygiene and urban facilities, changes in these domains inevitably affected the ragmen. The two phenomena that overwhelmed their world – the emergence of hierarchies in the economic situation and the liquidation of the large *cités* – resulted directly from the new sanitation trends: the regulation of 1883 signified a struggle against unsanitary rental dwellings and improvised habitats. The same urban environment grew increasingly intolerant of eccentric groups among the population: this striking logic applied in still greater measure to the working-class population overall, both at the time and in the long run.

Translated from the French by Lee Mitzman

NOTES ON CONTRIBUTORS

Shahid Amin, Department of History, Delhi University, Delhi 110007, India.

Alain Faure, Centre d'histoire de la France contemporaine et d'étude des croissances, Département d'histoire, Université de Paris X-Nanterre, 200 Avenue de la République, 92001 Nanterre Cedex, France.

Juan A. Giusti-Cordero, 1689 Cuernavaca Street, Urbanización Venus Gardens, 00926 Rio Piedras, Puerto Rico.

Madhavi Kale, Department of History, Bryn Mawr College, 101 North Merion Avenue, Bryn Mawr, PA 19010-2899, USA.

Erick D. Langer, Department of History, Carnegie Mellon University, Pittsburgh, PA 15213-3890, USA.

Marcel van der Linden, Internationaal Instituut voor Sociale Geschiedenis, Cruquiusweg 31, 1019 AT Amsterdam, The Netherlands.

Gyan Prakash, Department of History, Princeton University, 129 Dickinson Hall, Princeton, NJ 08544-1017, USA.

Samita Sen, Department of History, Calcutta University, 51/2 Hazra Road, Calcutta 700019, India.

Dilip Simeon, A-4 / 303, Ekta Gardens, 9 Patparganj, Delhi 11 00 92, India.

For EU product safety concerns, contact us at Calle de José Abascal, 56–1°, 28003 Madrid, Spain or eugpsr@cambridge.org.

www.ingramcontent.com/pod-product-compliance
Ingram Content Group UK Ltd.
Pitfield, Milton Keynes, MK11 3LW, UK
UKHW020349140625
459647UK00019B/2367

9 780521 589000